Instructor's Manual and Test Bank to Accompany

Mastering Communication in Contemporary America

and

Fundamentals of Human Communication

Nancy F. Burroughs
Patricia Kearney
Timothy G. Plax
Melvin L. DeFleur

This instructor's manual is designed to accompany both *Mastering Communication in Contemporary America* and *Fundamentals of Human Communication.*The first twelve chapters of these texts are identical; thus, references in the instructor's manual to these chapters apply to both texts. Chapters 13-15 are different, as the table of contents indicates.

Mayfield Publishing Company
Mountain View, California
London • Toronto

International Standard Book Number: 1-55934-229-3

Manufactured in the United States of America
10 9 8 7 6 5 4 3 2 1

Mayfield Publishing Company
1240 Villa Street
Mountain View, CA 94041

CONTENTS

INTRODUCTION

An introduction to communication course can be organized in a variety of ways, and the material in the text can be used in different ways by different teachers. As the teacher of record, you must decide how much emphasis to give each chapter. Moreover, you will need to decide how to balance the components of theory, research, and practice, and how much time to devote to lectures, class discussions, activities, and other assignments. The number of students in your course, the number of class meetings that will be held, and the special needs of your students will all ultimately influence how you organize your course. With you and your needs in mind then, we have put together some ideas and recommendations that you can use in preparing the basic course.

The instructor's manual for *Mastering Communication in Contemporary America: Theory, Research, and Practice* and *Fundamentals of Human Communication* is divided into five parts:

* Part I provides an overview of the course including sample syllabus, course outlines for the organization of the course based on either a semester or a quarter system, and general teaching tips or strategies for new teachers.

* In Part II we have provided a list of learning objectives that correspond to each chapter in the text. Moreover, we have included extended outlines for each chapter that you can follow in your own lectures.

* Part III includes over 600 examination questions: a mixture of multiple choice, true/false, and essay items. We wanted to make sure you had a large selection and a variety of items that you could use.

* Part IV contains a variety of suggestions for instructional activities to accompany text chapters.

* Part V is concerned with the evaluation of students and teachers. Included in this section is a discussion of how to write your own lecture-based examination questions for objective and essay testing; how to take the subjectivity out of grading essays; how to assign grades; how to measure effective teaching; and, finally, a reference list.

We hope that this organization will allow you to locate and use the information provided quickly and easily. We wish you and your students an enjoyable, stimulating course!

PART I

ORGANIZING THE COURSE

SAMPLE COURSE SYLLABUS

COURSE DESCRIPTION: In an effort to understand the role of communication in a variety of contexts, we will examine relevant theoretical and applied practices of human communication. SPCH 100 is a content-oriented class designed to introduce basic concepts involved in the communication process across a number of communication situations. [Refer to your department catalog description].

COURSE RATIONALE: No matter what business or vocation you choose, you will be expected to possess effective communication skills. In order to help you achieve this goal, we will discuss the human communication process in terms of its basics, contexts, personal skills, and public speaking applications. Throughout, we will not only discuss the concepts, principles, and theories of communication that have been developed by theorists and researchers, but we will also try to identify ways in which those ideas have practical application to communication problems in everyday life. [You may want to insert your own rationale here instead.]

INSTRUCTOR: Nancy F. Burroughs-Denhart [insert your name].

Office hours: MWF 1:00–2:00 P.M. [Every university has its own policy; check with your department.]

Office phone: (510) 869-1530 [insert your campus/office phone number].

TEXT: Defleur, M. L., Kearney, P., & Plax, T. G. (1992). *Mastering Communication in Contemporary America: Theory, Research, and Practice* or *Fundamentals of Human Communication.* Mountain View, CA: Mayfield.

COURSE REQUIREMENTS:

Attendance: You are expected to attend all classes. The success of your learning experience depends on the active contributions of everyone. Each unexcused absence after one week of classes will result in receiving one letter grade lower than you earned for the course. [This is a sample attendance policy; you may want to check your department's policy on attendance and revise accordingly.]

Testing: Three exams will be administered during the course. Each exam will include a variety of multiple choice, true/false, and essay questions. Each exam will include material from both lecture and assigned readings. Exams may not be taken late. [We recommend a variety of grading opportunities—three exams is a good number.]

Speeches/Assignments: Two major speeches and/or assignments will be required. You will be evaluated on your skills in researching, organizing, and effectively delivering your speech(es) and/or completing your assignments. Your improvement in presenting orally will also be evaluated. Criteria for each speech and/or assignment will be provided prior to each presentation/due date. [Once again, insert your own policy.]

Make-ups: Because you are enrolled on assigned dates and times in this course, you have a commitment and are expected to present speeches, turn in assignments, and take exams on assigned dates. Unexcused absences will result in no make-ups and a grade of zero will be given. Excused absences are only granted to students who verify their illness by a physician. Students with excused absences will make up their speech, assignment, or exam within *one week* at the instructor's convenience.

GRADES:
Points Possible

Exam 1	50 points
Exam 2	50 points
Exam 3	50 points
Speech 1	20 points
Speech 2	<u>30 points</u>
Total	200 points

Grading Scale	**Percent**
A = 180–200	90–100 %
B = 160–179	80–89 %
C = 140–159	70–79 %
D = 120–139	60–69 %
F = 119 and below	59% and below

TEACHING A SEMESTER COURSE
15 WEEKS: 45-HOUR SEMESTER
COURSE OUTLINE

Week	Topic	Readings
1	Introduction to Course: Syllabus, Overview, Purpose, and Course Requirements	
	The Communication Process: An Overview	Ch. 1
2	Verbal Communication	Ch. 2
3	Nonverbal Communication	Ch. 3
4	Listening as Communication	Ch. 4
5	Communicating Interpersonally	Ch. 5
6	Communicating in Small Groups	Ch. 6
7	Communicating in Organizations	Ch. 7
8	Communicating with Media	Ch. 8
9	Presenting One's Self Effectively	Ch. 9
10	Influencing Others	Ch. 10
11	Coping with Conflicts	Ch. 11
12	Overcoming Shyness and Apprehension	Ch. 12

Mastering Communication in Contemporary America:

Week	Topic	Readings
13	Preparing the Content	Ch. 13
14	Speaking Before a Group	Ch. 14
15*	Public Speaking: Polishing and Fine-Tuning Course Summary	Ch. 15

Fundamentals of Human Communication:

Week	Topic	Readings
13	Communicating in a Multicultural Society	Ch. 13
14	Understanding Mass Communication	Ch. 14
15	Conducting Communication Research Course Summary	Ch. 15

*Depending on the number of speeches or group activities assigned, you will want to rearrange your weekly course outline. For example, you may want to allow one 50-minute session for the presentation of *only* 6 or 7 student speeches, which are about 4–5 minutes in length.

[Be sure to include due dates for papers or other required activities/assignments. Also, indicate exam dates and times on this outline.]

TEACHING A QUARTER COURSE
10 WEEKS: 40-HOUR QUARTER
COURSE OUTLINE

Week	Topic	Read...
1	Introduction to Course: Syllabus, Overview, Purpose, and Course Requirements	
	The Communication Process: An Overview	Ch. 1
2	Verbal and Nonverbal Communication	Chs. 2–3
3	Listening as Communication Communicating Interpersonally	Chs. 4–5
4	Communicating in Small Groups and Organizations	Chs. 6–7
5	Communicating with Media	Ch. 8
6	Presenting One's Self Effectively Influencing Others	Chs. 9–10
7	Coping with Conflicts	Ch. 11

Mastering Communication in Contemporary America:

Week	Topic	Read...
8	Overcoming Shyness and Apprehension	Ch. 12
9	Preparing the Content and Speaking Before a Group	Chs. 13–14
10*	Public Speaking: Polishing and Fine-Tuning Course Summary	Ch. 15

Fundamentals of Human Communication:

Week	Topic	Read...
8	Overcoming Shyness and Apprehension Communicating in a Multicultural Society	Chs. 12–13
9	Understanding Mass Communication	Ch. 14
10	Conducting Communication Research	Ch. 15

*Depending on the number of speeches or group activities assigned, you will want to rearrange your weekly course outline. For example, you may want to allow one 50-minute session for the presentation of *only* 6 or 7 student speeches, which are about 4–5 minutes in length.

[Be sure to include due dates for papers or other required activities/assignments. Also, indicate exam dates and times on this outline.]

1 = PTaking Exercise
2 =
3 = NVC observation exercise
4 = attentional biases in listening

TEACHING TIPS FOR NEW TEACHERS

A GENERAL OVERVIEW OF TEACHING AND PLANNING

As a rule, many teachers are trained in subject or content competencies within their area of study, but few are required to have any formal background in teaching skills (McKeachie, 1986). Good and Brophy (1987) state that "many teachers fail to fulfill their potential . . . , not because they do not know the subject matter, but because they do not understand students or classrooms" (p. 3). They argue that more attention is needed in studying "action systems knowledge" rather than "subject matter knowledge." Action systems knowledge refers to skills for *planning* lessons, making decisions about lesson pace, explaining material clearly, and responding to individual differences in how students learn. In other words, there's more to teaching than the "what" of our content areas; we must also pay attention to "how" we relate that content to our students. We may all have a lot to teach, to say to our students, but we must also learn how to communicate what we know in our efforts to become more effective at what we do.

In this section we provide some general teaching tips or suggestions that will enable beginning teachers of the course to enter the classroom organized and prepared to meet the challenges of instruction. The key to good instruction is the ability to communicate effectively. Fortunately, that's our profession. Communication professionals like us have a "jumpstart" on teaching. Importantly, because we are communication specialists, our students will *expect* us to be excellent communicators and to provide them with communication role models for them to emulate. Every time we enter the classroom, then, we must remember to practice all that we know about interpersonal communication, small-group discussion, and public speaking.

LEARNING DOMAINS AND LEARNING OBJECTIVES

Learning Domains

In order to help teachers approach learning more systematically, types of learning can be grouped into three major categories: cognitive, affective, and psychomotor. These areas (or domains as they are generally called) are widely referred to in the literature that discusses learning objectives. Your understanding of the levels within each domain is important when planning a unit of instruction (Kemp, 1985). For your convenience, in Part II of this manual we have provided a list of learning objectives for each text chapter. Most of these objectives measure the cognitive domain of learning. However, you may wish to develop both affective and psychomotor learning objectives by incorporating activities and assignments to increase enjoyment of the topic and strengthen specific skills. To help you develop a better understanding of the use of learning objectives, we have provided a brief overview on learning domains and objectives.

The cognitive domain of learning focuses on intellectual abilities and skills. Six objectives are ordered in a hierarchy from simple to complex types of learning: knowledge, comprehension, application, analysis, synthesis, and evaluation (Bloom, Engelhart, Frost, Hill, & Krathwohl, 1956). Teachers tend to test this area more often as grade level increases. By the time students are in college, they are tested almost entirely on learning that occurs in this domain.

The affective domain focuses on students' attitudes toward the area of study and emphasizes the development of appreciation through changes in interests, attitudes, and values. That is, the objectives in the affective domain range from low levels of enjoyment or liking to higher levels of wanting to learn even more and applying the learning to other areas (Krathwohl, Bloom, & Masia, 1956). The hierarchy in the affective domain includes: receiving or attending to something; responding or showing some new behavior as a result of experience; valuing or showing some involvement or commitment; organization, or integrating a new value into one's general set of values; and characterization by value, which simply means the learner is acting consistently with the new value (Woolfolk & McCune-Nicolich, 1984). Unlike the cognitive domain, instruction in the affective domain is rarely strategically planned. However, students are likely to learn cognitively when they are predisposed to "like what they learn" as well (Kearney & McCroskey, 1980). By internalizing the value of specific content, students also tend to learn content-relevant (cognitive) information. Furthermore, the influence of affective goals often extends outside the classroom, such as positive attitudes toward the course, the course content, and the teacher. Consequently, teachers need to *plan* to enhance students' willingness or affective orientation to learn.

Until recently, the psychomotor domain has been overlooked by many teachers not involved in physical education. This domain of learning focuses on developing particular performance abilities or motor acts. Psychomotor outcomes include reflex movements (stretching), basic fundamental or inherent movements (walking), perceptual abilities (following verbal directions), physical abilities (distance running), skilled movements (dance), and nondiscursive communication (communication through movement; Harrow, 1972). Unless instruction is specifically directed toward the development of some movement or skill (welding, karate, or public speaking), the psychomotor domain is often dismissed, especially at the upper grade levels. Nevertheless, in skills-oriented communication courses, attention needs to be directed toward psychomotor outcomes of speech delivery, listening, and other verbal and nonverbal skills.

Because all three learning domains typically occur simultaneously, teachers need to recognize the importance of each outcome. Rather than restrict instruction to the cognitive domain, learning outcomes should result in a change in all three, including affective and psychomotor outcomes (Hurt, Scott, & McCroskey, 1978).

Learning Objectives

When instruction is based on the domains of learning, learning objectives should specifically define the desired/required behavior of the student. Behavioral objectives focus on observable changes, such as what the learner will be able to do: list, define, add, or calculate. Cognitive objectives are usually stated in terms of internal changes, such as understand, recognize, create, or apply. Nevertheless, both types of objectives are simply descriptions of changes in learners (Woolfolk & McCune-Nicolich, 1984). Therefore, if a student has "learned," he or she will be able to demonstrate the "defined" behavior.

Learning objectives serve several purposes: First, they provide a useful method of organizing course content. Second, they prescribe the level and type of learning requested from the student. And third, they assist in evaluation and test constructions (Woolfolk & McCune-Nicolich, 1984). Additional studies found that objectives serve as cues for learners to attend to relevant, as opposed to irrelevant or incidental, information (Kaplan, 1974; Kaplan & Rothkopf, 1974; Kaplan & Simmons, 1974; Rothkopf & Kaplan, 1972; cited in Lashbrook and Wheeless, 1978). Popham and Baker (1970) suggested that objectives may serve to increase student achievement while decreasing uncertainty and behavior problems. In summary, learning objectives clearly specify to the learner what is to be learned, how it is to be learned, and how he or she can be expected to be evaluated. Having a clear idea of what to focus on, students are more likely to spend more time studying. Therefore, they are more likely to achieve goals specified in the objectives (Woolfolk & McCune-Nicolich, 1984). Through such organization, the teacher and the students are better able to focus their attention and effort toward instruction and learning. Finally, evaluating instructor effectiveness and student learning becomes easier and more precise.

Writing learning objectives involves formulating a precise statement that answers the question "What should the learner have learned or be able to do upon completing the unit or chapter?" It is important to ask yourself this question each time you start to write an objective. To answer the question, it is necessary to write each learning objective with an *action verb* (to name, to operate, to compare), followed by the subject that describes the content being referenced (to name the parts of an informative speech). In some cases, you may want to be more specific by indicating the "performance standard" or any "conditions" under which evaluation will take place. For example: The student should be able to name the parts of an informative speech *in order* (performance standard) with 100% accuracy (conditions of evaluation). In many cases, the performance standards and conditions of evaluation are often understood by the teacher and the learner.

TESTING AND EVALUATION

Tests or exams are a very common method of evaluation, comprising a major part of students' total evaluation. When a teacher is measuring students on the cognitive domain, objective questions such as multiple choice, true/false, matching, and short answer are effective for measuring knowledge and comprehension. Such questions limit the number of possible interpretations at these lower cognitive levels. For this reason, responses to these questions are often easier to grade. Unfortunately, this is not the case for evaluating essays. Even so, we like to use essay questions because they effectively measure higher-order learning of application, synthesis, and evaluation.

Learning in the affective domain is also important to measure. Anonymous critiques, surveys, and feedback are effective means of gathering affective information. Because learning in this domain requires attitudinal and behavioral assessment, student anonymity is necessary to obtain truthful feedback (Katzer, Cook, & Crouch, 1982).

Through skill demonstration the psychomotor domain can be assessed. Performance tests that outline the skill(s) being evaluated can be administered along with or separate from other domain evaluations (e.g., speech criteria sheets).

All methods of evaluation are made easier when objectives are used to specify the expected learning outcomes. Specific test questions derived from learning objectives can be easily developed. Based on learning objectives, testing should occur frequently. This encourages the retention of information and appears to be more effective than simply spending a comparable amount of time reviewing and studying material (Nungester & Duchastel, 1982). Tests and other forms of evaluation (homework) indicate to the teacher if he or she has *successfully* taught. In turn, feedback from the teacher allows students to determine whether or not he or she has learned. Learning is enhanced by *immediate* feedback (Nash, Richmond, & Andriate, 1984; Woolfolk & McCune-Nicolich, 1984). That is, it is important to return examinations, papers, speech critiques, and assignments back to your students immediately (ASAP!).

Anxiety, an additional issue that concerns both students and teachers, is related to evaluation and feedback. A common occurrence in the classroom, fear of evaluation may inhibit learning (Hurt, Scott, & McCroskey, 1978; Woolfolk & McCune-Nicolich, 1984). Often the sources of anxieties experienced by students are beyond the teacher's control; that is, students may suffer from poor self-concepts, an overconcern for grades, negative reinforcement, repeated failure, or modeling behavior (Nash, Richmond, & Andriate, 1984). Instructors can help reduce evaluation anxiety by setting up situations that maximize the probability of success. By using learning objectives, numerous formative evaluations that have minor grade significance, advance study organizers for summative exams, and options within the exam to allow the students to demonstrate their best potential, instructors will help reduce students' anxiety.

Students are not the only people prone to evaluation anxiety. Instructors must deal with evaluations of their own performance from students, peers, society, and themselves (Branan, 1972; Mouly, 1973; Check, 1979). However, teachers can increase their chances of success, while decreasing their own level of anxiety, by planning and developing a sound and systematic course that includes learning objectives, numerous methods of student evaluation (exams, assignments, speeches, etc.), and well-developed lectures that are rehearsed.

GETTING STARTED: THE FIRST DAY/WEEK OF CLASSES

In this section, we briefly outline a list of issues and/or questions a new teacher may want to consider and answer before beginning the first day/week of class.

Teacher/Student Concerns

1. Teachers' special concerns
   a. Will they think I'm smart?
   b. Will they know how inexperienced I am?
   c. Will they do what I ask them to do?
   d. Will they like me/approve of me/be my friend?

2. Students' special concerns
   a. Will this be a "nice" teacher? Easy to talk to? Easily accessible?
   b. How hard will the class be? How much work do I have to do?
   c. Will this teacher be fair?
   d. Is this class going to be fun?
   e. How relevant is the information going to be?
   f. How will grades be determined?
   g. How many papers, speeches, and exams? What type of exams?

Getting Started on the Right Foot (Impression Formation)

1. Appearance (clothing and grooming)

   Our physical appearance or general attractiveness is one of the most influential cues for initial interactions. Within the classroom context, perceptions of both teacher and students are influenced by nonverbal messages revealed through our appearance. In general, informal but well-dressed teachers are perceived as more sympathetic, friendly, and flexible. On the other hand, teachers dressed formally (suits) are often viewed as being more knowledgeable, organized, and well prepared in the classroom. For most teachers, it is recommended that they start the semester/quarter dressed more formally and relax the dress code as time goes by. However, we warn against trying to dress too much like your students; your colleagues, and many of your students as well, will want you to look professional at all times.

2. Credibility induction

   Credibility refers to how believable a teacher is perceived to be. Within the instructional context, the believability of the teacher has a major impact on learning. Five dimensions of credibility have been identified: competence, character (trustworthy), sociability, extroversion, and composure. In general, teachers should strive to be perceived as knowledgeable, honest, friendly, outgoing, and relaxed.

3. Immediacy

   Immediacy is defined as the degree of perceived physical and psychological closeness between people (Mehrabian, 1971). In essence, immediate behaviors produce reciprocal liking. Both verbal and nonverbal behaviors have been linked to perceived immediacy of teachers in the classroom. Researchers found immediate teachers to communicate at closer distances, engage in more eye contact, smile, face students, use more gestures and overall body movements, touch others, have a relaxed body posture, and to be vocally expressive.

Teachers' verbal behaviors related to perceptions of immediacy include the following: using humor; praising students' work/actions or comments; initiating and/or being willing to become engaged in conversations with students before, after, or outside of class; self-disclosing; asking questions or encouraging students to talk; soliciting students' opinions; following up on student-initiated topics; referring to the class as "our" class and what "we" are doing; providing feedback on students' work; asking students how they feel about class procedures; inviting students to telephone or meet with them outside of class and using students' names.

Adding Students to Your Class

1. In theory (Check your department's policy and follow it.)
2. In practice (How can I say no when there's still physical space available?). Explain to your students that in order for you and your students to successfully complete the course requirements, only a limited number of students can be actively enrolled. Overenrolling your class only shortchanges your students.

Teaching the Syllabus

Explain to your students that the course syllabus is a written *contract* between you and your students. Be sure to "teach" or "explain" each and every detail of your course requirements! In fact, some institutions require that you go over the syllabus aloud with your students the first week of class to make sure they understand the rules and procedures of your course.

Components of a Syllabus (See Sample Syllabus)

1. Title of course, catalog course description
2. Course objectives and goals
3. Time and place course meets
4. Office location/office hours/phone
5. Textbook (complete APA reference)
6. Course requirements
   a. Attendance policy
   b Exams: number and types of questions
   c. Speeches: number and types of speeches
   d. Activities: number and types of activities
   e. Papers: number and types of papers
7. Excused/unexcused absences? Tardiness?
8. Should attendance be graded?
9. Should "class participation" be graded?
10. Extra credit assignments?
11. Make-ups?
12. Rewrites/respeak options?
13. Grading policy, point system, weighted grades
14. Topic/weekly outline
15. Reading assignments
16. Due dates: exams, speeches, assignments

Teacher Idiosyncratic Rules

Not all rules and procedures in a course have good, sound instructional reasons behind them. They should. But we recognize that we are only human and there are some behaviors or practices that may annoy us. For those behaviors you are unable to ignore or tolerate, be sure to tell your students what you prefer instead. Tell them your special concerns or requirements. You may want all papers turned in to be stapled; late students should knock before entering your room (or wait outside til the student speaker is finished). You may want them to call you by your professional title or by your first name. And so on. Whatever the idiosyncracy, tell them what you want instead. You'll save yourself a lot of hassle and your students some embarrassment if you both understand the rules and procedures of the course right away.

Setting the Tone/Pace of the First Day/Week

The first day/week of class is often characterized by a lot of administrative duties. Try to relax and enjoy yourself the first day/week of classes. Be firm but friendly. Get to know your students. Take time to learn their names, where they are from, why they are interested (or not interested) in taking your course. Find out if they have any special problems or concerns. Try to reduce their anxieties about taking your class.

At the same time, give them some information about yourself. Besides letting them know some of your own professional credentials (be careful not to brag, and yet, don't sell yourself short), tell them a little about your own life. Do you have children? How many? How old? What about pets? Hobbies? Favorite local restaurants and shops? When selecting what information to disclose and what information to withhold, keep in mind one important principle: Students like to hear good things about us—what we like, as opposed to what we don't like. They like for us to stimulate and promote a positive, warm, supportive climate.

PART II
LEARNING OBJECTIVES AND EXTENDED LECTURE OUTLINES

CHAPTER 1
THE COMMUNICATION PROCESS: AN OVERVIEW

LEARNING OBJECTIVES

After studying the chapter, the student should be able to:

- Understand and discuss how speech and language distinguish humans from animals.

- Discuss why effective communication skills are even more important today than in the past.

- Define the general or comparative perspective of communication.

- Define human communication and describe how it differs from the comparative definition.

- List and discuss the components of the human communication definition, such as process, symbols, nonverbal signs, contextual cues, and meanings.

- Understand and discuss the *linear model of communication*.

- Identify and discuss the five stages in the communication process.

- Define and discuss the term *meanings*.

- Distinguish between *traces* and *schemata*.

- Define and discuss the term *perception*.

- Define and discuss the term *feedback*.

- Understand and discuss the *simultaneous transactions model of communication*.

- Be familiar with the six basic propositions involved in the transactions model of communication.

- Understand and discuss the connection between accurate and distorted communication.

- Identify and explain the factors that create distortion.

- Explain the index of fidelity.

- Discuss how we can live with limited accuracy.

- Distinguish between surface and deep meanings.

EXTENDED CHAPTER OUTLINE

This chapter focuses on the basics of the communication process. A theoretical framework that integrates the "linear" and "transactions" models of communication is developed.

I. The significance of communication in contemporary life.
  A. Speech and language as the foundation for thought and society.
    1. The ability to use words to convey internal ideas from one person to another is what separates human beings from animals. Human beings are social by nature and they use language as a basis of their group life. Although sounds used by people may be imitated by some animals (parrots, for example), animals cannot use them to communicate in the same manner as human beings.
    2. The process of thinking for human beings is also dependent upon the use of words because they "stand as signs of internal conceptions." Consequently, the use of speech and language is a necessary condition for organizing human society, and for engaging in imagination and individual thought.
  B. Communication skills in an information society.
    1. In today's society a command of effective communication skills is critical. In fact, skills in communicating with others have become far more important than those skills that involve working with one's hands. Since the beginning of the 20th century, we have entered into the "information society." That is, people spend more time and energy manipulating symbols, words, and numbers than they do in manufacturing "things."
    2. In such an information society the ability to communicate effectively is vital to achieving success. Effective communication includes a command of skills related to the use of speech and language, and nonverbal components.
    3. Critical communication skills involve both sending and receiving messages, thus making both talking and listening equally important skills. Moreover, it is also important to understand that communication always occurs in some kind of context.
    4. One's communication style, habits, and abilities are built up over an entire lifetime and are resistant to change. However, with knowledge and practice, it is possible to learn to communicate more effectively.

II. Defining communication.
  A. General or comparative perspective: Communication occurs when one organism (the source) encodes information into a signal which passes to another organism (the receiver) who decodes the signal and is capable of responding appropriately.
  B. Human communication: A process during which source individuals initiate messages using conventionalized symbols, nonverbal signs, and contextual cues to express meanings by transmitting information in such a way that similar or parallel understandings are constructed by the receiving party or parties toward whom the messages are directed.
    1. Process: A series of stages in which something undergoes transformation at each step.
    2. Symbols: Words, numbers and other marks, objects, or signs to which we have learned to associate patterned meanings that by established conventions are shared by other members of our language community.
    3. Contextual cues: A physical setting and/or social situation in which communication takes place.

4. Meanings: Form of internal or subjective behavior that occurs as responses to words or other standardized signs and signals.
    a. Parallel: Occurs when the communication is accurate, similar in meaning.
    b. Distortion: Occurs when the communication is different in meaning, with limited accuracy.

III. Stages in the communication process: A linear model.

A linear model is a careful and succinct description that summarizes a process that moves like a straight line, from a beginning to an end through specific stages. Although the linear view is oversimplified, it provides a model to begin an analysis of the basic principles involved in communication. Essentially, the linear view of human communication involves the following five stages:

A. Deciding on the message.

A person who will serve as a source decides on a message to be sent to a receiver(s) so as to achieve a desired goal.

B. Encoding the intended meanings.

The source searches his or her memory for specific words and gestures and their associated meanings that can be put together in a pattern that will describe the desired facts, ideas, and images.

1. The meaning of meaning.

The nature of meaning is a subjective behavior, which cannot be directly observed. There are several assumptions that can help clarify the concept.
    a. One can experience (respond) to the reality firsthand through the senses.
    b. One can have similar experiences indirectly as a response to the symbol that labels that aspect of reality.
    c. Meanings defined: Subjective responses that individuals learn to make, either to objects, events, or situations in reality that they experience through their senses, or to socially shared symbols that are used to label those aspects of reality.

2. Symbols and meanings in memory.

A message is made up of a number of organized schemata, developed initially from the meanings associated with each word (traces), and put together in a combination that is assembled according to shared and understood rules of grammar and syntax.
    a. Traces are imprinted records of experiences registered in the brain by electro-chemical activities of its nerve cells.
    b. Schemata (schema) refers to a pattern or configuration of traces of meanings that have been put together in an organized way and recorded in a person's mental storage.

3. Role-taking to assess probable interpretations:

An activity of a sender by which the likelihood is assessed that a receiver will be able to interpret the intentions and meanings of a particular form of a message.

4. Encoding as automated behavior: The encoding process is fast and occurs unconsciously.

C. Transmitting the message.

The message is transformed by voice (or other means) into physical information (like sound waves) so that it can overcome distance. The message moves in this form from sender to receiver.

D. Receiving the message.

The receiver attends to the physical information as it arrives and identifies the symbols into which it has been encoded.

1. Receiver: A person who attends to, perceives, and interprets (decodes) the message information transmitted by a source.

2. Perception: The psychological process of seeing, hearing, or feeling something (with the senses) and then identifying it within the interpretations provided by one's language and culture.

E. Decoding, or interpreting, the message.

The receiver searches and compares the incoming symbols with meanings stored in her or his memory and selects those which seem best for interpreting the message.

1. Decodes: The assignment of meaning to symbols perceived by a receiver in the communication process.

2. Active reconstruction of meanings: Understandings and interpretations stored in the memory of the receiver.

3. Feedback: Messages provided in an ongoing manner by a receiver in response to a message being transmitted by a source or sender. Such messages may be verbal or nonverbal.

IV. Interactive communication: A simultaneous transactions model.

Any kind of exchange—that is, an activity that occurs between, and mutually influences, all parties acting together in some way at the same time. Six basic propositions can be used to sum up the simultaneous transactions model:

A. Simultaneous encoding and decoding: All of the involved parties act as both senders and receivers at the same time.

B. Simultaneous role-taking and feedback: These processes take place as each party decodes messages and encodes replies at the same time.

C. Simultaneous influences of prior communication: What people say to each other and the way they respond during a given transaction depends greatly on what has been said previously.

D. Simultaneous influences of physical settings: People communicate differently in distinct kinds of places.

E. Simultaneous influences of social situations: What people say is almost always a part of an ongoing social situation, such as a date, family dinner, or work activity.

F. Simultaneous influences of social relationships: Both long-term relationships between marrieds or friends as well as newly established relationships among strangers or coworkers, will have a significant influence on their transaction.

V. Achieving accurate communication.

Totally accurate communication is rarely achieved. Complete and accurate communication occurs only if the total combination of traits and schematic configurations of meanings intended and developed by a source is identical to the combination constructed and experienced by a receiver.

A. Factors creating distortion.

1. Defining distortion: An outcome of communication in which meanings intended by the source become compounded with, or displaced by, unintended implications as the meanings of the message are constructed by a receiver.

2. Verbal: Poor choices of spoken, written, or printed symbols and patterns (grammar and syntax).

3. Nonverbal communication: Both intentional and unintentional body language and facial cues are easily misinterpreted.

4. Context: The social and physical setting within which communication takes place can introduce cues into the process, which may modify any given communication interaction.

B. An index of fidelity: A conceptual model that measures the degree to which the sender's and receiver's combinations of memory traces and schemata for encoding and decoding are identical or alike.

C. Living with limited accuracy: Perfect accuracy is not necessary in most situations. This is because most message transactions result in arousal of deep meaning that serves the practical needs of the communicator. In any message there is both a surface meaning and a deep meaning.

1. Surface meaning: The entire set of meanings that are encoded into a source's message, whether they are essential to understanding its basic ideas or not.

2. Deep meaning: The basic ideas implied by a message that can be understood well enough for practical purposes.

VI. Chapter review.

CHAPTER 2
VERBAL COMMUNICATION

LEARNING OBJECTIVES

After studying the chapter, the student should be able to:

- Define and discuss how the *phylogenetic continuum* is related to human beings and language.
- Understand and discuss how communication based on *inherited behavior systems* differs from communication *learned* through signs and symbols.
- Explain how animals may use their *senses* to communicate.
- Define and explain *instinctual communication*.
- Distinguish between *signs* and *symbols*.
- Explain how meanings for *natural signs* are acquired.
- Discuss the implications of animal studies with regard to *language* and *communication*.
- Define and discuss the term *semantics*.
- Discuss how *meanings* are acquired.
- Define and discuss how *concepts* are configurations of meanings.
- Explain how concepts are related to *perceptions*.
- Define and discuss the term *symbols*.
- Understand and discuss the principle of *arbitrary selection*.
- Understand and discuss the principle of *conventions*.
- Explain the *meaning triangle*.
- Distinguish between *denotative* and *connotative* meanings.
- Discuss the *structural features* of language (vocabulary, grammar, syntax, and redundancy).
- Discuss the conclusions you can draw regarding language and communication by human beings and animals.

EXTENDED CHAPTER OUTLINE

This chapter compares and contrasts human and animal communication. It clarifies the nature of language and shows in detail how human beings uniquely use symbolic processes to arouse and share parallel meanings.

I. Communicating without language.

Virtually every creature in the world uses some set of techniques to communicate. There are essentially two ways in which they do this: Some animals inherit their communication abilities through genetic endowment, whereas others learn to communicate through signs and signals. This unit discusses both inherited and learned skills.

Early in the 20th century, a controversy developed over whether or not animals could use language. By 1866, the evolutionary theory of a phylogenetic continuum developed, which states that animals can be arranged along a kind of scale in terms of the complexity of their bodily structures and organization. Soon numerous comparative studies were done to determine how human beings were positioned on that continuum relative to animals. Consequently, an examination of the phylogenetic continuum provides an important comparison and contrast with the tools of communication used by human beings.

A. Communicating with inherited behavior systems.

Animal communication based on inherited biological systems is common and effective for survival. Insects are good examples of animals that communicate effectively with one another to find food, protect themselves from danger, and provide for reproduction. A distinction between the use of senses and genetically determined abilities can be argued.

1. The use of senses.
    a. Sense of smell: Insects, like humans, depend upon their senses in order to communicate. They receive sounds, see light, feel objects, and detect odors. For the insect species, the sense of smell is the most important sense for communication. Chemical secretions (called pheromones) are used by insects and other animals in the communication process. These pheromones are released in the air, or deliberately used to mark trails, territory, or readiness for mating.
    b. Sense of sight: Insects, especially bees, depend heavily on sight. For example, bees perform a variety of "dances" to indicate the distance and direction to food sources.
    c. In comparison, the senses of human beings are not as keen as those of insects. Humans' most acute sense is sight, which is used to detect nonverbal cues. However, our verbal communication is based primarily on the production and detection of sound. Because humans also use the senses of touch and smell, as well as sight and sound, to communicate with other individuals, in some ways human and insect communication are similar.

2. Genetically determined abilities.

Adaptive behavior patterns that are inherited, unlearned, and universal in a species are often called *instincts*. The nearly total dependence on instinctual forms of communication makes insects unlike other animals along the phylogenetic continuum. While higher animals may use some instinctual patterns in many aspects of their behavior, they are much more dependent upon learning in order to adapt to their environment.

B. Communicating with learned signs and signals.

1. Learning to signal.
    a. Sign: An event in the environment that animals (and human beings) learn to associate with and use to anticipate subsequent events.
    b. Signal: A noise or patterned movement that animals can make to which animals like themselves can respond.
    c. While instincts are very important to many animals, communication is limited to signs based on patterned movements and sounds that may be acquired in part by learning but which are limited by inheritance.

2. Acquiring meanings for natural signs.
   a. Many animals can detect a large number of complex natural signs to which they learn appropriate responses. Natural signs are simply those signs or associations that occur in the species' environments, such as danger or the presence of food.
   b. Natural signs used by animals are not arbitrarily selected by the animals, nor are their meanings shared by conventions among themselves.
   c. Thus, human language has technical features (such as words, rules, and patterns) that set it apart from the communication systems used by even the highest animal on the continuum. Left on their own, animals have never developed language. They communicate by other means, such as pheromones, inherited behavior patterns, learned natural signs, or a combination of all three.

II. The controversy over whether animals can use language.
A. Intelligent creatures in the sea.

The category of mammals known as cetaceans, which includes large and small whales, porpoises, and dolphins, has been studied by many to determine if their "noises" are in fact a secret language.

1. Communication among whales.

Although many would like to believe that whales have their own language and are very intelligent, little scientific evidence has been established to date.

2. Dolphins as communicators.

In particular, bottlenose dolphins have been studied extensively. Several studies have demonstrated that dolphins have the ability to mimic human vocal sounds and to associate word-sounds with ideas, such as "fetch the hoop from the bottom." Consequently, we can assume that these mammals are intelligent by comparison with other members of the animal kingdom, but we cannot assume they approach human beings. They do respond to signs in complex ways, but there is little evidence to suggest that they use a secret language.

B. Trying to teach apes to talk.

1. Assessing ape intelligence.

The classic study by Wolfgang Kohler examined the problem-solving abilities of chimpanzees. Although he found that chimps could solve a number of problems, such as stacking boxes to reach for food and breaking off or using a tree branch to rake a banana to a cage, and solve a number of similar spatial and tool-using problems, he concluded that they are far behind human beings in levels of intelligence.

2. The early language experiments.

Several studies were performed by scientists to see if a chimpanzee could learn to speak. Scientists initially argued that the reason chimps could not speak naturally was because they are not raised in a language environment. Thus, researchers attempted to raise chimps in homes. The home-rearing experiments with Gua and Vicki clearly demonstrated that the animals have difficulty speaking because their vocal physiology is not up to forming speech sounds. Quite simply, apes are not going to learn to talk; their bodies are not designed for it.

3. Ameslan and Yerkish.

Although apes are not up to speaking, they are better at manual dexterity than young human beings. Consequently, numerous studies attempted to teach apes "sign" language (Ameslan = American Sign Language or Yerkish = an artificial language used with a computer keyboard). Results indicated that apes could learn to sign, but were restricted to the here and now, never referring to the past or future. In addition, no evidence illustrated that they could understand syntax. Sign language for apes seems to be an adaptive behavior used for achieving specific goals.

C. Implications of the animal studies.

Attempts to teach animals like chimpanzees to talk have not been successful. They cannot generate the complex sounds required. Numerous attempts have been made to communicate with primates. Such efforts have based communication on movements or actions animals can make, such as signing in the manner of the deaf, using plastic symbols or even computerized systems to probe the potentials of primate ability to communicate with something like language. All such attempts are mired in deep controversy. Statistical analysis of patterns of "words" put together by chimps in experiments shows random distributions. At present it seems there is no convincing evidence for language ability among animals. While animals do communicate extensively, and often very effectively for the purposes they need in life, they do so in ways that do not parallel those used by people.

D. Human beings without language.

Human beings require language in order to develop normally. If they are denied such an environment, thought, perceptions, and social relationships are impaired. Thus, they remain at an animal-like level.

Two important lessons are derived from the two examples listed below. First, human beings, like animals, are limited in their development of communication skills by their inherited capacities. Second, high learning capacity is not enough. The ability to use speech develops only in the social environment of a language community. Even an intelligent human being reared in isolation will be unable to communicate beyond an animal level if she/he is denied access to a language culture.

1. The case of "Anna." See pages 47–48.
2. The case of "Isabelle." See pages 48–49.

III. The semantics of human communication with language.

Semantics is the study of relationships between words and their meanings, and of rules that can add meaning when human beings use language for verbal communication.

A. The world outside and the meanings in our heads.

Knowing "reality" means acquiring internal and subjective experiences, images, or understandings—that is, personal meanings that are our responses to objects, events, and situations existing outside our heads. However, verbal communication also requires a system of symbols. Symbols are verbal labels that are used by participants within a language community to arouse standardized meanings for aspects of reality.

1. How meanings are acquired.

Learning is the basis for language use. The internal images and other experiences we have for aspects of reality are acquired by both systematic and random experiences. Meanings are made up of remembered aspects of things, events, or situations that exist outside ourselves. Those aspects of reality are recorded and stored for later recovery in biochemical processes governed by the brain. As a result, "traces" are imprinted in our brain. Traces are those elements of meaning that we associate with an external object and with a label for that object. For instance, color, sound, or picture may be traces for a television.

2. Concepts as configurations of meanings.

A concept is a label that stands for and signifies a set of objects, situations, or events that can logically be grouped together and thought of as making up a class or category because they share similar properties or attributes, such as a word. By using symbols, human beings attach labels to concepts. The use of concepts is at the heart of the human ability to communicate with the use of language.

Concepts differ from schema or meanings in that concepts imply a process of abstraction. Concepts are also shared with other individuals who have parallel or similar sets of meanings for labeled classes. Therefore, an extended concept can be defined as a set or configuration of attributes by which any particular instance of a whole class of similar objects or events can be recognized.

3. Concepts as the basis of perception.

Individuals recognize instances of concepts in the process of perception, or "attach meaning" to stimuli which have come in contact with their senses. However, meanings can also be aroused by hearing a word or concept, reading about it, or even thinking about it.

B. Symbols and their referents.

1. Symbols as labels for meanings.

Symbols are socially agreed upon labels that we use to arouse meanings for concepts stored in schemata within our memory system. Symbols include nonverbal symbols and signs.

2. The principle of arbitrary selection.

The sounds and/or letters used to form words that refer to particular meanings within a given language are not initially selected by clear rules; instead, words are selected at random or even in capricious ways. Once selected and established in use, however, the relationship between word and referent becomes fixed.

3. The principle of conventions.

A convention is a rule that people of a given language community agree to follow. Therefore, once an association between a symbol and its referent has been established, it becomes fixed by convention. To establish such conventions and preserve them over time, dictionaries are used to provide relatively fixed meanings for symbols. See the meaning triangle (pages 56–58) for further elaboration.

4. Denotative versus connotative meanings.
   a. Denotative meanings, established by conventions, are aroused and experienced by a particular symbol. Also known as standardized meanings.
   b. Connotative meanings are personal or unshared meanings that an individual uniquely associates with a referent because of past experiences.

C. Structural features of language.

1. Vocabulary: The building blocks of language.

Every known language has an extensive vocabulary—a long list of symbol-referent conventions for communicating about various aspects of the physical and social world.

2. Grammar: Rules for constructing conventional patterns.

Grammar rules are the formation of different variants of symbols (tenses, verb forms, and so on) into grammatically acceptable forms, and are used for arranging them into conventionalized sequences.

3. Syntax: The architecture of language.

   Syntax refers to rules for ordering words in a sentence or an expression in such a way that their meaning is clear.
4. Redundancy.

   Redundancy in language occurs when one uses more words in a message than are actually needed to express deep meanings. A condition of excess, duplication, or abundance.

IV. Chapter review.

CHAPTER 3
NONVERBAL COMMUNICATION

LEARNING OBJECTIVES

After studying the chapter, the student should be able to:

- Understand and discuss the relationship between *verbal* and *nonverbal* communication.

- Define and discuss the term *nonverbal communication*.

- Explain the mystique surrounding nonverbal communication and our *true feelings*.

- Identify and discuss the four functions of nonverbal communication commonly used with our verbal messages (complementing, regulating, substituting, and contradicting).

- Explain what is meant by *framing* our verbalization.

- Define and explain the term *symbiosis*.

- Discuss and provide examples of how the *body* communicates messages.

- Define and discuss the term *artifacts*.

- Explain how *artifacts* are used to communicate meanings to others about our personal and social attributes.

- Discuss how *clothing* is used to communicate status and power, social acceptability, occupational roles, sexual attractiveness, and inner feelings.

- Define and discuss the terms *kinesics, vocalics, oculesics, proxemics, haptics,* and *chronemics*.

- Distinguish among *emblems, illustrators,* and *adapters*.

- Discuss how accents and tone of voice influence our judgments about others.

- Explain how eye contact can communicate both positive and negative feelings toward others.

- Discuss how feelings of embarrassment, guilt, and sadness are communicated through eye contact.

- Distinguish between *territoriality* and *personal space*.

- Differentiate between *primary or exclusive space* and *temporary space*.

- Identify Edward T. Hall's four zones of *interpersonal distance*.

- Explain how distances are used differently according to various age, gender, cultural, and socioeconomic groups.

- Explain and discuss *encroachment*.

- Discuss the effects of *touch deprivation* on human beings.

- Discuss how the amount of touch changes throughout one's life.

- Identify and explain the benefits of touch to human beings.

- Discuss some of the dangers of touch.

- Understand and discuss the terms *touch avoiders* and *touch approachers*.

- Distinguish between *biological* and *psychological* time orientations.

- Describe *temporal* time and time *intervals*.

- Understand and discuss communication as an integrated process.

- Define and discuss *nonverbal immediacy*.

- Identify and list those nonverbal behaviors that lead to nonverbal immediacy.

- Understand and discuss the *immediacy principle*.

- Explain how the immediacy principle may be applied.

- Identify the two drawbacks of using immediacy behaviors.

EXTENDED CHAPTER OUTLINE

This chapter discusses how nonverbal signs and signals function in the simultaneous transactions model of human communication. The chapter will review how all parties in communication transactions use nonverbal cues to modify meanings in messages conveyed by words.

I. The relationship between verbal and nonverbal communication.

Nonverbal communication can be defined as the *deliberate or unintentional use of objects, actions, sounds, time, and space so as to arouse meanings in others.* Nonverbal communication provides meanings that alter, amplify, or limit people's understandings of the words they use. Nonverbal behaviors, like our words, are part of the human communication process—one that cannot be separated from our spoken language.

Although some scholars argue that meanings transmitted by nonverbal means may contribute as much as 90% to our interpretations of the behavior of others, we argue that neither the verbal nor the nonverbal dimension of communication should be interpreted at the expense of the other.

There is also a mystique surrounding nonverbal communication. This idea claims that nonverbal behaviors reveal our "true" feelings and intentions while our words tend to hide the truth. Importantly, this idea is not supported in fact. Verbal and nonverbal transmission rely on an interrelated system of symbols and signals with which people communicate their meanings to others. The following four functions demonstrate how nonverbal cues are commonly used to extend, enrich, or modify our verbal messages to others:

A. Complementing our verbal meanings.

The most frequently obtained relationship between verbal and nonverbal communication is that the two complement, supplement, or reinforce each other.

1. Framing: Nonverbal communication serves to "frame" our verbalization. That is, the use of nonverbal gestures or other actions while talking emphasizes, complements, and reinforces what we are saying (for example, rolling our eyes or shrugging our shoulders). Framing assists others in understanding the emotional meanings that we attach to the messages we are sending.

B. Regulating verbal interaction.

While supplementing the meanings of our verbal messages may be the most obvious use of nonverbal behaviors, one of the most subtle is in the regulation of our conversations. Regulating involves using nonverbal signs and signals as informal "rules of order" to regulate the flow of talk among people who are communicating verbally.

For example, we use turn-taking and turn-yielding cues to decide whose turn it is to talk, when to start, or when to stop. Specific examples include looking at or looking away, a change in voice tempo and volume, or a hand gesture to slow down or speed up.

C. Substituting actions for words.

Occasionally we substitute actions for words. For example, people commonly use facial expressions or nonverbal gestures to communicate such emotions as disgust, hostility, or love. In American society, many nonverbal gestures have straightforward meanings that can be translated into direct verbal terms, known as "emblems." (This is discussed further under "kinesics.")

D. Contradicting our verbal meanings.

Sometimes our nonverbal actions or expressions openly contradict what we are transmitting verbally. Rather than being "accidental," this form of nonverbal communication is usually deliberate. That is, people are usually aware when they are sending or receiving contradictory nonverbal cues.

Some people believe that our nonverbal messages are both unwitting and unintentional. This leads them to believe that the "true" meanings of our verbal messages are revealed by nonverbal cues. However, the reliance on nonverbal cues can lead to both uncertainty and misunderstandings.

Deception detection is another area that focuses on nonverbal cues that somehow "leak" the truth. Some people maintain that it is possible to identify nonverbal gestures, expressions, and postures that indicate when an individual is lying (such as using a polygraph test). However, research results are inconsistent.

Sarcasm is a way in which verbal and nonverbal messages can convey different meanings. Adults understand this mode of communication very well, but children and adolescents are unskilled in identifying true meanings and interpret the "literal" meaning of the message.

E. Interpreting nonverbal communication.

The relationship between verbal and nonverbal communication is primarily one of *symbiosis*, that is, mutual dependence. Understanding the process of nonverbal communication can help us to communicate more effectively. Not understanding the importance of nonverbal communication can lead to confusion and misunderstandings.

One reason that speaking as a mode of communication is often more effective than written messages is that we can include nonverbal cues to enrich and to add emphasis to our meanings. That is, when written communication is used, the *absence* of nonverbal communication can pose problems. However, the absence of nonverbal cues on even the most basic level of interactions can leave us insecure and without complete understanding.

II. The use of "things" in nonverbal communication.

Three major nonverbal strategies are used to indicate to others information about ourselves or about some other topic that we want them to interpret. All three strategies involve the use of *things*, which may be manipulated, modified, selected, or excluded by the sender to communicate an intended message.

A. The body as message.

The body itself is at center stage in our nonverbal communication with others. Our body is available to us as a communication device. While some body-related messages can be controlled through various means (e.g., diet, exercise, surgery, cosmetics, and/or medications), others (e.g., age, height, skin color, general body configuration, and in some cases weight) are not subject to voluntary change but still carry nonverbal messages. Consequently, the amount of manipulation and change possible depends on how far an individual wants to go and what he or she wants to communicate to others.

B. Arousing meaning with artifacts.

Artifacts are those physical objects we possess, such as jewelry, handbags, pens, and briefcases (or even homes, cars, and offices), that provide meanings to others about our personal and social attributes. Artifacts are used in our society to signal one's position in the social order. This translates for the most part into messages about wealth, status, and power.

Artifacts or objects we use to arouse such meanings are the various things we buy, use, and display, which may include expensive homes, furniture, and automobiles. On a smaller scale, artifacts may include eyeglasses, jewelry (rings, earrings, or necklaces/chains), and briefcases. These items communicate to others where we belong in the social class system, something about our financial resources, background, hobbies, and interests.

C. The social meaning of clothing.

Clothing is one of the most meaningful artifacts we use to communicate nonverbally. Since the dawn of history, people have defined their rank, power, resources, personal tastes, and group membership with the clothing they wear. Today, we dress to communicate such meanings as status and power, social acceptability, occupational roles, sexual attractiveness, and inner feelings.

1. Communicating status and power.

Subtle codes of dress have come into use for both women and men. Clothing distinguishes between those who perceive themselves to have more refined tastes and those who do not understand or who choose to ignore the rules of "proper" dress. For example, in business men and women have "rules" for proper attire (e.g., dark business suit, conservative blouse, hosiery, and plain shoes with high heels for women; somber gray or dark blue suit, subdued tie, knee stockings and shoes that match the suit for men).

The men and women who feel that appropriate dress is important are likely to be the ones who are "in charge." The way in which we dress may influence the way we are treated even in the most casual encounters (in stores, banks, car dealerships, etc.).

2. Dressing to fit in.

Besides dressing to communicate status and power, we dress to be socially acceptable— to fit in with different kinds of groups. Some examples include those occupational categories that require uniforms (nurses, police officers, and airline pilots). However, informal "uniforms" are worn by those involved in recreational activities (e.g., tennis, sailing, riding, and hunting), which require different "costumes."

3. Personal attire and sexual attractiveness.

Using clothing to try to communicate sexual attractiveness is still common today. Although we may argue that we dress to please ourselves, take a look at the clothing we choose to wear (e.g., shoes, ties, button-up shirts, etc.).

4. Communicating inner feelings.

Clothing is often used to communicate how we feel—or at least how we want others to think we feel. For example, we wear black to funerals to communicate grief and respect and conservative clothes to church to communicate religious concern; or consider the politician who wears a farm jacket and feed-company hat to look like one of the plain folks.

Generally, clothing is far more than something we wear for modesty or protection from the cold. The nonverbal use of clothing is governed by conventions that define what is acceptable or unacceptable attire for hundreds of professions, situations, and social activities. It can be used to enhance sexual attractiveness, and on many occasions, it sends messages about our inner feelings.

III. "Actions" that communicate.

A number of actions, postures, and activities are part of the nonverbal dimension of human communication.

A. Body movements and gestures: Kinesics.

The study of body movements, including gestures, posture, and facial expressions, is called *kinesics*. A person's overall body orientation or posture typically communicates his or her level of interest, liking, and openness.

1. Emblems: A category of nonverbal gestures that has established conventions of meaning providing direct verbal translations (e.g., putting your index finger to your lips = be quiet).

2. Illustrators: A category of nonverbal gestures that includes hand and arm movements which demonstrate and reinforce meanings intended by verbal messages (e.g., using your hands and arms to show just how "big" the fish was that got away!).

3. Adapters: A category of nonverbal gestures that includes unintentional hand, arm, leg, or other body movements used to reduce stress or relieve boredom (e.g., pencil tapping or nail biting while waiting in a doctor's office).

B. Nonverbal uses of the voice: Vocalics.

The study of the nonverbal uses of the voice is known as vocalics. Simply stated, how you say something can at times be as important as what you say. Nonverbal cues can take many forms—pitch, tone, rate, volume, and accent patterns in speech all make big differences in how verbal messages are interpreted. Accents, for example, can cause numerous problems in judging the intelligence, emotions, and personalities of people who speak in ways that seem different and strange to us. In fact, people who have either a midwestern or southern accent are often characterized as lazy or ignorant. However, no relationship between regional and ethnic accent and level of intelligence exists. Finally, tone of voice influences the judgments we make about people's emotional states. Research suggests that negative emotions (anger, disappointment, sadness) are more easily identified from vocal cues than are positive emotions (happiness, relief, excitement).

C. Eye contact as communication: Oculesics.

Oculesics refers to the study of eye contact and pupil dilation in nonverbal communication. People use their eyes to indicate their degree of interest, openness, and even arousal as they communicate. Even though eye contact generally communicates positive feelings toward another, lengthy eye gaze or staring can be interpreted as a sign of hostility or aggression. Because we can communicate both emotional extremes (anger or love) we have to look to other communicative behaviors to determine the particular emotion revealed.

Research in deception detection has failed to support the popular lore that the lack of eye contact is a certain clue that someone is lying. However, we do gaze at others less when we feel embarrassment, guilt, or sadness. Another effect of eye contact on others is that it obligates them to talk. For example, when a professor asks a question in class, a student can avoid answering by quickly looking away.

D. Using space and distance: Proxemics.

The study of the meanings communicated by space and distance is called proxemics. Two uses of space are important in understanding human communication behavior: territoriality and personal space.

1. Territoriality: A tendency common to both animals and human beings in which they define some fixed or semifixed space to claim or stake out as their own. As individuals, we feel that some territory belongs to us exclusively, but we willingly share other territory with family and friends (e.g., our room, our side of the bed, our chair). Still other territory involves temporary ownership, which is more public, such as a parking spot, a seat or desk in a classroom, or a table reserved at a restaurant.

2. Personal space: The immediate zone we carry around with us during our daily interactions with others. It is like a "bubble" that moves with us. The degree of personal space one allows with others is determined by the nature of the relationship, the topic under discussion, gender, age, and cultural background.

   a. Edward T. Hall's zones of interpersonal distance:
      1. Intimate: 0–18 inches
      2. Casual-personal: 18 inches to 4 feet
      3. Socio-consultative: 4 to 8 feet
      4. Public: beyond 8 feet

   b. Gender and age.
      Females tend to interact at a closer distance with other females than males do with each other. However, mixed-sex dyads (male/female couples) interact at closer distances than either same-sex dyad. Furthermore, children comprise the greatest number of "space invaders." As they get older, they learn to follow distance rules.

   c. Cultural differences.
      Rules governing proxemics differ by culture. People in the United States are considered *noncontact-oriented* people. That is, we avoid spatial closeness (intimate zone) except with members of our immediate family or circle of close friends. However, other people, such as Latin Americans and southern Europeans are more *contact-oriented*.

   d. Socioeconomic status.
      Proxemic differences have been found among African-Americans, whites, and Hispanics. Research suggests that such variations are more a function of socioeconomic status than of either racial or ethnic identification. No differences were found when people interacting were all middle class or from lower strata in the social system.

   e. Encroachment, or space invasion.
      People respond to space invasion in one of two ways—fight or flight. The most common response to encroachment upon public or more temporary territory is flight. Fight responses are more common when invasions occur within primary or exclusive territory.

E. Communicating with touch: Haptics.

The study of touch as a means of nonverbal communication is called haptics. Haptics is a logical extension of proxemics. That is, in order to touch someone, you must be physically close to that person.

1. Touch deprivation: The importance of touching begins early in life. Studies have shown that a positive relationship exists between touch deprivation (little or no touching) and infant mortality rate. Furthermore, infants who had been touch deprived and survived typically became maladjusted or retarded.

2. Amount of touch: Infants who develop under normal family circumstances are touched very often until they are about 2 years old. Then the frequency of touch begins to decline. In fact, senior citizens may be touched very little or not at all. However, people of all ages continue to enjoy being touched and touching others.

3. Benefits of touch: A number of studies suggest that health problems often arise when people fail to get their quota of touch. Allergies, skin diseases, and speech development may be affected by lack of touch. Most important, without touch we are likely to succumb to stress in our daily lives. Therefore, touch can help improve both our health and our state of mind.

4. Dangers of touch: Depending on the kind of touch used, such actions can communicate dislike and aggression. In general, we touch those we like and avoid touching or being touched by those we don't.

5. Touch avoiders/approachers: "Touch avoiders" are those people who feel very uncomfortable touching or being touched by others, whereas "touch approachers" enjoy touching and being touched by others. In any case, understanding the rules of touching is critical in relating to others.

F. Meaning associated with time: Chronemics.

The study of the way in which people use time to transmit nonverbal messages is called chronemics.

1. Biological time: Individual personality differences in people's tolerance for early and late time schedules.
   a. Owls: People who prefer late afternoon and evenings to accomplish tasks.
   b. Sparrows: People who prefer early morning and afternoon to accomplish tasks.
2. Temporal time: Informal usage of time.
3. Time intervals: The amount of time.
4. Psychological time orientation: Society's orientation toward time in terms of the past, present, and future.

IV. Communication as an integrated process.

All of the nonverbal uses discussed above need to be considered as a system of factors that act in a simultaneous transaction with one other. Their influence on meanings for both sender and receiver is not element-by-element but is a kind of integrated package. When people communicate they do so as persons in a particular context.

A. The importance of nonverbal immediacy.

The use of nonverbal signals and actions that promote physical and psychological closeness with others is referred to by communication specialists as "immediacy" behaviors. Many of the actions that we use in nonverbal communication—especially proxemics, kinesics, haptics, and oculesics behaviors—aid in establishing and maintaining closeness with others. These immediacy behaviors include eye contact, touch, forward leaning, head nodding, smiling, open gestures, standing close to someone, and other behaviors.

    1. The immediacy principle: People approach things and others they like or prefer and avoid things/others they don't like or don't prefer.

B. Application of the immediacy principle.

When people engage in the immediacy behaviors of approach, they are perceived by others to be more popular, well liked, responsive, and sensitive. Those who behave in opposite ways are likely to be labeled as aloof, unresponsive, tense, awkward, and insensitive.

    1. Drawbacks of using immediacy behaviors: Some people may misperceive nonverbal attempts at eliciting psychological closeness as flirting or even a blatant sexual "come-on." Another potential problem of using immediacy behaviors is that immediacy often results in more, not less, communication with others.

V.   Chapter review.

CHAPTER 4
LISTENING AS COMMUNICATION

LEARNING OBJECTIVES

After studying the chapter, the student should be able to:

- Define and discuss the term *listening*.

- Differentiate between *listening* and *hearing*.

- Discuss the four purposes listening serves in our lives.

- Distinguish between what is meant by *active* versus *passive* reception or listening.

- Explain why a necessary condition for effective listening is being perceived and classified by others as a good listener on the basis of observable signs and behaviors.

- Identify some *observable* behaviors or actions that differentiate good from bad listeners.

- Discuss the two ways why looking like a good listener may contribute to effective listening.

- Define and discuss *adaptation* in relation to the listening encounter.

- Define and discuss what is meant by *sender/receiver reciprocity*.

- Discuss the five responsibilities of senders.

- Discuss the five responsibilities of receivers.

- Define and discuss what is meant by *sender/receiver similarity*.

- List and discuss the four inaccurate assumptions about listening.

- Define and discuss the term *barrier*.

- Identify and discuss the four broad categories of *barriers* to effective listening.

- Discuss why *planning* is so important to effective listening.

- Identify and describe the seven activities that help improve one's *competence* in listening.

EXTENDED CHAPTER OUTLINE

This chapter focuses on the receiver as an essential part of the human communication process. An overall analysis and description of the listening process, the characteristics of good and bad listening, the sources of many kinds of listening problems, and suggestions for improving our listening skills will be discussed.

I. The listening process.
   A. Listening as behavior.

   Listening can be defined as: An active form of behavior in which individuals attempt to maximize their attention to, and comprehension of, what is being communicated to them through the use of words, actions, and things by one or more people in their immediate environment.

   Although most people think of listening in terms of using their ears, it also involves monitoring nonverbal and contextual messages. Therefore, listening includes attending to and interpreting all the ways in which people use words, actions, and things intended to arouse meanings in their receivers.

   Successful attending to and comprehending what is communicated to us will be achieved only if it is deliberately set as a key objective.

   Finally, an important prerequisite to effective listening is the acquisition of skills in *discriminating* between what is important and what is unimportant.

   B. What we gain from effective listening. Listening serves four primary purposes in our lives:
      1. Acquiring needed information.

      Some information is important to our well-being, whereas other kinds may be trivial. Our ability to discriminate as, or even before, we listen will determine the degree to which we can successfully screen important from trivial information and thus successfully attend to and comprehend relevant, needed information.

      2. Evaluating and screening messages.

      The second reason people listen is to evaluate information. Because we receive so much information daily, we must be able to sort through and evaluate quickly both the relevance and the accuracy of the information we receive when interacting with others. In order to accomplish this selection activity effectively, we need a set of criteria according to which judgments can be made.
         a. Source credibility: Believability of the source must be evaluated. That is, we must decide whether the source (speaker) is trustworthy.
         b. Message characteristics: Believability and importance of what is being said must be evaluated against whatever we have selected as standards for judgment. That is, we must decide whether what the person (source) is saying is believable and whether or not the message is important to us in any way.

      3. Listening as recreation.

      A great deal of our listening comes under the heading of amusement, fun, or diversion. We engage in this form of listening when we socialize with others, attend concerts, turn on our stereo, or watch television. However, classifying certain kinds of listening as recreational can be damaging. When we are in this mode of communication, it is likely that we are not alert and may miss important information that comes our way. For example, if a teacher uses a lot of entertaining jokes and illustrations in her or his lectures, students may not actively attend to the important points of the presentations and therefore may suffer the consequences.

      4. Listening as a requirement for social efficacy.

      Social efficacy means being competent as a social person—being able to form, manage, and maintain all kinds of social relationships effectively. Good listening skills are practical tools for developing smooth and comfortable social relationships on which professional success often depends.

C. Actions required of an effective listener.
   1. Active versus passive reception.
      a. Passive listening occurs when little or no effort is exerted by the receiver. Usually, passiveness stems from conditions as basic as boredom, hunger, disinterest, and apathy. Of the four, lack of interest is probably the most frequent.
      b. Active listening occurs when substantial effort is exerted by a receiver. When a receiver makes an effort to listen, the likely result is not only greater attention and comprehension on the part of the receiver but greater enthusiasm and appreciation on the part of the source as well. Our "activity imperative" can also be a beginning point for conflict resolution.
   2. Listening as observable action.
      Effort and activity while listening operate as internal motivators. That is, they are factors that operate "in our heads" to influence us as good listeners. Such internal states are not observable by others. However, the characteristics of an effective listener can also be discussed as *observable actions* that make us "look the part."
      Subtle nonverbal skills of good listeners can be observed: forward body leaning, eyes fixed on the speaker, and perhaps occasional nodding in agreement from time to time. The opposite is to stare off in the distance, with eyelids partially closed, perhaps arms crossed, leaning backward, and with a bored look or slight frown.
      Therefore, a necessary condition for effective listening is being *perceived* and *classified* by others as a good listener on the basis of observable signs and behaviors. Looking like a good listener may contribute to effective listening in two ways:
      a. Adaption: When someone is perceived to be a good listener, the person doing the talking is likely to feel sympathetic toward that individual. Both senders and receivers may modify how they think about and behave toward each other.
      b. Habitual behavior transformation: Conducting one's self in ways necessary to be perceived by others as a good listener requires that certain standards of good listening conduct be met. If the appropriate kinds of actions can be initiated and performed, a real transformation can take place. New listening behaviors can displace the habitual ones.

II. The listening encounter.
The behaviors of both senders and receivers are important to the listening process. But it is the receiver of the message who carries most of the burden in accomplishing the actual level of listening effectiveness.
   However, if accuracy of communication is to be high, both of the individuals participating in an encounter must *adapt* to each other. Active attempts to adapt can produce a number of positive outcomes for listening: Adaptation helps promote and maintain attention, which in turn can improve both message comprehension and communication accuracy.
A. Sender/receiver reciprocity.
   By engaging in both role-taking and feedback simultaneously, successful adaptation can occur. Such adaptation is also known as "interpersonal adjustment." Reciprocity is the combined influences of such behaviors on *both* parties as they adjust to each other, whereas adaptation only involves the various ways in which both message senders and receivers *independently* modify their actions. Understanding the need for reciprocity helps in understanding the "responsibilities" of both sources and receivers.

1. Responsibilities of senders.
   a. Consider *what content* is to be communicated. That is, senders must think through what is to be sent before any communication takes place.
   b. Consider the *way* a message is to be communicated. Deciding how a message will be sent will influence a receiver's ability to listen to it.
   c. Consider *where* a message will be communicated. The context can control both how a message is interpreted and whether listening occurs successfully. Therefore, the sender must make sure the content is appropriate for the message to be communicated.
   d. Consider *who* is to receive the message. Individuals sending messages to others should be sure that the nature of the receiver is considered in the design of the message. Often senders ignore or are totally insensitive to their audience.
   e. Consider the *consequences* of a message prior to transmission. Remember: Communication is irrevocable.
2. Responsibilities of receivers.
   a. Consider the amount of effort necessary for maximum understanding and comprehension of what is communicated. This type of decision involves discriminating carefully among the goals of information seeking, evaluation, and recreational listening.
   b. Understand the *intent* of the source. Receivers should be able to understand the reason or reasons why a particular message is being communicated. That is, receivers need to be able to distinguish important from unimportant information.
   c. Consider *where* they are when interpreting a given message. In order to be effective listeners, we need to be able to discriminate competently among the communication contexts.
   d. Consider *who* is communicating the message when interpreting it. Source credibility and message credibility should be considered.
   e. Avoid *overreacting* to either what is being said or how something is being communicated.
B. Sender/receiver similarity.

This is a condition in which both the message sender and the receiver have had sufficiently similar learning experiences in their language community so as to have acquired parallel meanings for verbal and nonverbal signs and symbols. Listening cannot be effective unless we can experience some degree of shared meaning with the individual transmitting the message. Importantly, effective listening is easy or difficult depending on the degree to which the sender and receiver are similar kinds of people. The degree of similarity (or differences) in our experiences will help or hamper our understanding.

III. Barriers and misconceptions that impair listening.
A. Inaccurate assumptions about listening.

The following are four common misconceptions made by poor listeners:

1. Listening is easy. Effective listening is a complex activity that requires effort. Good listeners are not "born"; they are made—through hard work.
2. It is just a matter of intelligence. Good or bad listeners cannot be distinguished on the basis of their levels of intelligence. Effective listening is neutral in regard to intelligence.

3. Listening requires no planning. Effective listening follows from having planned carefully, not just from the sheer frequency of doing it.

4. Read better, listen better. Listening and reading are not based upon enough common skills to allow for a simple transfer of skills.

B. Barriers to effective listening.

A barrier is any condition in the physical setting or that is personal to the listener which functions to reduce accuracy in communication. Most barriers to effective listening can be grouped into the following four broad categories:

1. Physical conditions. Noise interference can come from any number of causes external to listeners, and often beyond their control. These include sounds caused by printers, aircraft, lawn mowers, or any other source that physically interferes with our ability to hear.

2. Personal problems. These may be either physical or psychological. Physical problems may be due to sickness, exhaustion, overindulgence in food or drink. Psychological problems include things we have on our mind that distract us—financial problems, a sick child, a stressful relationship with a loved one, or a preoccupation with the future.

3. Prejudices. Barriers to effective listening also include negative attitudes that lead us to "prejudge" the characteristics, abilities, or intentions of some categories of senders, regardless of what particular individuals are doing or saying. Our "prejudices" interfere with our ability to listen objectively to others toward whom we hold a particular bias. Biases are not restricted to race or ethnicity but may also include women, younger or older individuals, or those perceived as physically unattractive.

4. Connotative meanings. Connotative meanings are those personal, subjective, and unshared interpretations we have for verbal and nonverbal symbols and signs. An erosion of accuracy in communication may be due to different connotative meanings in the encoding/decoding processes of sender and receiver.

IV. Planning for effective listening.

Effective listening is a critical communication skill; it can be learned; and it requires both effort and planning.

A. The importance of planning.

In today's complex world, *social* skills are far more important than manual or even technical ones. It is individuals with high competency in relating to and influencing others who become leaders in their fields. Those social skills depend heavily on being able to communicate effectively, which as the transactions model shows, includes being a first-rate receiver and listener.

B. Features of a sound plan.

Listed below are seven specific activities that provide broad guidelines for improving competence in listening:

1. Understand our current listening skills. Before we can begin to refine our listening skills, we need to identify our current strengths and weaknesses as listeners—receiver eccentricities. *Receiver eccentricities* are those personal attributes and individual differences that help or hinder our capacity to receive and interpret messages accurately.

2. Prepare ourselves to listen. Preparing ourselves for listening requires that we be open and sensitive in relating to others.

3. Control concentration. We need to expend effort to be a good listener. Listening requires that we deliberately and consciously attend to and try to comprehend what is being communicated to us.

4. Show alertness and interest. Effective listening requires that we appear to be listening. How we engage in specific kinds of overt behaviors leads senders to believe that we are listening intently to what is being said.

5. Search actively for meaning. The fifth step in a listening plan is to provide for deliberate concentration on the intended meaning of messages. That is, we need to look for every clue as to what a person is trying to say. Here we take into account the individual's personal characteristics, possible connotative meanings, and implications of the setting or context.

6. Keep active while listening. We need to consider ways that will help us maintain a high level of activity during listening. In the context of listening, our efforts to attend to and comprehend messages need to last the duration of the entire encounter.

7. Suspend judgments about message and source. We need to recognize and minimize any tendency we might have to make premature judgments about either the source or intended message.

V. Chapter review.

CHAPTER 5
COMMUNICATING INTERPERSONALLY

LEARNING OBJECTIVES

After studying the chapter, the student should be able to:

- Identify and discuss the three *basic features* of context.

- Define *interpersonal communication*. How does it differ from other forms of human communication?

- Explain the two major *background features* of interpersonal communication.

- Identify and discuss the *six characteristics* of interpersonal communication.

- Define and explain what is meant by the term *self*.

- Describe the *six images or personas* involved in any communication transaction.

- Explain how interpersonal communication is *fully transactional*.

- Explain the *cost/benefit ratio* principle. Why is this principle relevant to interpersonal communication?

- Identify and discuss the *three reasons* for engaging in lasting interpersonal relationships.

- Describe the *cushioning* function.

- Explain the principle of *utilitarianism* and the principle of *utility*.

- Describe the *critical first moments* of engagement.

- Discuss the stages of *small talk*.

- Identify and discuss the six *skills of small talk*.

- Explain *exchange theory*.

- Distinguish between a *reservoir of rewards/costs* and the *principle of delayed gratification*.

- Discuss the three methods of revealing *core* information about self.

- Discuss some of the *communication norms* that develop between intimates (such as intimate idioms and inside humor).

- Explain the definition of the *situation principle*. Compare this idea with the *social construction of reality* theory.

- Discuss the causes of *relational disengagement*.

- Discuss how *language* in relational disengagement changes when saying goodbye.

- Explain the *two-fold* process of saying goodbye (*distancing* versus *disassociation*).

- Identify and discuss *Baxter's* four main strategies to terminate friendships.

EXTENDED CHAPTER OUTLINE

This chapter focuses on the features that make up any type of context and how these influence interpersonal communication. The chapter looks at the kinds of messages people use when they want to develop, maintain, and disengage from valued relationships.

I.   Basic features of a context.

Three features of the transactions model are discussed in terms of describing what is meant by the *context* in the study of communication.

A. Physical settings: How places influence communication.

People act out their parts in physical surroundings that serve as a kind of "stage." The physical stage includes buildings, parks, and beaches. The physical stage also includes props and artifacts, such as clothing, automobiles, and furnishings. These "nonverbal" things provide meanings as part of the physical context. The physical context shapes communication insofar as either inhibiting or encouraging certain kinds of messages.

B. Social situations: How goals influence communication.

People get together with other individuals so that they can accomplish goals in social situations that they could not achieve by individual action alone. Therefore, social situations are organized around goals people pursue through communicating with each other, and the goals shape the general content of their messages.

C. Social relationships: How rules influence communication.

The rules of interaction in a given situation are general norms that all parties are expected to follow, the specialized roles that they play in the division of labor, the ways in which ranks define each participant's authority, power and prestige, and the social controls that are exercised by both verbal and nonverbal communication.

II. Communication is an interpersonal context.

Interpersonal communication is defined as the process of transmitting messages between people through the use of language and actions that are intended to arouse meanings intended by the source. This form of human communication focuses on *interactions between two people*. In the systematic study of interpersonal communication, researchers recognize that interpersonal affiliations are not static; they are constantly being modified. This chapter discusses the engagement, management, and disengagement of interpersonal relationships.

A. Characteristics of interpersonal communication.

Two background features frame the discussion of interpersonal communication. The first is that interpersonal communication takes place in the dyad. The second major feature is that as individuals involved come to know one another better, their relationship tends to move from impersonal to personal. With these two features in mind, six key characteristics of interpersonal communication can be identified.

   1. Interpersonal communication begins with the "self."

      a. The term *self* is defined as that pattern of beliefs, meanings, and understandings each individual develops concerning her or his own personal characteristics, capacities, limitations, and worth as a human being. In other words, the self consists of our personal conceptions of who we are, what we are, and where we are in the social order.

b. In the process of interpersonal communication, we can recognize six images or personas (the central and unique characteristics of an individual that set him or her off from others) involved in any communication transaction. These images of self and other help shape what is said and what is understood. The six images include:
   (1) My self-image
   (2) My image of the other
   (3) The other's self-image
   (4) The other's image of me
   (5) What you think your image is in the mind of the other person
   (6) What that person feels is the image that you have constructed about her or him

2. Interpersonal communication is fully transactional.

   More than in any other, the communication involved in interpersonal contexts is based on the simultaneous transactions model. Each party simultaneously influences the other's behavior while being affected in return.

3. Interpersonal communicators share physical proximity.

   Interpersonal communication takes place with two individuals engaging in face-to-face interaction. Simply put, people have to be near each other in space to engage in interpersonal communication. By being in close physical proximity, communicators are able to increase their chances for understanding each other accurately and efficiently by having access to immediate feedback.

4. Interpersonal communication is shaped by social roles.

   When people are engaging in interpersonal communication, the content can be interpreted only within the context of the roles that define their overall relationships. Both content and relational messages interact together in determining the meaning of any interpersonal exchange.

5. Interpersonal communication is uniquely irreversible.

   As pointed out earlier in Chapter 1, there is no way to erase an unfortunate message. Interpersonal communication cannot be undone, it is by nature irreversible.

6. Interpersonal communication is unrepeatable.

   We all know that we cannot go back and attempt to relive the exact same communication experiences again.

7. These six characteristics taken together distinguish interpersonal communication from other forms of human communication.

B. Reasons for initiating and maintaining relationships.

Interpersonal relationships can be examined in terms of a cost/benefit ratio (amount of effort exerted and rewards acquired). Interpersonal communication is the foundation on which intimate human bonds are formed. Consequently, there are three broad reasons for engaging in lasting interpersonal relationships.

1. Constructing and maintaining a positive self-image. By careful screening and recruiting accommodating associates, we can build and maintain a satisfying self-image. Consequently, relationships allow us to learn more about how others perceive and feel about us.

2. Coping with daily problems.

   While we rely on others to help with our self-image, we also need them for many kinds of practical reasons. In essence, we rely heavily on friends, family members, and other intimate associates to help us solve a number of problems of everyday living that would be difficult to handle alone. These friends and family members often serve a *cushioning* function—supplying emotional support when we are anxious or afraid, when tragedy strikes, or even when we are just feeling down.

3. Maximizing rewards and minimizing punishments.

    Based on Bentham's (1748–1832) theories of "utilitarianism" and "the principle of utility," people engage in those behaviors that maximize pleasure and avoid those that result in pain. Consequently, close personal relationships are developed with people whose company and behavior are the least punishing and because of the rewards that they provide.

III. Engagement: The decision to encounter.

Moving from the very first moments in the history of an encounter to the decision to try to develop into a closer relationship involves a set of regular stages.

A. The critical first moments.

1. Our first impressions are often based on nonverbal cues—the person's overall physical appearance, clothing, and other "packaging."

2. Next, we engage in "scripted" conversations. These conversations can be called "stereotypic" in that they are highly standardized and predictable. Conversations can be classified as stereotypic if they follow clear, rigid rules in certain well-defined situations. Examples include our initial "Hello, how are you?" with a normative reply such as "Fine, and how are you?" Research indicates that new acquaintances almost always exchange factual, nonopinionated (safe) and relatively superficial information. Exceptions occur when we reveal intimate disclosures to strangers with whom we do not expect to develop social ties; this is known as the "stranger on the plane" phenomenon.

B. Small talk as big talk.

Small talk may be the most important communication skill we can possibly master. Every dyadic social relationship develops through a stage of small talk.

1. Auditioning for friendship.

    Individuals look over one another in an effort to determine whether or not a relationship is worth establishing.

2. Controlling self-disclosure.

    Small talk also allows us to reveal a bit of who we are to others cautiously and in a safe way.

3. Painless interaction.

    Small talk serves what Knapp refers to as an "interpersonal pacifier." Small talk is easy and is relatively painless. Often, the type of information exchanged between new acquaintances is basic biographical data, such as "My name is Diane."

C. The skills of small talk.

1. The importance of eye contact.

    Eye contact is mandatory for effectively initiating encounters with others.

2. Providing nonverbal immediacy.

    Use of nonverbal immediacy cues can communicate interest and liking.

3. The importance of name.

    Be sure to remember and use the other's name to communicate interest.

4. Drawing out the other person.

Get the other person to talk about himself or herself. Use follow-up questions or comments that relate directly or indirectly to what the person just said. Avoid random topic switching.

5. Keeping it light.

Avoid jumping too quickly to heavy issues early in a relationship; the other person is likely to feel threatened if this happens.

6. Accentuating the positive.

Negative talk can be perceived as a "downer." Commenting negatively about others can lead to some destructive, disagreeable interactions, especially if your conversation partners find the same person attractive.

IV. Management: The decision to linger.

The decision to continue a relationship depends on the rewards versus the benefits we think we have gained, or suspect we will gain from the affiliation.

Based on "exchange theory," a cost/benefit ratio can be calculated to determine whether or not to maintain or to terminate the relationship. That is, when rewards outweigh the costs for both individuals, then the relationship is likely to survive and gain momentum. In contrast, if one or both partners perceive the relationship as too costly, the relationship is likely to terminate.

Although some argue that the cost/benefit principle is overly simple, we know for a fact that most of us prefer to be around individuals who make us feel good (rewarding experience). Similarly, we do not like to be around persons who make us feel bad (cost/punishing experience). Therefore, the balance of rewards and punishments is an exchange—still a viable idea that can predict the fate of a relationship.

A. Assessing the rewards and costs.

This ratio of costs and benefits is a long-term matter. In lasting interpersonal relationships we find that individuals involved are likely to have accumulated a kind of "reservoir" of rewards that can be drawn upon in troubled times. It is this reservoir that maintains the relationship and is critical for relational management.

"The principle of delayed gratification" is an exception to the cost/benefit ratio principle. That is, many people will put up with a great deal of costs as long as they can predict that significant rewards will follow. Such costs may involve financial strain, isolation, career interruptions, or even physical or psychological abuse.

B. Revealing "core" information about self.

When a relationship is rewarding, both parties find themselves sharing private information with each other that is usually reserved for a few individuals who know each other very well. Such "core" information involves risks because it requires disclosure of very personal matters.

1. Testing the water.

As we begin the process of mutual self-disclosure, individuals test the water by revealing something indirect. The goal is to observe the reaction of the partner. This process is simply a matter of trust—that is, whether or not we can trust the other to respond sensitively to our personal attributes, our secrets, and our deep feelings. If we are satisfied that our partner will remain sympathetic and supportive, we intensify the relationship (as long as both partners have tested the water—the reciprocal process).

2. Labeling the relationship.

We provide our relationships with labels. This labeling process is important because it attaches specific and culturally defined meanings to the relationship. This labeling process changes everyone's perceptions of the persons involved and alters the responses of other people toward them. At each movement toward intimacy, individuals employ "secret tests" to check out the level of commitment each feels to the other.

3. Achieving full disclosure.

Once the foundation of trust is established and we reach a state of full disclosure (exposing more and more about ourselves), we have become an intimate pair, who are seen as such by ourselves and others.

C. Communicating with an intimate other.

Many of the communication norms that develop between intimates are unique to that specific relationship between those two particular individuals. Whatever they may be, such rules tend to be both personal and private. Some rules may be explicit, whereas others are implicit and are assumed by one another.

Another characteristic of participants in close relationships is their use of "intimate idioms" and "inside" humor. That is, couples often share words, nonverbal gestures, and meanings for situations that others may not understand, recognize, or know about.

V. Disengagement: The decision to leave.

Up to this point, we've focused primarily on relationships in which both partners choose to move forward toward greater intimacy. Now we will turn to the opposite kind of process—termination.

The *definition of the situation* principle states that if people believe something to be real, they will act as though it were real. This is really the idea of *social construction of reality,* where people's beliefs are derived from their interactions with others. In essence, when people go through the process of disengagement, they create, as a result of communication with others, their own individual interpretations of what they believe to be the real cause of the disengagement.

A. Causes of relationship disengagement.

1. The pressure for an explanation.

Friends and family need, want, and expect us to give them an accounting of what happened. Ideally, there has to be "blame."

2. Acceptable assignment of blame.

One of the first requirements of a story that will be accepted is the justification for leaving (not to blame). We need an explanation in which we are seen as the moral party. Another important requirement for a story explaining a disengagement is that it should reflect a sense of emotional maturity and recognition that it "takes two" to make and to break a relationship.

B. Saying goodbye.

The language of individuals involved in relational disengagement reflects a dramatic change. Couples revert back to first names and the stereotypic language of strangers. Their conversations become hesitant and awkward as they hold back disclosure. Couples begin to disengage by a two-fold process:

1. Establishing distance.

Both physical and psychological distance may be achieved through both verbal and nonverbal messages. Individuals may start spending time apart or simply put up barriers to replace the close association that had been maintained earlier.

2. Disassociation.

The term *disassociation* refers to reducing the use of the unit-implying pronoun "we" and reverting back to the individualistic "you" and "I." Messages about the future become transformed into messages about the past. Throughout the disassociation process, differences, rather than similarities, are emphasized. Disengagers spend an increasing amount of time and energy avoiding contact and stressing dissimilarities. While intimates talk about togetherness, coupling, and attachment, disengagers frequently communicate separateness, autonomy, and detachment.

C. Fifty ways to leave your lover.

The majority of attempts to disengage from relationships can be characterized as nondirect.

Baxter categorized college students' attempts to terminate close friendships into four main strategies:

1. Withdrawal/avoidance.

This indirect approach avoids confrontation, letting the relationship simply "fade away." This method may work for unwanted friendships but may be difficult to employ for married couples.

2. Ending on a positive tone.

This strategy represents a socially "appropriate" means of ending relationships. Couples who use this strategy show concern and regard for one another by being "nice" to each other. In some instances, couples attempt to remain friends.

3. Machiavellianism.

This strategy involves manipulation and deception. This strategy seeks to convince the partner that relational termination was his or her idea and that it is in the partner's best interest. Individuals may violate a relational rule, or provoke an argument, then encourage the other partner to leave.

4. Open confrontation.

As the name implies, this approach involves facing the partner, disclosing that the relationship is over, explaining why this is so, and coping with the resulting emotional uproar that will follow.

5. In reality, the disengagement of a couple may involve more than one, or perhaps all, of these strategies for termination. Disengagement leaves people drained, sad, and often bitter. At the same time, the personal and emotional ratio of costs versus benefits may make it the only way out.

VI. Chapter review.

CHAPTER 6
COMMUNICATING IN SMALL GROUPS

LEARNING OBJECTIVES

After studying the chapter, the student should be able to:

- Define and explain the term *group*.

- Discuss some of the reasons why people become members of groups and maintain their membership.

- Discuss the influence of *group size* on group discussions.

- Identify the optimal number of group members for effective group discussion and participation.

- Distinguish between *intimate* and *task-oriented* groups.

- Compare and contrast task-oriented groups such as discussion, experiential, and decision-making groups.

- Discuss the *communication goals* in intimate groups.

- Differentiate between the three aspects of *human development* and *socialization* (personality, social understandings, and enculturation).

- Identify the three broad types of *task-oriented groups* (discussion, self-improvement, and decision-making).

- Identify and discuss the various types of *discussion groups*.

- Identify and discuss the four types of *self-improvement and task-oriented groups* (therapy, encounter, assertiveness, and consciousness-raising).

- Explain the purpose of *decision-making groups*.

- Discuss the four kinds of *judgments* decision-making groups commonly deliberate.

- Identify and discuss the stages of *group development*.

- Distinguish among communication *norms, roles, social ranking*, and *subtle social controls* in intimate groups.

- Differentiate among the three *styles of leadership* (authoritarian, democratic, and laissez-faire).

- Identify the two factors that influence *leadership emergence*.

- Discuss the influence of *power* and *authority* on communication in small groups.

- Define *formal communication*.

- Discuss how communication codes are established, delineated, and controlled in formal decision-making groups.

- Define *group cohesion* and its effect on group processes.

- Distinguish among *sentiment-based, reward-based,* and *assignment-based cohesion* in decision-making groups.

- Discuss the three potential sources of *group disorganization* (norm confusion, role confusion, and legitimacy of ranks).

EXTENDED CHAPTER OUTLINES

This chapter describes how the transactions model, along with considerations of basis and size of membership and the nature of cohesion, aids in the understanding of how people communicate in different types of small groups, and the consequences of their exchanges.

I. The nature of small groups.

A context includes three components: some physical setting in which communication takes place, a social situation in which participants are engaging, and a set of social relationships that prevail among them. However, in the study of small groups we must also add two factors: (1) the basis and size of membership and (2) an explanation of group cohesion—that which holds a group together as a functioning unit.

A. Basic features of a group.

1. Group defined: A group consists of two or more people who repeatedly interact together, regulating their conduct and communication within some set of rules that they mutually recognize and follow.

2. People become members of groups and maintain their membership for many reasons. Basically, they participate in groups in order to accomplish goals that they could not achieve by acting alone.

a. Some people voluntarily seek individual satisfaction that cannot be met in solitary behavior (e.g., by marrying or finding friends).

b. Some people become members involuntarily (e.g., by being born into a particular family, by being drafted, or even by being sent to prison).

c. Some people become members because someone assigns them the task, or it's in their best interest to take part (e.g., serving on a jury or being asked by the boss to serve on a committee).

B. The influence of group size.

In the study of small groups, communication is influenced by the sheer number of people who participate in the process. As a result, as size increases, communication patterns in a group undergo significant qualitative changes, and groups that exceed about a dozen members or so do not provide the same communicative experiences as do those that are smaller. Many communication specialists maintain that an optimal size for discussion and getting decisions made in a small group with all members participating fully is about five (with 10 pairs).

C. Types of small groups.

1. Intimate groups.

This category includes both the human family and peer groups of close friends. Individuals in this type of group are often referred to as "primary" groups, both because they are earliest in our experiences and because they play a critical part in our psychological and social development.

2. Task-oriented groups.

People who participate in this type of group do so to get something done through group participation, achieve some goal that they have mutually set as an objective. Listed below are several types of task-oriented groups.

  a. Discussion groups: Discussion groups may be formal, informal, public, or private.
  b. Experiential groups: The principal goal of participation is to make people feel better. Examples include therapy groups (drug or alcohol abuse), consciousness-raising groups (sex discrimination), and sensitivity-training groups (relating to rape victims or resolving domestic conflicts).
  c. Decision-making: The goal of this group is to make orderly judgments achieved on the basis of discussion. Many of these groups communicate in private settings to allocate scarce resources, evaluate people's performance, and achieve consensus about what is or is not true. Examples include standing university committees, juries within the justice system, or corporation boards of directors.

II. Social situations: Why people communicate in small groups.
  A. Communication goals in intimate groups.

  Our family and our innermost cliques of friends share the goal of shaping our psychological and social development in a variety of ways.

    1. Communicating in family situations.

    The family is the primary group in the communication experiences of the human individual. Thus, the family is the principal source for learning vocabulary, the linking of symbols, meanings, and referents.

      a. Learning experiences that take place as the person is maturing can be discussed together under the broad concept of "socialization." The term refers to those long-term processes of communication within which deliberate or indirect lessons are internalized, enabling the person to become a unique human being, a functioning member of society, and a participant in its general culture. Three aspects of human development summed up in the above definition represent our initial source of personality, social understandings, and enculturation.
        (1) Personality refers to *the individual's more or less enduring organization of meanings, motivations, emotional patterns, orientations, skills, and other attributes that make that person different in psychological makeup from all others.* In other words, personality is composed of the "individual's distinctive, consistent, patterned methods of relating to the environment." Personality is not inherited but is learned through social experiences.
        (2) Social understandings. Socialization is also the source of social understandings, that is, our insights into how to behave in group situations. By participating in social situations, the norms, roles, ranks, and controls of various groups become understood by the individual.
        (3) Enculturation takes place through the process of socialization. Enculturation is defined as the process of acquiring understandings of the general culture of a person's society, including not only language skills but also shared beliefs, emotional orientations, attitudes, values, and everything that makes a person an accepted human being who "fits in."

    2. Communicating in peer group situations.

    This communication experience begins within the intimate groups of friends that are formed outside the family during early childhood. Through communication in peer groups, individuals improve their role-taking skills and their ability to interpret feedback.

Late in adulthood, membership in peer groups communicate among themselves simply for the pleasure, personal fulfillment, and companionship the process provides. The goals of such communication are the satisfactions provided by the communication.

B. Communicating in task-oriented groups.

Included in this category are three types of small groups that accomplish particular goals for group participants. One category is devoted to conducting some type of *discussion*; another is aimed at helping people *improve themselves;* and still another has the purpose of orderly *decision-making.*

1. Conducting a discussion. Many kinds of groups can be identified as having discussion-related goals. These range from informal to formal and private to public.

   a. *Private, informal, and casual discussions.* A small group of friends may get together casually and find themselves discussing a problem that seems to be troubling all of them.

   b. *Private, informal but deliberate discussions.* A group of people who share a problem may deliberately call an informal meeting to try to find a solution. They may achieve consensus on a solution and end the process, or ask someone to coordinate the group for further meetings.

   c. *Private and formal discussion group.* A group of people may decide to organize a formal group. They may elect a president, a secretary, and a treasurer. Then they may design a set of bylaws and formulate an agenda of long-range issues to be solved.

   d. *The round table.* A group where diverse views on a topic or issue are discussed among a small group of participants. In a round table, no audience is present and communication proceeds informally.

   e. *The panel.* A panel resembles a round table, but it is public rather than private. Here the participants tend to be experts or representatives of some sort. The panel is usually coordinated in a formal way by a moderator, and the discussion usually takes place before a live audience.

   f. *The symposium.* This is a very formal and public kind of group. Usually, a symposium has some unifying theme—a problem or issue being addressed. The participants are usually a small group of experts who are knowledgeable about the theme. They are individually introduced by the moderator, and each then makes a speech about the theme.

   g. *The seminar.* Seminars usually have regular meetings over a lengthy period of time and a clear organization with an intellectual leader who coordinates the discussions of students.

   h. *The forum.* This format of small-group discussion combines features of the round table, panel, and symposium. In a forum there is usually a brief presentation by a small group who are introduced by a chairperson. The presentations are usually followed by audience participation.

   i. *The conference.* Several participants are brought together, usually under private conditions, to share technical information or to discuss a problem in their area of expertise. Such conferences are common among people who work in a particular corporation or field, where solutions can be worked out together. Video tele-conferencing is now becoming popular.

   j. *Specialized small-group discussions.* A long list of groups that are found in one setting or another can be collapsed into this category. Examples include buzz groups, brainstorming sessions, quality control circles, and focus groups.

2. Helping people improve themselves.

Two different but related specialized types are involved in helping people to improve themselves. One is the small group in which people get together so as to learn to cope with a serious personal problem, such as a therapy or encounter group. A second type of group is devoted not to helping with a personal problem but to reaching a goal of personal or social improvement, such as educational or training groups.

a. *The therapy group.* These groups are widely used for assisting people who have personal problems. Participants meet with a coordinator who usually has some special insight into their problems. The underlying assumption is that if people who share a common problem get together and disclose their experiences, thoughts, and feelings to each other it will help them feel better. The presumed benefits are that the participants will gain insight into their difficulty and learn to cope with it more effectively.

b. *The encounter group.* Many discussion groups are organized for the purpose of identifying and coping with difficulties experienced in daily life. A common example is a weekend "retreat" where people go away from the distraction of their daily environment.

c. *The assertiveness training group.* Training goals are often sought in a small-group format. For example, assertiveness training groups function to give instruction in ways in which people can stand up for their rights and be more demanding in ensuring that they are treated with dignity and respect. Other specialized training groups teach people technical skills such as word-processing and how to handle hazardous wastes.

d. *The consciousness-raising group.* Another type of training goal is sought in groups by participants who feel disadvantaged in society. In the consciousness-raising group, participants present positions, exchange views, and gain insights into a topic of mutual concern.

3. Reaching important decisions.

Formal decision-making groups are deliberately formed to serve the decision-making needs of an organization or larger social system within which they operate. Members of formal decision-making groups are selected intentionally. They are requested, assigned, or ordered to participate after some sort of screening. Examples include a board of directors, a jury, a committee, or a council of qualified members. The kinds of judgments that are made fall into the four categories listed below.

a. *Allocating scarce resources.* Committees are often formed to handle the problem of designating who should get resources that are in short supply, such as space, time, effort, money, or some other valued commodity.

b. *Evaluating performance.* A very difficult kind of decision that must be made in larger systems is deciding who meets designated standards of performance, also called assessing merit.

c. *Formulating or changing policies.* Establishing or changing the formal rules that guide how organizations do things is still another task that is often assigned to formal decision-making small groups. This may involve planning the objectives, strategies, and directions that a large organization will take.

d. *Deciding what is true.* Our society operates with small groups that weigh facts and reach truths. The most obvious group is the jury in the American court system. Other fact-reviewing and truth-seeking small groups include those that investigate facts concerning plane crashes, new drugs, insecticides, and land-use proposals.

III. Social relationships: Rules for communicating.

Social relationships between members of a group are controlled and defined by its rules of communication. Such rules become part of the group's culture. Once in place, these rules serve as guides as to whether those relationships are informal or formal.

A. Stages in group development.

Many of the task-oriented groups discussed undergo a series of *stages* after the members first come together during which the organization of rules for communicating emerge and become stabilized.

1. Forming: The stage of initial orientation.

This "orientation" stage is one of uncertainty, probing, and trial. It is in this stage that rules which will govern communication are first tried out: The norms and roles (specialized parts) start to take definition. Individuals start to take on the roles of leaders, clowns, socio-emotional facilitator, and so on. Status, power, and control messages are often common in this early stage.

2. Storming: The stage of emerging conflict.

The orientation activities of the storming stage shift into one where conflict emerges. People begin to disagree about power, status, and control roles within the group. Moreover, a leader emerges and style of leadership becomes established.

3. Norming: The stage of stabilization.

After the group works its way through whatever conflicts arise, the members will have worked out at least the initial "images" they have of each other. Members can now turn away from the process of sizing up one another and begin resolving the conflicts that were generated in the earlier stages. They can now deal with the group as an existing and predictable pattern of social relationships and turn to the task.

4. Performing: The stage of task achievement.

With the group stabilized in terms of its rules of communication, the task for which the participants came together can now be addressed fully. Participants at this stage have examined various proposed solutions, and they come together in consensus about the one they believe to be the best.

B. Informal rules for communicating in intimate groups.

1. Communication norms in intimate groups.

Communication norms are general rules that each member is expected to follow in regard to what issues and topics and modes of transmission are acceptable within the group.

2. Communication roles in intimate groups.

Communication roles are a cluster of rules in a group that define who has the right to transmit particular kinds of messages and who must pay attention to them. The role system that exists in a particular group is an adaptation of the general cultural model that has been shaped, modified, extended, and adapted to the needs of the unique individuals who make up the group. Each group must work out its own pattern of communication rules.

3. Variations in social ranking.

Communication ranks are the rules that define communication patterns based on authority, power, and privilege within a group: for example, who can issue orders, who must always listen to whom, who has a right to speak first or last, and whose messages are regarded as more or less important.

4. Subtle social controls.

The rules for communicating in small groups are maintained through messages that provide "sanctions"—that is, meaning of rewards for compliance and punishment for deviance. The process can range from nonverbal signals of approval or disapproval to shouted praise or shrieking verbal abuse. The communication of social controls in intimate groups tends to be subtle and not heavy or obvious.

C. Rules for communicating in task-oriented groups.

1. Communication norms in task-oriented groups.

The communication norms that are adopted and used within a particular task-oriented group will be some mix of the traditional patterns that are applicable to that type of group (panel, seminar, therapy group, etc.) and the personal styles of each participant.

2. Leadership and other communication roles.

a. Three general categories of communication roles have been identified.

(1) Group task roles include "opinion leader," "initiator," and "energizer."

(2) Group building and maintenance roles include "encourager," "harmonizer," and "gatekeeper."

(3) Individual roles include "aggressor," "help-seeker," and "recognition-seeker."

b. Classic research suggests that three basic styles of leadership can be found in task-oriented groups.

(1) Authoritarian style: This type of leader sets the goal, decides on who will do what to get there, and defines the techniques or methods by which success will be achieved. Policies, and steps to implement them, are determined solely by the leader. It is the authoritarian group that gets the most done in the shortest time, but members tend to achieve their goals in less original ways and there is much less member satisfaction.

(2) Democratic style: Policies are discussed and determined by discussion and voting. Basically, the democratic leader takes people where they already want to go. He or she helps them to determine what that is and the best steps to take to get there—then coordinates their efforts so that the goal will be achieved. Cohesiveness tends to be greatest in this group because the experience results in greater member satisfaction.

(3) Laissez-faire leaders are "laid back" and do little to interfere with the choices or activities of members. Little visible authority and power is exercised, and the leader does not provide much in the way of reward or criticism. Questions are answered and advice is given only when asked. The laissez-faire style is less efficient than the other two, and it tends to produce the lowest levels of member satisfaction.

c. Two factors that influence leadership emergence:

(1) Leadership traits. These are special personal qualities that people admire and respect, attributes of personality that are the basis of leadership.

(2) Situation. A second explanation is that situations, rather than traits, determine leadership and that different types of people will be successful leaders in distinctive social situations.

3. Communication power and authority.

In more formally organized groups, members with formal roles of leadership and coordination are obviously in a position to control the flow of messages. Also, the social position and prestige of group members *outside* the group determine rank within a discussion group.

4. Enforcing the communication rules.

The principles of verbal and nonverbal communication outlined previously govern the enforcement of who can say what in a task-oriented group. The rules are enforced with feedback.

D. Communication codes in formal decision-making groups.

Formal communication can be defined as: controlled communication between parties who are allowed or required by the group's coded rules to transmit particular kinds of messages to specific receivers using officially designated rules. The most widely used "official" version of rules for formal communication is *Roberts' Rules of Order*. This book quickly became the world's standard of rules for decision-making.

1. Official requirements for communicating.

What started out as convenient guidelines have become quasi-legal restrictions that not only govern communication behavior in certain kinds of decision-making groups but also have implications for the quality of the conclusions that are reached.

2. Clearly delineated communication roles.

In decision-making groups following rules, the role of the leader is termed the "chair." Others in the group are "delegates," or "representatives." Formal terms of address related to these roles are deemed appropriate. Proposals for actions, or possible solutions to problems, must be communicated to the group in the form of a "motion," after recognition by the chair. The official rules tightly control both the nature and flow of messages between people in specific roles.

3. A hierarchy of power in controlling communication.

Ranks in a formal decision-making group are well defined. Power in the group is not uniformly distributed. The greatest power is vested in the chair. The chair controls the agenda, has the power to recognize members to speak, and has the power to break a tie.

4. Explicit controls.

Official codes make ample provisions for controlling their members with the use of explicit messages. For example, "resolution": commending a member may be brought to a vote. A member judged to be a deviant may be criticized in a motion of "censure" that may be placed in the official minutes. Beyond that, resignations are sometimes requested, or the sergeant of arms may have to eject an offender from a meeting.

IV. Group cohesion and disorganization.

Group cohesion involves the set of factors in every kind of group, large or small, intimate or formal, that move the participants to maintain their membership and to perform the activities required of them. As long as the basis of that cohesion is present, members will maintain their memberships and try to achieve whatever goals they are collectively pursuing. If the basis of that cohesion erodes, the group will break down. Thus, group disorganization often stems from "bad" communication processes rather than from "bad" people.

A. Distinct bases of cohesion.

1. Sentiment-based cohesion in intimate groups.

This type of cohesion is based on bonds of affection generated with the group. Group members feel tied to each other by their feelings. In a highly cohesive group, the members feel a deep sense of loyalty and obligation to other members. In such a group, commitment to the group's goal is very strong.

2. Reward-based cohesion in discussion groups.

   Here, member satisfaction of a personal or individual nature is the key factor. People continue in therapy groups, consciousness-raising groups, or encounter groups because they derive personal benefits—rewards—by maintaining membership. By participating they feel better, learn important things, or gain beneficial skills.

3. Assignment-based cohesion in decision-making groups.

   This type of cohesion is based on the fact that members of a group have been asked (or ordered) to serve by their boss, are voted into membership by a valued constituency, or must serve for some other valid obligation or duty. Assignment-based cohesion is a condition binding a person to a group based on willingness to work with others to accomplish goals because that has been defined as one's duty.

B. Communication breakdown and group disorganization.

Whether a group is large or small, intimate or impersonal, spontaneous or deliberately designed, a loss of cohesion can occur if members of a group are unclear about its communication norms.

1. Normative confusion takes place when communication norms have not been effectively clarified, or if consensus breaks down about what kind of messages, topics, or issues are approved and disapproved. This condition can be serious and can quickly result in group disorganization.

2. Role confusion is another potential source of disorganization. Role confusion refers to a situation in which shared understandings are inadequate, ineffective, or unclear about who should transmit what kind of messages to whom.

3. Legitimacy of ranks is another source of potential group disorganization. If members of a group come to believe that the messages transmitted by those in positions of power and authority lack legitimacy, the ranking system will be ineffective. Thus, the basis of effective control over communication behavior in a group lies in shared beliefs accepted by group members that breaking the rules will bring disapproval and rejection, and that conforming to them in an exemplary manner will result in approval and honor.

V. Chapter review.

CHAPTER 7
COMMUNICATING WITHIN ORGANIZATIONS

LEARNING OBJECTIVES

After studying the chapter, the student should be able to:

- Define *organizational communication*.
- Discuss why people communicate in organizations.
- Identify and discuss the five basic *social institutions*.
- Define and explain *bureaucracy*.
- Identify and discuss Weber's principles of bureaucracy.
- Distinguish among the three general theories of management: *human use, human relations,* and *human resources*.
- Explain the *wage formula* from classical economics.
- Discuss the era of *scientific management*.
- Discuss the *universal principles of management*.
- Discuss the legacy of the *Hawthorne studies*.
- Explain why the human relations concept declined after the 1960s.
- Explain why *quality control circles* are effective.
- Distinguish between *formal* and *informal* communication flow in large organizations.
- Discuss the four issues that need to be considered in describing information flow with organizations: *vertical transmission, message content, accuracy versus distortion,* and *consequences*.
- Distinguish between the kinds of messages that flow upward and downward.
- Discuss how messages flowing upward may become distorted.
- Discuss how downward messages may become distorted.
- Explain how informal messages operate within an organization in terms of capacity, flexibility, and speed.
- Explain how *embedding* and *compounding* patterns of distortion work together in the transmission of rumors through the grapevine.
- Distinguish among the three forms of distortion that often characterize the content of a message: *leveling, sharpening,* and *assimilation*.

- Define and explain organizational subcultures. Explain how organizational subcultures develop.

- Discuss the terms *organizational cohesion* and *dependency-based cohesion*. How are they related?

EXTENDED CHAPTER OUTLINE

This chapter focuses on the unique communication processes found in organizations. An *organization* is a human group that has been deliberately designed so as to achieve a desired objective. *Organizational communication* is the transmission of messages through both the formal and informal channels of a relatively large, deliberately designed group, resulting in the construction of meanings that have influences on its members, both as individuals and on the group as a whole.

I.   Social situations: Why people communicate in organizations.
  A. From an economic framework, organizations served needs more efficiently in the public sector (to develop and distribute consumer products) and at higher profit levels in the private sector.
  B. Society's need for organizations.
     The basic needs of a population are met by its social institutions. A social institution can be defined as: a rather broad configuration of closely related cultural elements and organized social activities that are essential to fulfilling a perceived basic need of the social order. In other words, organized social life requires that new members born into society be systematically introduced to its ways and requirements.
       In every society there are basic social institutions:
     1. Government: order, predictability, and security in social life.
     2. Religious institutions organized around the need to understand and try to influence the supernatural.
     3. Economic institutions evolved to handle the production and distribution of goods and services.
     4. Family—the oldest and most fundamental institution—was established for bearing and rearing of children within responsible and stable groups.
     5. In modern urban-industrial societies there are many other social institutions such as medicine, science, spectator sports, and mass media.
  C. Bureaucracy as a prerequisite.
     A technical definition of bureaucracy is a deliberately designed plan of the goals, norms, roles, ranks, and controls in an organization. The need for bureaucracy as an organizational plan that controls the formal routing of messages within any large-scale group comes about for two reasons:
     1. One is group size: As the number of members of a group increases arithmetically, the problem of maintaining face-to-face communication among members grows geometrically.
     2. Second, the complexity of the tasks a group must pursue to achieve its goals.
II. The classical theory of bureaucracy.
     The systematic study and analysis of the basic principles of organizational design began in the early part of the 20th century, by Max Weber, a German social scientist.

A. The emergence of a rational society.

Weber believed that social order was held together by society's trend toward rationality and an increasing understanding of the nature of leadership that made such organizations work. In his analysis of authority, Weber concluded that leadership and authority in modern urban-industrial societies were based on legal-rational power, as opposed to previous authority sources of tradition or charisma. That is, leaders in the organizations that provide for institutional needs are usually selected or appointed because they possess technical managerial skills, rather than because they have a "legitimate" right or a unique personal quality.

B. Weber's principle.

Weber set forth a number of basic principles that should be present in the operation of a well-designed bureaucratic organization. Weber maintained that a bureaucratic organization should have:

1. Fixed rules: Stable norms for all forms of behaviors that apply equally to everyone and can be learned and followed.
2. A rationally defined division of labor. Each position within an organization is mapped out with specific duties.
3. A clear graded hierarchy of power and authority. A chain of command set forth in an official plan that shows superior/subordinate relationships.
4. A fixed and universalistic system of sanction. All employees should be hired, promoted, rewarded, reprimanded, or separated solely on the basis of competence and performance.

III. Management-oriented approaches to organizational communication.

The study of organizational communication today focuses heavily on the problems of management and the design of production-oriented groups. In this section, a brief review is made of three general theories that focus on strategies of organizational design, management, and communication.

A. *The human use perspective* (developed between the early 1800s and the late 1920s). In the first decades of the Industrial Revolution, workers were not thought of in humanitarian terms, but simply as one more thing that had to be "used" along with machinery and exploited like raw materials. Communication within the 19th-century organization often seemed like military commands.

1. Wage formula from classical economics.

Wages were considered to be the only means thought to be available as messages from managers to motivate employees. Therefore, "wage incentive systems" were designed. That is, piece-work formulas were developed so that wages were tied to personal output. Production norms were established for a standard day's work, and bonuses were added as motivating controls to stimulate workers to exceed those norms.

2. The era of "scientific management."

Frederick Taylor developed a refinement of the human use approach for controlling workers. With a stopwatch in hand, Taylor's "time and motion" studies swept the industrial world. It was the first time that experiments, systematic observation, and detailed studies had been used to achieve rational designs in production-oriented large organizations.

3. Universal principles of management.

Henri Fayol, a French engineer, contributed the "organizational chart." Such a chart communicates in graphic terms the chain of authority and command, and thereby the flow of formal messages. In terms of vertical communication, Fayol maintained that communication should be restricted to the tasks and operations related to the work being done. In times of crisis, "a bridge" may be used to bypass those formal channels creating rapid message transmission.

4. The classical bureaucratic theory developed by Weber and modified by Taylor and Fayol focused attention on the essential nature of deliberate planning.

B. *The human relations perspective.*

1. The Hawthorne studies and their legacy.

A number of scientific management experiments began in November 1924 at the Western Electric Company in Cicero, Illinois. The first studies focused on the effects of illumination and varying working conditions (lengths of rest periods, lengths of workday, and number of days worked in a week) on worker output. Results from these studies were surprising for the experimenters. The scientific management perspective had regarded assembly line workers as basically interchangeable—easily replaceable units that merely needed to be controlled and motivated by communicating simple economic incentives or other measurable factors. However, the results of the Hawthorne studies provided the evidence that the personal and social characteristics of workers as individual human beings are critical factors in the work process. In both experiments, the illumination and the Relay Assembly Room, increased worker efficiency was found to be related to perceived attention and concern given to employees. When lighting or working conditions were improved, output increased, but output also increased when lighting was dimmed or working conditions were restricted.

The Hawthorne experimenters discovered that people at work are complex human beings. Through the process of informal communication, they develop peer groups, which become important to them, and they come to be influenced by the shared meanings that they find at work. Consequently, management needed to find new ways to increase worker efficiency by finding messages that would motivate, encourage, and foster performance by taking advantage of factors in individual personality and human relationships. This is the human relations perspective. This perspective demanded that managers design communication systems in organizations that would produce high job satisfaction. The assumption was that satisfaction would lead to improved work performance.

2. The decline of the human relations theories.

The human relations concept remained the dominant perspective until the 1960s. While the idea that a happy worker is a productive worker sounded wonderful, it frequently failed in the tougher environment of the factory and corporation. Managers found that the principles of the human relations approach were difficult to implement. That is, supervisors who tried to be "caring" and "sympathetic" were often perceived as weak and indecisive. Also, sharing the decision making, policy formation, and power sharing with the rank and file became difficult, often creating unwanted tensions and conflicts. For many managers, the human relations perspective seemed unrealistic and idealistic. Consequently, a new perspective emerged: the human resources perspective.

C. *The human resources perspective.*

Although it is not widely known, the fundamental principle of industrial production that has made Japanese organizations famous was actually invented by W. Edward Deming, an American statistician and management consultant. Dr. Deming was brought to Japan at the close of World War II to help Japan rebuild and establish a solid manufacturing economy. Dr. Deming's primary objective was to produce goods of *maximum quality*. Essentially, Japan had implemented the human resources perspective in its design of production organizations. The Japanese realized that workers on the line have insights and a grasp of the production process that cannot be developed by executives far removed from day-to-day operations. For that reason, they created small groups of workers called *quality control circles*. These are composed of individuals from particular units right on the line whose members all face the same production task. They meet weekly as discussion groups and are coordinated by their supervisor, who takes their solutions seriously. The Japanese quality control circles effectively use the human resources—the insights, talents, skills, and loyalties of workers—to improve both efficiency of production and to maintain very high standards in the products produced. The channels of communication between workers and management are deliberately kept flexible and open.

In summary, the human resources approach is related to the human relations theory, but there are important differences between them. The human resources approach is more complex: It sees employees as major potential resources for the organization in terms of talent, energy, dedication, and pride in work. The tasks of management are to design a system that will minimize communication barriers and lead to high performance by workers while maximizing factors that will motivate them to work at a high level of quality. In recent times, American managers have been scrambling to apply both Deming's ideas and Japanese organizational communication ideas to production processes. However, because of differences in culture and tradition, they do not always fit.

IV. The flow of messages in large organizations.

One of the most important kinds of behavior constrained by an organizational design is formal communication. An important function of the social plan of any organization is to direct the way in which messages can flow through the system. A simple way of describing formal communication in an organization is to say that the design for the content, transmission, and reception of messages dictates *who* can say *what* to be received by *whom* about specific kinds of *topics* by communicating with what *medium* in order to achieve specified types of *goals*.

Because official channels of formal communication are rigid, more flexible and open channels for *informal* communication develop. People working in groups need to communicate in a variety of ways about a number of topics. For that reason, the "grapevine" and other similar systems develop and are used to convey a great deal of information without noticeable restrictions on their transmissions.

A. Formal communication through official channels.

Four issues that need to be considered in describing the flow of official messages through the organization are the channels, the kinds of topics, the quality of communication, and the consequences of both limitations and restrictions on accuracy produced by the formal system.

1. Vertical transmission.

As can be seen on most organizational charts, the hierarchical structure implies vertical communication. That is, in a group with clearly graded levels of power and authority, communication must flow either up or down in the system.

2. Message content in formal communication.

There is a similarity in the topics that flow both upward and downward through formal channels in almost all organizations, regardless of their goals.
   a. Kinds of messages that flow upward:
      (1) Routine operational messages
      (2) Assessment by experts
      (3) Feedback on completion of tasks
      (4) Reports on problems
   b. Kinds of messages that flow downward:
      (1) Requests
      (2) Specific orders and instructions
      (3) Operating guidelines
      (4) Policy-shift directives
   c. A major point to be made in considering the flow of organizational communication, either upward or downward, is that the messages that move within the formal channels can be, and often are, *critically* important to both the people who send them and those who receive them. People's jobs can depend on what they receive in the way of orders, assessments, directives, reports, requests, and instructions.

3. Accuracy versus distortion up and down the line.

As pointed out in previous chapters dealing more generally with the basic nature of the communication process—in terms of both its verbal and its nonverbal aspects—many factors can distort and limit the paralleling of meaning between communicating parties. This is as true in the organizational setting as it is anywhere, and with greater force.
   a. Upward communication accuracy and distortion.
      (1) *Condensed*: Messages tend to get shorter and more concise as they travel from one level to another.
      (2) *Simplified*: Details are selectively dropped out of complex messages or reports. They are organized around the most salient details.
      (3) *Standardization*: Messages are couched in terms of standard terms familiar within the organization's special argot or jargon.
      (4) *Idealized*: A message transmitted to a higher level may be rephrased so as to cast the person below in the best possible light.
      (5) *Synthesized*: The message transmitted may be combined with additional details so as to form a more understandable overall picture—even when the added meanings were never part of the original event.
   b. Downward communication accuracy and distortion.
      (1) *Selective exposure:* Messages get misfiled, misplaced, or accidentally thrown away because the entire message may not be read or heard for a variety of reasons.
      (2) *Selective attention and listening:* Even if a person hears or reads a message in full, attention can wander and listening can deteriorate.
      (3) *Selective perception:* The psychological process of organizing incoming message symbols into associated meanings is a complex activity. To a considerable extent, those psychological factors can reshape meanings to fit with what the receiver hopes for, wants, fears, or likes. A situation in which meaning in a message is transformed by a receiver in such a way as to minimize a potential threat is referred to as a *perceptual defense*. Another kind of transformation of meaning can occur because of *perceptual set*, where a receiver

is expecting a particular meaning to be implied in a message. Consequently, selective perception may operate to modify meanings received, even via channels of formal communication that have been carefully designed to minimize misinterpretations.

(4) *Selective retention and recall:* No one's memory is perfect. People tend to remember good or rewarding parts of messages and "repress" those parts that seem stressful, punishing, or difficult.

(5) *Selective action:* Even if a message is perceived and interpreted accurately and remembered fully, this does not mean that it will be fully acted upon as requested or ordered. Circumstances at the times may require that some of the ordered actions be postponed, carried out in a modified manner, or simply ignored.

(6) *Vocabulary differences:* Well-educated managers and less-educated lower supervisors do not always have the same vocabulary or have the same meaning for words they do share.

B. Informal communication in organizational settings.

The de facto organization is made up of not only its deliberately designed structure but also the social ties existing among the many small and intimate groups of peers that are found in any large group. Thus, messages flow not only through the official channels prescribed for formal communication but also through grapevines—complex social pathways in a network of intimate groups.

1. Socially validated constructions of meanings.

It is through this network that rumors are retold, gossip is exchanged, and word-of-mouth diffusion of important information is transmitted. This sharing validates meanings, giving them social legitimacy.

2. Capacity, flexibility, and speed.

Generally, informal communication networks within an organization convey a great number and variety of messages on a day-to-day basis, with a great deal of flexibility in channels used and move without restrictions up and down the ranks, and horizontally within a given stratum. Because of these conditions of few barriers, many channels, and virtually no restrictions on content, informal communication can flow very swiftly to surprisingly large numbers of people.

The kinds of messages carried on the grapevine consist of *rumors, gossip* about individuals or events within the organization, *speculation* about what is going to take place as a result of some planned or suspected change, and *interpretations* of the nature and meanings of actions taken by those in power.

C. Distortion of messages in the grapevine.

While an organizational grapevine may provide for swift communication flow to a large number of people, the accuracy of this type of communication can be very low (except for short messages). Two general patterns of distortion have been found that characterize the spread of rumors, the movement of news from one person to another, and similar interpersonal transmission of verbal messages. In reality, the embedding and compounding patterns tend to work together in the actual transmission of rumors through a grapevine.

1. The "embedding" pattern.

Refers to a particular set of distortions in a message that may occur when it is transmitted orally from one person to another to the next in a kind of serial pattern. Three forms of distortion that often characterize the content of a message as it moves along a chain of tellers and retellers:

a. *Leveling* refers to a general shortening of the original account, rumor, or story.

b. *Sharpening* is the counterpart of leveling. As the story or account shrinks, it becomes organized around its most central or "salient" details. This results in a dropping away of original richness of detail, and consequent distortion creeps in as the message is repackaged into briefer and briefer versions.

c. *Assimilation* is the process by which the message is reshaped by the psychological characteristics and culturally learned habits of the person who hears it.

d. Through leveling, sharpening, and assimilation, then, the embedding process can produce many unexpected and unusual changes in the content of a message as it moves by informal word-of-mouth communication through the grapevine in an organization.

2. The "compounding" pattern.

A substantial body of research has revealed a pattern whereby an original message passed by informal communication in a grapevine gains additional details and interpretations that were never part of the original message. These tended to happen under two conditions: first, if the original story is relatively brief, and second, if it was of a *threatening* or disturbing nature.

D. Consequences of formal and informal communication.

1. Organizational subcultures.

Within organizations, a subculture develops that is unique to each particular group. While it includes all of the physical objects used in achieving the goals of the organization, it also includes all of the attitudes, values, beliefs, sentiments, rules, special language, and everything else that is produced and shared by its members.

The organization subculture develops from two basic sources: One is the official organization as it functions with its carefully defined channels of formal communication. The other is the micro subcultures of the many spontaneously formed peer groups that develop among work associates at all levels of the ranking structure.

2. Conflicting subcultures.

There is always the potential that differences between subcultures within a diverse organization will become pronounced. That is, the beliefs, attitudes, language, and so on, of some may become incomprehensible to the others. If that happens, barriers to effective communication, even of the formal type, exist and limit the degree to which the group can achieve its goals.

3. Organizational cohesion.

Organizational cohesion is different than personal satisfaction. Such cohesion is based on features of the organization itself that keep it together as a whole. What keeps an organization together is called *dependency-based cohesion.* This type of cohesion is based on the complex division of labor that produces a strong pattern of dependencies between individuals and even units within an organization. Individuals are in a relationship of mutual task dependency that holds the overall group together so that it can function as a unit.

What coordinates the activities within this division of interdependent labor is formal communication. Throughout the system, a flow of formal communication provides vital instructions that coordinate subgroups and individuals performing specialized tasks within the structure. Thus, formal communication is the basis on which dependency-based cohesion is established and maintained.

V. Chapter review.

CHAPTER 8
COMMUNICATING WITH MEDIA

LEARNING OBJECTIVES

After studying the chapter, the student should be able to:

- Compare and contrast the similarities and differences between *face-to-face* and *mediated* communication.

- Discuss the personal and social influence of *new media*.

- Identify the advantages and disadvantages of *letters*.

- Explain how a *memorandum* differs from a *letter*.

- Identify and discuss the advantages and disadvantages of using *memoranda*.

- Discuss the importance of the *telephone* for communication.

- Discuss telephone etiquette for business and personal calls.

- Discuss the use of *answering machines, voice-mail networks,* and *facsimile (fax)*.

- Explain how *computer networks* are being used to link together local, national, and multinational communication systems.

- Explain *electronic mail* and its advantages and disadvantages. Also discuss e-mail norms.

- Define and discuss *teleconferencing*.

- Compare and contrast *computer conferencing, audio conferencing,* and *video conferencing*.

EXTENDED CHAPTER OUTLINE

This chapter will focus on the human communication process as it takes place with the use of several types of media. These include not only traditional written media—letters and memoranda—but also contemporary electronic systems that move information almost instantaneously from message senders to receivers.

I.   Face-to-face versus mediated communication.
    A. Why media matter.
       A medium is simply a device that moves information over distance so that people who are apart can communicate. All of the media that are in wide use today are designed to move information. Does the process of using media to move information alter the correspondence in intended and constructed meanings? YES! Each medium places its own demands on both the source person and the receiver, and mediated communication is both similar to and different from that which takes place when people are face-to-face.
       The major similarity between mediated and face-to-face communication lies in the fact that there are people at each end. Thus, contemporary media systems, such as cellular telephones, answering machines, facsimile, and computers linked by satellite relays, continue

to make use of the basic features of human communication that have been discussed previously. These features are verbal and written symbols based on language, at least some nonverbal cues and signals, transactional constructions of meanings, and all the rest.

In spite of the similarities in the underlying principles of all forms of human communication, there are important differences. Some have to do with modifications of the social relationships that link senders and receivers. Others have to do with technical features of various kinds of media themselves; and some media can be used to transmit messages of subtle and sensitive interpretations, whereas others are severely limited to concise denotative meanings.

1. Media limit effective role-taking.

    One of the alterations in the social relationship between senders and receivers that occurs when media are used is the limitation of role-taking. Effective role-taking is far less possible where persons who transmit a message cannot observe (face-to-face) or are not well acquainted with the receivers. Role-taking can be accomplished reasonably well with some media, such as a private letter between people who know each other intimately. However, when huge numbers of strangers are in an audience and a message source can make only limited predictions as to how each member of the audience will react to his or her message, role-taking becomes almost impossible.

2. Media limit the adequacy of feedback.

    Here, more depends on the nature of the medium than on the existing relationship between the communicating parties. For example, in a telephone conversation, some immediate feedback is possible, but it is not as rich in nonverbal feedback as it is in face-to-face communication. Consequently, the accuracy, or the "index of fidelity," is almost automatically reduced by limitations that are imposed by the use of media. Nothing beats face-to-face communication when accuracy is desired or influence is an important goal.

B. The personal and social influence of new media.

The widespread adoption of new technologies of communication has always altered the communication process itself. This is because each new medium:

1. Imposes its own special requirements on the ways in which messages are formulated.
2. Governs the speed and convenience with which message transmission takes place.
3. Influences the ways in which receivers reconstruct meaning from what is sent to them.
4. Creates significant changes in the social, economic, and cultural processes within which it is used (e.g., the telegraph had subtle and long-lasting effects on the entire society).

II. Traditional written media.

The present analysis will not be concerned with the print mass media—books, magazines, and newspapers—but will focus on written transmissions that originate with a single individual who wants to transmit a message to either one person, a small group, or a large number of receivers. This kind of written communication takes place when people write letters or memoranda.

A. Letters.
    1. Advantages:
        a. Portable: All a sender needs is a pen or pencil, writing paper, an envelope, and a stamp. A letter can be read almost anywhere.
        b. Hard copy: It can be placed in a file, saved, read, and reread at the recipient's own pace.
        c. Required action: It implies that the recipient should take some action or do something (at least send a written reply).

d. It can be composed at the writer's own convenience and pace.
e. Privacy is ensured by the U.S. Postal Service. Strict federal laws forbid tampering with a person's mail.

2. Disadvantages:
a. Inconvenience, limitations on length, and slow speed of composing and sending a letter.
b. Intellectual capacity and some skill with words may be in short supply. The norms for writing letters are complex. A few basic rules of thumb have been identified that can help in the preparation of any business letter so that it will be more favorably received and better understood:
    (1) General features: Correct grammar, spelling, and punctuation are absolute requirements. Neatness and "letterhead" stationery are suggested.
    (2) Format: There are a variety of acceptable business-letter formats for positioning the address, the salutation, the body of the letter, and the signature.
    (3) Formulating an appropriate message: Selection of appropriate strategies will depend on the goal the sending person is trying to achieve (applying for a job, persuading a receiver to buy a product; informing someone of favorable or unfavorable decisions, such as a promotion or a rejection of a credit application).
    (4) Whatever the purpose, an effective letter must express sincerity and concern, must be readable and concise, and must emphasize the main points in the message. Finally, it must never contain sexist language (women make up half of our labor force).

B. Memoranda.

A memorandum is very different from a letter, and it serves a restricted purpose. It is a widely used medium for written communication between members *within* an organization, particularly where a permanent record seems desirable.

The memorandum is a very stylized medium. It follows a standardized format that has evolved as a form of organizational communication over many decades (see page 231 of your text, for example).

1. Advantages:
a. Leaves a memory or paper trail in an organization. A memorandum, like a letter, is a "hard copy" that can be saved or filed. Such files often develop around sensitive transactions (performance evaluations). If that file needs to be reviewed, proof is there that communication took place and the nature of the messages transmitted or received is clear. Therefore, memoranda preserve messages through time in an effective way.
b. Most memoranda are brief and concise.

2. Disadvantages:
a. Memoranda lack legal protection. In other words, memoranda lack the official protection and deterrents applicable to letters that are sent through the U.S. mail.
b. Memoranda are often interpreted as unimportant—especially those that are addressed to "staff" or "all personnel."
c. They also suffer from the same limitations on role-taking and immediate feedback as other media. Because they need to be concise, with messages formulated in official language, they are phrased in terms that might not characterize a conversation or even a lengthier written document.

3. Despite these disadvantages, the memorandum remains an important medium in organization communication. In particular it retains the advantage of leaving a "memory-record." For this reason, it is not likely that it will be easily replaced.

III. Telephone and related systems.

The telephone continues to be, and will remain, one of the most important media. Today, we use the telephone so often, we often take it for granted. Americans make an estimated 800 million telephone calls a day—but we seldom take the time to plan a telephone message or worry that we are following the best procedures. However, there is a reasonably well-understood set of norms that thoughtful senders and receivers follow.

  A. Using the phone.

    1. Telephone norms: Much depends on whether we are sending or receiving a business call or a personal call.

      a. Etiquette for business calls:

        (1) Business calls should be restricted to business hours.
        (2) Nothing is more thoughtless and obnoxious than a call that interrupts a meal.
        (3) Do not let a telephone call take priority.
        (4) Return telephone calls promptly.
        (5) Identify who you are when calling; do the same as a receiver.
        (6) If you want to chat, ask if the receiver has time.
        (7) Keep in mind that business phones are not always private.

      b. Etiquette for personal calls:

        (1) Think carefully before letting young children answer the phone.
        (2) Callers should consult their watch (or time zone) before calling.
        (3) Apply the suggestions for business calls, such as identifying yourself.

    2. Answering machines.

       These devices are becoming increasingly adopted for both business and home use. They serve the purpose of recording messages so that calls can be returned. However, many people use them to "screen" calls. There is a great variety in types of recording one hears when one's phone is answered by a machine. Such variation in messages send their own nonverbal messages.

    3. Voice-mail networks.

       An elaboration of the answering machine in a organizational setting is a central computer-operated answering machine that serves everyone on a network of users.

  B. Using fax.

     A telephone-based medium of great significance is facsimile transmission—or "fax" as it is more popularly called. Facsimile is a telecommunication system by which exact copies of a document or even photographs can be sent via phone lines. The greatest advantages of a fax are speed and cost. Fax is relatively inexpensive to send and arrives immediately. However, one limitation of the fax is that it is not very private. Fax transmissions should always include a cover sheet indicating clearly the number of pages being sent, who originated the transmission, and to whom it is addressed.

IV. Computer networks.

Today, networks of computers, linked together in local, national, and international systems, are creating a quiet but profound communication revolution. Many observers have noted that these computerized communication technologies have changed the United States into an "information society" (where more labor force time is spent in communicating and processing symbols than in agriculture or manufacturing).

A. Types of networks.

1. Localm area networks (LANs).

   A local area network is a set of linked computers (usually of the desktop variety) that are confined to a limited physical area, such as an office or group of offices. This allows individuals at each "station" to send and receive messages; to share programs, software, data files, storage space, and expensive equipment.

2. Large-scale networks.

   Large "super-networks" are also in place. These are networks of networks. BITNET is an example. This system connects the local area networks of hundreds of universities and research organizations in the nation into a single system.

3. On-line information services.

   Of increasing importance in the U.S. are various on-line information services provided for both organizations and consumers by commercial vendors. Examples are CompuServe and Prodigy. For various fees, a user can subscribe to such a service, access it from a desktop computer equipped with a modem, and obtain information from hundreds of databases containing an incredible variety of information. Some on-line systems provide electronic "bulletin boards" where users can leave messages for others to read.

B. Electronic mail.

   E-mail is the name given to messages sent from one computer to another by combining word-processing software with the nearly instantaneous transmission speed of computers linked by phone-linked networks.

1. Advantages: E-mail allows people to send various kinds of print messages without having to stuff and address an envelope or wait several days for delivery. Instead, the message is typed on a computer screen, along with the receiver's electronic address on a local or national network. The source's computer transmits the information directly to the recipient's computer. Messages do not have to filter through secretaries or administrators (like many faxes do) before reaching the intended person. Copies of a message can be sent to a single receiver or several people at the same time. E-mail also maintains its own archives. That is, most systems have both a temporary "reader file" for recent messages that have not been read yet and a "notebook" file where all past messages that have been sent or received are permanently stored on disc or tape. If a "hard copy" is needed at a later date it can be printed out.

   From these characteristics it can be seen that e-mail has great advantages. It is incredibly fast and efficient. Network e-mail also saves labor costs (reducing the number of people needed to do typing, filing, etc.).

2. Disadvantages: With e-mail, messages do not signal their arrival (as is the case with the phone). Thus the sender is at the mercy of the receiver's schedule for reviewing e-mail messages.

   Another problem with e-mail is that it is not totally private. Sometimes an e-mail address or a user-identification code is shared by a group of people, rather than just one person. There is usually no way for a message source to know in advance, without knowing the local situation in detail. This means that one ought to think twice before transmitting highly sensitive or potentially embarrassing personal information.

3. E-mail norms.

E-mail, like other forms of communication, provides clues about the person sending the message. That is, even when communicating by an electronic medium, message content and style play a part in the "presentation of self" by which receivers form opinions about and assessments of the personal qualities of the transmitting person. Therefore, concern should be devoted to grammar, punctuation, and spelling (as in letters). Also, one should be aware of the potential nonverbal messages sent by "all caps" or abbreviated messages. In addition, electronic mail, like other forms of communication, is irretrievable; once it is sent, it cannot be retracted. Finally, e-mail users must consider the issue of privacy—others may "open" a receiver's mail. Currently, ownership of e-mail messages is being debated.

V. Teleconferencing.

The term *teleconferencing* comes from the Greek word *tele*, meaning "at a distance." Today it refers to the use of several different media systems to overcome distance and to link spatially dispersed people together for the purpose of conducting a formal or informal meeting. There are a number of ways to accomplish this goal—some more effective than others.

A. Computer conferencing.

A simple and limited form of conferencing can be based on e-mail exchanges through computer-linked networks. However, computer conferencing is not flexible (being restricted to typed messages). It is both linear and cumbersome in that participants have to wait until others type and send their messages. And it obviously provides only minimal role-taking and feedback because senders and receivers neither see nor hear the others. Thus, a computer conference would be unsuitable when sensitive discussions are needed or in situations where parties have to be persuaded to reach consensus through the use of subtle arguments. However, computer conferencing can be arranged with very little lead time and with participants remaining at their work stations. In addition, it has the great advantage of being cheap.

B. Audio conferencing.

This is an older and familiar form of teleconferencing. Conference calls occur when people in several locations use telephones to engage in group discussions. More formal audio conferences often take place in special rooms, one at each site, with participants seated around tables communicating via telephone lines. Such rooms are often equipped with speakers and microphones for high-quality voice transmission.

While they are more expensive than simple computer conferences, audio conferences provide for rich communication experiences. They can be set up with only minor lead time and little disruption to participants' normal work schedules. However, audio conferences suffer all the limitations of any other form of telephone communication (limited role-taking and visual nonverbal signals cannot be read). In spite of these limitations, audio conferencing provides a comparatively inexpensive and flexible system permitting people to engage in group discussion.

C. Video conferencing.

One of the fastest-growing forms of mediated communication is video conferencing. In its most sophisticated form, it brings together video cameras, interactive satellite transmission, and television receivers. Video conferencing is by far the most expensive of the various forms of teleconferencing systems. Many American businesses find it efficient to use as compared to trying to get people together in person (face-to-face).

The advantages of the video conference over any of the other methods lie in the fact that it provides richer messages with both verbal and nonverbal elements. Plus, it is relatively effective for role-taking, feedback, and the use of nonverbal cues. Also, video permits people to see various kinds of graphics, film clips, and displays of physical objects.

The video conference is an effective system in cases where the issues under discussion are time-sensitive, where interactivity is both important and useful, and where the discussion can be significantly enhanced by the video. On the other hand, it requires expensive equipment and trained technical personnel. Finally, it is sensitive to weather conditions and needs up to 3 hours of lead time to set up the video facility.

VI. Chapter review.

CHAPTER 9
PRESENTING ONESELF EFFECTIVELY

LEARNING OBJECTIVES

After studying the chapter, the student should be able to:

- Define and explain the concept *person perception*.

- Discuss the idea of *presentation of self*.

- Explain what is meant by *impression management* and *effective self-presentation*.

- Explain and discuss the *principle of rapid impression formation*.

- Explain and discuss the *principle of the salient characteristic*.

- Explain and discuss the *labeling principle*.

- Explain and discuss the *implicit personality principle*.

- Discuss the common problems in initial encounters.

- Discuss the typical problems that are created when more than two persons are present and how they affect impression formation.

- Discuss how the contextual issue of where people meet can influence initial encounters.

- Discuss the importance of *planning* and *goal clarification* on self-presentation.

- Discuss the significance of *selective perception* on self-presentation.

- Identify and discuss the principles that can be used in preselecting an impression.

- Define and explain the concept of *attribution*.

- Distinguish between *internal* and *external* attributions.

- Describe how *typical* behaviors are used as the basis of attributions.

- Discuss the influence of *social constraints* on attributions.

- Identify and discuss the six steps that can assist in gathering information for and reduce uncertainties about self-presentation.

- Explain the concept of *affinity-seeking* and its relationship to self-presentation.

- Define and discuss the concept of *self-disclosure*.

- Distinguish between depth and breadth of self-disclosure.

- Identify the type of self-disclosure that may be undesirable and risky to initial encounters.

- Distinguish among the three kinds of messages that create opportunities for self-disclosure: *greeting*, *small talk*, and *the main topic*.

- Define and explain *credibility* and its relationship to self-presentation.

- Explain the inflexible nature of pre-existing impressions.

- Distinguish among the three factors that influence attributions: *distinctiveness, consistency,* and *consensus.*

- Discuss the *principle of covariance.*

- Discuss how one may construct new realities.

EXTENDED CHAPTER OUTLINE

The foci of this chapter are on answering four major questions: First, how do people form initial impressions of others? Second, how can we influence the impressions others form about us? Third, what specifically can we communicate, both verbally and nonverbally, to make favorable impressions? Finally, what can be done to change unfavorable impressions?

I.   The impressions we make in initial encounters.

    A. What research tells us about initial impressions.

Person perception is the broad area of investigation that focuses on the general stages people pass through when they meet and develop initial impressions of each other. More specifically, Tagiuri defines the concept as "the process by which a person comes to know and to think about other persons, their characteristics, qualities, and inner states." Because this definition is broad, the locus of this chapter is specifically on the steps involved in what has been called *presentation of self.*

      1. The process of presenting one's self.

The idea of "presentation of self" refers to formulating and transmitting verbal and nonverbal messages to other people about what kind of person we are. Our transmissions concerning ourselves may be deliberate or completely unconscious.

In our initial encounters, we do not always intend to get other individuals to evaluate us in a particular way. However, if we want to, it is possible to *plan* a communication strategy and transmit verbal and nonverbal messages that are deliberately designed to create a particular set of first impressions. This process is referred to as *impression management.* In this chapter, this management process is referred to as *effective self-presentation.*

      2. The principle of rapid impression formation.

The pioneering research by Solomon Asch on impression formation demonstrated that (1) subjects quickly form elaborate impressions of the target after receiving only limited information about the individual; and (2) if the target was thought to have one set of favorable qualities (being intelligent, skillful, determined, and practical), subjects believed the target had other such qualities (being generous, good-natured, happy, and important).

      3. The principle of the salient characteristic.

Once again, Asch found that by adding a single characteristic, such as either "warm" or "cold," to a list of descriptive terms, subjects reorganized their overall impression of the target to coincide with the characteristic. In other words, when we meet someone who seems to have many positive, attractive qualities, our initial impression is usually positive. Then, a single additional revelation (or characteristic) may suddenly change the impression drastically. Such a salient characteristic (or revelation) might be that the person has a serious disease, uses drugs, or has a criminal record. Upon fitting that "characteristic" into our mental configuration, our impressions switch immediately to a negative pattern.

    4. The labeling principle.

    The labeling principle is essentially the same idea as Asch's "salient characteristic" principle. The basic idea is that one critical piece of information about a person can communicate a powerful message. Labels often supply such information, regardless of whether they are right or wrong. Any negative label, like "former mental patient," "suspected sex offender," or "cheater," can have a dramatic and negative influence on the impression people form of another person.

    5. The "implicit personality" principle.

    "Personality" refers to a pattern of psychological attributes that makes each individual human being different and unique, and those traits are thought to shape people's responses to their physical and social worlds. Thus, the reason we form impressions of another person, constructing our interpretations of their "implicit" personality, is that we are trying to predict in our own minds how they will behave toward us and others.

    An investigation by Wishner clearly illustrates implicit personality research. Wishner had a group of college students rate their professors on a list of personal characteristics. The terms "warm" and "cold" were added (as in the Asch experiments). The results of Wishner's experiments imply that the overall pattern of impressions of a particular individual can be predicted from the *relationship* between the lists of characteristics that the target person is first thought to possess (friendly or unfriendly). In other words, people construct a relatively well-organized pattern of what they think is important about someone on the basis of very few facts. Furthermore, certain kinds of characteristics have a truly powerful influence on the "implicit personality" that people project onto the target person.

  B. Problems in initial encounters.

    1. Common difficulties when meeting people:
      a. Finding things in common with strangers
      b. Finding things to say to strangers
      c. Not knowing how to say things appropriately
      d. Meeting people you just don't like
      e. Meeting people who just don't like you
      f. Adjusting to language differences
      g. Adjusting to different backgrounds of experience
      h. One- or two-way communication apprehension
      i. Feeling generally awkward
      j. Feeling self-conscious
      k. Feeling alienated from others
      l. Worrying about saying the wrong thing

    2. Meeting one individual versus several people.

    The inclusion of additional individuals in a situation can influence perception, evaluation, and the messages that are exchanged. Below is a list of typical problems that are created when more than two persons are present:
      a. Fragmenting participation and focuses of attention
      b. The problem of "you can't please everybody"
      c. Individual differences create difficulties

      d. Perceptions of favoritism
      e. Speaking generally versus specifically to one person
      f. Coalitions among pairs
      g. Conversational intrusions and interruptions

3. Familiar versus unfamiliar places.

The contextual issue of *where* we meet is the third and final contingency which needs to be considered among the factors that shape initial encounters. Generally, we are more at ease in familiar surroundings. The importance of location is that the physical surroundings where a person meets others can have a dramatic effect on how *capable* and *confident* the individual feels during the meeting. When manifested in behaviors, those feelings can serve as salient characteristics that help observers organize the pattern of personality characteristics that they project onto the individual. Thus, persons who are seen as at ease, capable, and confident are also perceived in more positive terms overall than those who are seen as inept and nervous. In this way, then, physical setting can help or hinder the outcome of self-presentation.

II. Presenting yourself in encounters that really matter.

A. Goals in first meetings.

Meetings can be either intentional or accidental. Whatever the nature of the meeting, having a clear idea as to *why* the meeting has been initiated can help in the selection of strategies, content, and style of delivery. If the encounter is a critical one, *planning* in advance for self-presentation can lead to a more certain outcome.

Developing a strategy for initiating and engaging in an encounter involves two things: First, before the encounter takes place, the *goals* that are to be achieved must be clarified. Second, attention must be given to setting the stage to accomplish those goals.

What are the goals to be achieved in a critical encounter? If we want that outcome to be favorable, there are three goals we need to consider ahead of time. That is, we can plan ahead to achieve effective control over:

1. The earliest impressions formed during initial moments of contact.

2. The expanding configuration of impressions organized as our presentation of self unfolds.

3. The lasting patterns of impressions that the other party finally takes away.

(Goal clarification can help us identify the impressions that are more likely to contribute to success.)

B. Pre-selecting your impressions.

In some first meetings, what you really want (goal) and how you want to be perceived may be virtually the same thing. It is important, then, to communicate those characteristics that count in the situation so that they will be quickly and unmistakenly perceived and understood by those on the receiving end.

There are two major reasons why pre-selection of qualities that create positive impression is not all that difficult: First, everyone has many positive qualities. Second, most people tend to like other people. An important part of the task of effective self-presentation is to minimize potentially negative influences and to maximize the positive features, or salient characteristics, that are so important in initial impression formation.

1. The significance of selective perception.

The term *perception* refers to "making sense of" or "attaching meaning to" some aspect of reality. Perception is a critical process in forming impressions of other people, and there are easily understood reasons why it is inevitably a "selective" activity. Every person perceives and experiences the world through his or her own internalized meanings, dispositions, emotional states, and needs. *Selective perception, then, refers to the unique way people interpret what they observe.* It is the basis for the selection of some salient characteristic around which an observer can create a complex initial set of impressions about what we are really like.

2. Developing a preliminary game plan.

   Strategies of effective self-presentation consist of using such nonverbal forms of communication as clothing, mannerisms, gestures, posture, and demeanor, plus verbal messages with specific content delivered with a particular style and level of vocabulary. However, perhaps the best guide to which strategies to select is based on common sense. That is, one should avoid doing or saying anything to others that might be perceived selectively and used as a basis to construct a negative "implicit personality."

   Certain principles can be used in preselecting the kinds of impression that one may want to create during a particular initial encounter. For example, consider the following:

   a. Size up the people to whom you are making a self- presentation.
   b. Appraise the physical setting carefully.
   c. Do not misrepresent yourself.
   d. Use all communication channels open to you to get your positive qualities across.
   e. Look very closely for feedback messages.

   In essence, careful assessment of the people, the situation, the channels of communication available, and the nature of feedback messages transmitted during the encounter is far more likely to result in an effective self-presentation than is one that consists of just "letting things proceed naturally."

C. Sizing up people.

   The central factor in any encounter is, of course, the people. One must have enough knowledge about them to engage in effective role-taking, to have a good idea about how they are going to interpret your presentation and how they are likely to respond to you (favorably or unfavorably).

   1. Attributing motives to others.

      Attribution can be defined as *the selection and assignment to another individual various personal qualities, conditions, or dispositions that we believe are the causes of or influences on some aspect of that person's behavior.* Some of those attributed causes or influences are seen as within or "internal" to the person (e.g., attitudes, values, and motivations). Other influences are seen as "external" to the individual (e.g., requirements of social organization or other aspects of the surrounding situation). Thus, when we "size people up," we are making inferences about them in two ways: (1) how they are likely to react to us and (2) why that will probably be the case.

   2. "Typical" behaviors as a basis for attribution.

      One source of information that can be used for attributions about other people is their membership in significant social categories (e.g., males, children, educated people, working class, farmers, etc.) Often, people in such categories are said to be characterized by certain regularities in their behavior. We all make predictions on the basis of "typical" interests of people in specific social categories. However, carried to extremes, rigidly held assumptions, categorical attributions, and unfounded forecasts can become *stereotypes*.

3. Social constraints as factors in attribution.

External to the individual, but very influential on behavior, are social constraints that dictate at particular times how the individual has to evaluate and respond to your self-presentation, regardless of his or her inner feelings and attitudes. For example, individuals in positions of power and authority have to think and act according to the mandates of those positions at times.

The following list includes simple and effective steps that can assist, both in the gathering of personal information about others and in reducing uncertainties about their probable reactions and behaviors:

    a. Look carefully at people to identify any obvious verbal and nonverbal behavior that communicates psychological characteristics (attitudes, intelligence, emotions, etc.).

    b. Observe people interacting to see how they respond to each other (aggressively, politely, formally, warmly, etc.).

    c. Ask questions about your potential audience (if possible) so as to understand as much as you can about who they are and where they come from, both geographically and socially.

    d. Compare the people with individuals you know. If they seem alike, they may think and behave similarly.

    e. Gather whatever information you can about social category membership (education, occupation, age, race, ethnicity, religion, etc.).

    f. Review carefully the social constraints that are on them at the time of the encounter, or other requirements they have to meet, and assess what these require them to do.

    g. Review everything you have learned and try to put together a composite—an organized prediction—of how they will respond to various aspects of your self-presentation and why.

D. Getting people to like you.

In recent years, social scientists have done extensive research defining strategies that people use to try to get others to like them, otherwise known as "affinity-seeking."

1. Affinity-seeking strategies.

Refer to Table 9.1 (pages 268–269), which refers to 25 specific strategies that people report to use to get others to like them. Actually, the consolidation of patterns may produce over 40 million combinations. It is clear, then, that numerous strategies can be used to get people to like you—the problem becomes not whether affinity-seeking strategies are available but which one(s) to select.

2. Selecting strategies.

A "one size fits all" rule cannot be applied to the selection of affinity-seeking strategies. A person's selection of a strategy, or some combination of strategies, must be based in part on that individual's gender, personal preferences, and familiarity with the situation, plus a combination of personality characteristics.

III. Deciding what to say.

A. Self-disclosure in initial encounters.

Self-disclosure (revealing information about ourselves) is an important part of what goes on in any self-presentation. The actual content of our self-disclosure is dependent on both the depth (intimacy) and breadth (amount) of what we communicate about ourselves. It is suggested that in initial encounters, we should be cautious about what we self-disclose. Because of selective perception, early disclosures communicated to strangers are highly susceptible to misinterpretation. Furthermore, self-disclosing information that is other than what is obvious is likely to be misinterpreted, and that which is too intense and revealing for strangers is both undesirable and highly risky. For these reasons, it is suggested that effective self-disclosure aimed at creating positive impressions must be provided carefully, gradually, and systematically.

B. Talking with new people.

Three kinds of messages create opportunities for self-disclosure in initial encounters: greetings, small talk, and the main topic of the encounter.

1. Greetings.

Under the heading of greetings we can include all of the salutations that are employed when individuals recognize and acknowledge each other. They can be verbal, nonverbal, or both.

2. Small talk.

Generally, integrating small talk into the situation helps people feel more at ease in a first encounter.

3. The main topic.

If the occasion of an encounter is informal, there will be no main topic to discuss. In contrast, in a formal encounter (such as an interview, a sales presentation, or a committee meeting), the stages are different. After a greeting and a certain amount of small talk, the participants must "get down to business" and communicate about the subject matter that brought them together in the first place.

Furthermore, the perceived personal *credibility* can have a strong influence on the interpretation of the main topic under discussion. That is, the information communicated may be judged within a framework of important dimensions—as valuable or worthless, critical or trivial, true or false—depending on the perceived sincerity and honesty of the presenter as evaluated by the audience.

IV. Changing old impressions.

Changing someone's entrenched convictions and impressions is a very difficult task that requires that the individual erase the existing impression and then recreate a new one by effective communication of fresh messages. However, older negative impressions can be changed, though it will not be easy.

A. The inflexible nature of pre-existing impressions.

A plan to extinguish a pre-existing impression begins with an understanding of the way we make attributions about ourselves. Research indicates that when we engage in an activity which we perceive as unacceptable to others, we tend to attribute the cause of that behavior to *external* causes that are beyond our control, rather than to our own *internal* preferences and desires that we can control. However, when other people observe us engaging in that unacceptable activity, they make just the opposite attribution.

What can we do to change an impression? The basic goal is to suppress the existing impression and help the target rebuild a new one that includes greater credibility and more favorable attributions to you. Once again, we must plan what we are going to say and how we are going to say it.

According to one well-known investigator, attributions concerning our behavior are a function of three factors:

1. Distinctiveness
2. Consistency
3. Consensus

Research on such factors has identified what is called the *principle of covariance*, which is defined as a general rule regarding the attribution of internal and external causes to a person's pattern of behavior. That is, if the behavior is disapproved by others, they will tend to attribute it to negative personal qualities (an internal cause). If the behavior is approved, they will attribute it to external factors beyond your control.

B. Resistance to change.

Because long-term habits of meaning can be deeply rooted and thus highly durable, one must first consider whether it is realistically possible to change a person's impression. Second, one must evaluate whether it is worth the effort (assessment of cost versus benefits).

C. Constructing new realities.

If one decides that change is possible and worth the effort, the process of reconstructing a person's impressions and attributions by self-presentation should begin by carefully considering the objectives. The task of restructuring is to communicate unmistakably favorable (distinctive) meanings that are shared by others (consensus). This needs to be done over and over again (consistency). By actions and comments, skillfully communicated, it can be made clear that others regard you favorably, respect your judgment, believe you to be trustworthy, and so on. In essence, it is important to communicate *only that which contributes to the creation of a supportive climate for interaction.*

V. Chapter review.

CHAPTER 10
INFLUENCING OTHERS

LEARNING OBJECTIVES

After studying the chapter, the student should be able to:

- Discuss the importance of persuasion in everyday life.

- Explain how persuasive messages are seen as *magic bullets*.

- Discuss the process of communication as a *transaction*.

- Define and discuss the concept of *persuasion*.

- Explain how *coercion* can be used to gain compliance.

- Explain how people can be persuaded to conform to *social expectations*.

- Explain how *cognitive reorganization* can be used to achieve behavioral change.

- Describe the process of employing *psychodynamic strategies* to persuade.

- Discuss how meanings are constructed or reconstructed to influence change.

- Explain how shaping or altering beliefs can influence change.

- Define the term *belief*. Be sure to distinguish between factual and affective beliefs. Furthermore, explain how beliefs are related to action/behavior.

- Define the term *attitude*.

- Discuss the relationship between attitudes and behavior. Consider the roles of topic importance, social pressures, and action constraints in this relationship.

- Explain Brehm's theory of *psychological reactance*.

- Distinguish between *destructive* and *constructive* resistance.

- Compare and contrast among the types of yielding: *compliance, identification,* and *internalization*.

- Explain the concept of *receiver susceptibility*.

- Discuss the relationship of receiver susceptibility to gender and various personality characteristics.

- Discuss the five features of effective messages: sidedness, message ordering, fear appeals, behavior-alternation techniques, and nonverbal cues.

- Define and discuss the term *credibility*.

- Identify and discuss the five dimensions of credibility: *competence, trustworthiness, extroversion, composure,* and *sociability*.

EXTENDED CHAPTER OUTLINE

In this chapter, the process of influencing others within the perspective of communication will be discussed. More specifically, the principle of communication underlying persuasion will be examined.

I. The importance of persuasion in everyday life.

Persuasion is one of the most pervasive communication processes in modern life. Persuasion for commercial purposes is used to sell and market a vast array of consumer products. It is a basic part of government; politicians use it in their campaigns for re-election and to establish support for legislative policies. Persuasion also plays a key role in religion, education, and public health. In short, it is widely found in virtually every aspect of life where someone wants to shape or modify the ideas, feelings, or actions of someone else in a specific way.

Most of the persuasion processes that come immediately to mind are associated with the world of mass communication. However, there is another, less obvious kind of persuasion that each of us must deal with directly every day. That is, in almost every significant face-to-face human encounter, people initiate communication for the purpose of modifying the beliefs, attitudes, or behavior of someone else. It is this type of persuasion that is the focus of this unit.

II. Formulating a definition.

A. Linear versus transactional views of persuasion.

Persuasion can be viewed as either a "one-way" process or an "interactive" exchange between the parties.

1. *Persuasive messages as magic bullets.*

In this view, the message transmitted by the sender in the persuasion process is seen as aimed at the person selected as the target. The components of the message are seen as "magic bullets," impinging on the receiver and having an effect. In other words, a source organizes a message with clever words, arguments, and appeals, then aims these at the person to be persuaded. Once the bullet arrives, the receiver undergoes the alterations desired by the source. Thus, the message organization and appeals cause some form of change of belief, attitude, or behavior.

2. *Persuasion as communication transaction.*

A second interpretation of the way in which persuasion works indicates that the receiver of a message plays as active a part in achieving whatever changes takes place as does the source. This view of persuasion as a transaction has now become the way in which most communication scholars think about it.

B. A formal definition.

Persuasion can be defined as *a communicative transaction in which a source constructs and transmits messages designed to influence a receiving person's constructions of meanings in ways that will lead to change (desired by the sender) in the receiver's beliefs, attitudes, or behavior.*

III. The dynamics of influence.

A. Using coercion to gain compliance.

The term *coercion* refers to compelling someone to do something, or restraining them from acting in some way, by threatening them with consequences that they find unacceptable.

B. Persuading people to conform to social expectations.

The organizing factors of all kinds of human social behavior in group settings are the kinds of shared rules we have referred to as *norms, roles, ranks,* and *controls.* The key here is that persuasive messages define the kind of behavior that is permitted and expected by members of a group. This "social expectations" approach to persuasion can be an effective strategy in getting people to change their behavior. The process of sociocultural persuasion based on social expectations is a complex process in which norms, roles, ranks, and social controls all play a part in defining what is *acceptable* versus what is *deviant* behavior.

C. Cognitive reorganization to achieve behavioral change.

Several terms needs to be clarified: *Cognitive functioning* refers to what used to be called thinking, interpreting, and knowing. *Cognitive organization* refers to the structure of one's beliefs, attitudes, and values. Finally, *cognitive processing* includes perceiving, interpreting, remembering, and recalling.

Cognitive organization (or structure) is important in discussing persuasion. According to the *psychodynamic strategy,* the route to achieving behavioral change lies in achieving cognitive reorganization. That is, if carefully designed messages can change the way people believe or feel about a topic, such changes will result in modifications in the way they act toward the object of the communication.

1. *Constructing or reconstructing meanings.*

One important way in which cognitive organizations can be influenced is by providing people with *meanings* for objects, situations, and events that they have to interpret and react or respond to. People trying to persuade others often make use of connotative meanings to influence the interpretations that receivers make of a particular message. It is a process of establishing, extending, substituting, and stabilizing meanings that are associated with particular words, concepts, events, or situations.

2. *Shaping or altering beliefs.*

A belief is defined as *a kind of statement of truth that an individual accepts about some object, situation, or event.* Some beliefs are factual, others are affective (emotional quality that implies such feelings as like, dislike, acceptance, rejection, approval, or disapproval).

The psychodynamic strategy of shaping or altering beliefs focuses mainly on *affective* truth statements. The reason is that they are closely linked to the kinds of actions often sought in persuasion—that is, accepting or rejecting something, or acting positively or negatively toward it in some other way. Our affective beliefs seem as valid and compelling to us as do those that incorporate only emotionally neutral facts.

The reason that altering beliefs is a goal of psychodynamic persuasion is that beliefs—both factual and affective—are *guides to actions.* This link between belief and behavior provides the foundation for one of the most important assumptions underlying the entire field of persuasive communication: It is assumed that persuasive messages can be designed to alter people's beliefs—factual or affective. If they do indeed achieve that objective, and the person does modify his or her beliefs, then it follows that their *actions* may also change. In essence, messages are designed to change beliefs, which will then serve to modify behavior.

3. *Creating or modifying attitudes.*

An attitude can be defined as *a relatively enduring organization of affective beliefs about some broad object (such as a policy, social category of people or situation) that increases the probability that an individual will respond to that object in a manner consistent with those beliefs.* Attitudes are learned and developed through experiences.

4. *The relationship between attitudes and behavior.*

   Although a substantial controversy exists among researchers, there is general agreement that in fact *there is often little direct association between attitudes and behavior in most real-life situations.* The probability of acting in accord with one's attitude is dependent on the presence or absence of several limiting and facilitating factors, such as *topic importance, social pressures, and action constraints.*

   Generally, even if a person has a strongly held attitude toward a topic he or she regards as important, and even when inhibiting social pressures are completely absent, there may still be numerous factors in a real-life situation that will prevent corresponding action from taking place. Therefore, it is unrealistic to expect that, if persuasive messages do succeed in bringing about attitude change, there will be a corresponding change in behavior with attitudes and actions remaining in accordance.

IV. Understanding resistance and yielding.

   As human beings, we are universally *resistant to change.*

   A. Resistance as reaction to persuasion attempts.

      Jack Brehm's *theory of psychological reactance* states that a person is motivated to "rebel" when his or her freedom to choose a particular way of acting is threatened by persuasion. Thus, our need to be in *control,* plus a strong desire for a stable and balanced life, provides the foundation for reactance. That is, as adults we expect and like the freedom, the importance of that freedom, and many other closely related issues, all of which motivate us to resist particular influence attempts.

   B. Types of resistance

      1. *Destructive resistance.*

         Extreme destructive resistance is characterized as disagreeable, negative, subversive, or even rebellious behavior. From this perspective, resistance is misbehavior—disobedience or corruption of authority. This type of resistance clearly illustrates a contempt for authority figures or for authority itself.

      2. *Constructive resistance.*

         Constructive resistance can be explained as resistance to persuasion that contributes positively to a situation, especially when the behavior being solicited is against ethical norms. In reality, the boundaries between constructive and destructive resistance can be very cloudy. What seems constructive to one group may be interpreted as destructive by another. This is important because to develop a strategy for the reduction of resistance, it is important to understand whether, from the standpoint of the person, it is seen as constructive.

   C. Types of yielding.

      Although the most predictable reaction to an influence attempt is resistance, sometimes it is neither possible nor appropriate. That is, there are a variety of circumstances in which we might want to yield in a particular situation. Kelman has described three types of yielding: *compliance, identification,* and *internalization.*

      1. *Compliance.*

         This refers to yielding publicly or observably to an influence attempt—but in this case, without actually accepting the change privately. Compliance lasts only as long as the influencing agent is visibly present. Compliance as a form of yielding is based on the expectation of gaining rewards or avoiding punishment.

2. *Identification.*

Kelman's second type of yielding to influence is that which occurs because of our desire to emulate a particular individual. Yielding of this type is based on our wish to gain satisfaction in being "like" an individual or a group that we want to imitate, or that we admire.

3. *Internalization.*

This third type of yielding to influence indicates that we do so because it is personally rewarding or useful. More important, people yield in this manner so as to be consistent with their values. *Values* refer to whatever an individual deeply believes to be important in life. Internalization is the result of a rational decision to yield because the change fits into the individual's system of values.

V.   Communication strategies for influencing people.
  A. Recognizing receiver characteristics.

   As in all communication, persuasion strategies require some knowledge of the receiver target for change. There are a variety of ways we can acquire information about people we want to influence (as mentioned in Chapter 9). One additional consideration is *receiver susceptibility,* which refers to the degree to which an individual's personal characteristics make him or her either more or less easily influenced by others. Such attributes are important in deciding the best ways to influence receivers.

   1. *Gender differences.*

   Early studies supported the assumption that females were more easily influenced than males. By the late 1970s, however, researchers had concluded that there probably are no *major* gender differences in susceptibility to persuasion. Contemporary investigations indicate that there are certain things about more "traditional" males and females that probably do affect the degree to which they are susceptible to influence.

   2. *Personality characteristics.*

   Large numbers of researchers have investigated whether differences in personality characteristics among human beings are related to susceptibility to persuasion. One study found that change is clearly tied to particular receiver personality profiles. Specifically, large amounts of change occurred with receivers who were obliging, changeable, dependent, and unstable. Minimum change occurred among those who were aggressive, unchanging, forceful, efficient, and well informed.

  B. Features of effective messages.

   Of all the potential "keys" examined in thousands of studies, only a few even come close to working. These "keys" are more accurately called features of effective messages. Five features have been identified:

   1. *Sidedness.*

   Results of a number of studies support the use of a two-sided message strategy that refutes the other's position.

   2. *Message ordering.*

   A substantial amount of research has examined whether the *first* side of an argument presented or the most *recent* side carries the most influence. This is what is usually referred to as the *primacy-recency* question. Results indicate no universal law of primacy-recency, and one's choice should depend on what conditions exist at the time of the influence attempt.

3. *Fear appeals.*

The original research examining the effectiveness of using fear-arousing appeals to influence change indicated that large amounts of change are produced with weak fear appeals and little or no change results from strong appeals that aroused high levels of fear. More recent fear-appeal studies suggest that the opposite is the case. That is, strong fear appeals do work, producing more yielding than weak appeals. There seems to be a point at which too much fear in a message causes people to avoid or disregard the message or to do both. As with other strategies described, one must consider both the target and the situation carefully prior to trying this strategy.

4. *Behavior-alteration techniques.*

This refers to a set of message techniques rather than a single persuasion strategy. Investigations of these techniques indicate that using several behavior-alteration procedures appears to be effective in motivating a person to yield in a particular influence attempt.

Recent examinations indicate that the original techniques can be categorized into two general types: prosocial and antisocial.

5. *Using nonverbal cues.*

Nonverbal immediacy can be extremely important to influencing people. The effects of immediacy are based on the "principle of utility." In brief, we tend to approach people we like physically and psychologically, and we tend to avoid behaving in these ways toward people we don't like. People understand this, and therefore, signals of nonverbal immediacy are an effective form of persuasive communication.

C. Credibility of the source.

Credibility refers to "how believable a person believes a message source to be." Furthermore, credibility is something that is perceived—in the eye of the beholder. Second, to be credible, one must be believable. Believability refers to the combination of five separate dimensions: competence, trustworthiness, extroversion, composure, and sociability.

1. *Competence* refers to how knowledgeable or expert a source is thought to be in a given content area.

2. *Trustworthiness* refers to whether people believe us to be an honest person.

3. *Extroversion* refers to the degree to which the source is believed to be talkative, bold, dynamic, and outgoing.

4. *Composure* refers to the degree to which a source is in control of his or her emotions. Composed individuals are seen as poised, relaxed, and confident.

5. *Sociability* refers to how likable and friendly one seems.

6. Taken together, all five dimensions interconnect to influence people's perceptions of credibility. It should be noted that too much extroversion can be perceived as oppressive; too much composure can be perceived as not caring, and so on. Therefore, the best combination is to try to control how you are perceived so as to possess moderate to high levels of each of the five dimensions.

VI. Chapter review.

CHAPTER 11
COPING WITH CONFLICTS

LEARNING OBJECTIVES

After studying the chapter, the student should be able to:

- Identify and discuss the two characteristics of conflict.

- Define and explain the term *conflict*.

- Explain how the definition of conflict represents an *economic model* of conflict.

- Explain why conflicts are not, in and of themselves, either productive or unproductive.

- Identify and discuss the symptoms of *unproductive* and *productive* conflict.

- Define *conflict styles*.

- Identify and discuss the five conflict styles (strategies) for coping with conflict.

- Discuss the common causes of conflict (meanings and contextual factors).

- Define and explain the term *negotiation*.

- Identify and discuss the *method of principled negotiation*. Include in your discussion the eight recommendations that can lead to successful negotiation and conflict resolution.

EXTENDED CHAPTER OUTLINE

This chapter focuses on the nature of conflict, the strategies for coping with conflict, common causes of conflict, and successful conflict negotiation.

I.   The nature of conflict.

Conflicts are inevitable, recurring, and normal in human social life. Moreover, they come in many forms; they arise in virtually every type of social situation; and they can occur between people in all kinds of social relationships.

Two characteristics of conflict need to be recognized. First, conflicts can range from trivial, as in minor competitions, to devastating clashes that may become brutal and destructive. This chapter does not discuss the truly violent conflicts (gang wars, police shoot-outs, or barroom brawls) but discusses conflicts that occur between people in everyday walks of life, such as in the family, at work, among neighbors, or at school.

A second major characteristic of conflict can best be understood within a cultural perspective. That is, as Americans we exhibit a *culturally approved readiness* toward engaging in conflict. Being a good fighter is perceived by Americans as good, whereas avoiding or shrinking from conflict is regarded as bad or wimpy. In many ways, this orientation toward conflict is an extension of cultural roots to *succeed in life*. By succeeding, we mean "getting ahead of someone else." To act in ways consistent with this aspect of our culture, we must engage in a lifetime of competitive conflicts.

A. Formulating a definition.

For the purposes of this text, the authors define conflict as *a dispute in which different values result in claims to rewards or resources that are in limited supply, and where the main objective of the people engaged in the process is to either neutralize or eliminate the prospects of their opponent to win what is at stake.* Stated more simply, participants in a conflict are in *competition* with each other over something important to them.

The above definition states a kind of "economic model" of the causes of conflict. This definition explains that conflicts develop over some "commodity" (reward or resource) that all participants desire but not all can have. It is the scarcity of the rewards and resources that are valued in the specific situation which serves as an important beginning point for the development of conflict.

Furthermore, the above definition identifies that the main objective of the protagonists is to either neutralize or eliminate the prospects of their opponent. However, it is not acceptable in our society to literally damage, or even destroy or discredit, our opponent in some completely destructive way. Our culture requires that what is done must be within ethical standards. There are ways to neutralize one's competition in a conflict while remaining ethical and constructive. In other words, conflicts are not *inherently* negative or adverse. In fact, conflicts can range along a continuum from positive through neutral to negative.

B. Consequences of conflicts.

Conflicts are not, in and of themselves, either productive or unproductive. What is important is how people behave during a conflict and especially the specific *consequences* of the process. It is the people who initiate and engage in a conflict who determine whether it will ultimately be productive or destructive.

1. Conflicts that produce bad feelings and unproductive results tend to be those that just seem to get out of hand. Examples of conflicts which often end up being unproductive are those that center on divorce, child custody, job termination, disputes between family members, and union-management impasses.

   a. It is important to keep in mind that uncontrolled escalation of a competitive encounter can change minor disagreements into something that resembles World War III. Thus, we need to learn to recognize the *symptoms* of disagreement that potentially lead to escalating and unproductive conflicts. The easiest class of identifiers of potentially good or bad conflicts is characteristics of people. Specifically, people who show signs of stress are likely to escalate a conflict and cause unproductive outcomes.

   b. Symptoms of stress are:
      (1) Loss of energy or dedication
      (2) Rapid conversation
      (3) Noticeable indications of anxiety
      (4) Various forms of compulsive behaviors, such as overeating, excessive consumption of alcohol or drugs
      (5) Inappropriate use of time
      (6) Irrational use of resources (to undermine an opponent at the expense of getting the work done)

2. Productive conflicts can also be identified by a different set of signs. As in the case with unproductive conflicts, the most important signs are the characteristics and actions of the participants. The most obvious include friendly conversations between the opponents and friendly versus threatening nonverbal signs (smiles, friendly gestures, and close interpersonal distance).

II. Strategies for coping with conflict.

Most human behavior is relatively predictable because it follows patterns of action and reaction deeply established in our culture. Therefore, it is possible to predict with some degree of accuracy how people will try to deal with various kinds of conflict situations. These can be described in terms of what communication researchers refer to as personal *conflict styles*. Based on Ralph Kilman and Kenneth Thomas's classification system, our personal style of handling conflicts is based on our *concern for self* and *concern for our opponent*. This formulation allows for the assessment of five distinct conflict styles (or coping strategies).

A. *The competitive style.* A strategy for handling conflicts in which people narrowly view all conflicts as win-lose events. They believe that winning is their only goal and that having a concern for their opponent is both unnecessary and unimportant.

B. *The collaborative style.* A strategy for handling conflicts in which people work jointly or willingly in cooperation with an opponent. The collaborative style is characteristic of persons who are not only seeking self-related goals in a conflict situation but also have sincere concern for their opponents.

C. *The compromising style.* A strategy for handling conflicts in which participants reach agreement by making mutual concessions.

D. *The avoidance style.* A strategy for handling conflicts in which a potential participant chooses not to be a part of the confrontation but chooses to stay away from situations where disagreements and disputes are likely to occur.

E. *The accommodation style.* A strategy for handling conflicts in which people "give in" to their opponents. Accommodators are the opposite of competitors. They tend to be passive, foregoing their personal goal and preferring to let their opponents reach their objectives.

III. Common causes of conflict.

Aside from the five styles reviewed above for keeping conflict going or bringing it to termination, we need to comprehend some of the common *causes* of conflicts in social life. Earlier, conflict was defined with an "economic" model of the basis of conflict. It stressed that conflicts arise when there is a scarcity of some value over which competition develops. This is one explanation, but *two* other major factors also play a part in generating conflicts between people. One is meanings and the other is the context.

A. Meaning as a primary cause.

The meanings people construct during the processes of communication can be a primary cause of conflict. That is, unless people communicate with each other, there is simply no way for them to initiate or engage in conflict. By the same reasoning, it is our ability to communicate fully and effectively that enables us to *resolve* conflicts.

Generally, problems of meaning are at the heart of virtually any conflict. The construction of meaning by communicating parties assumes a *primary instrumental role* in generating and escalating conflict. Another problem is that a *low index of fidelity* (low accuracy) is likely to characterize messages transmitted and interpreted by communicators who are in the process of conflict development. These two conditions (construction of meanings and low accuracy) work together as central causal factors in producing and intensifying controversies.

B. Contextual factors that can generate conflict.

Here, as the general transactional model suggests, both the *social situations* in which the people are involved and the *social relationships* that exist between them play parts in shaping the meanings they construct as they communicate.

IV. Successful conflict negotiation.

A. Defining negotiation.

The term *negotiation* refers to *the process of communicating proposed solutions back and forth between opponents for the purpose of reaching a joint agreement and thus resolving a conflict.* The effective negotiation of a conflict cannot begin until all of the individuals involved agree on their primary objective—to reach an agreement as an end product of negotiations.

B. The Harvard Negotiation Project.

Over the past several decades, a group of researchers at Harvard University has studied the process of conflict negotiation extensively. The results of their efforts have been the identification of the method entitled "principled negotiation." The recommendations of the method involve eight points, which if applied correctly, lead to successful negotiation and thus conflict resolution.

1. *Don't bargain over positions.*

People trying to negotiate should never attempt to "bargain" over, that is, explain or justify—the different positions they hold on the issue of disagreement. Trying to defend very different positions on a point or issue can only contribute to opponents' greater and more heated separation on that issue.

2. *Separate the people from the problem.*

Participants need to look beyond the personal characteristics and suspected motives of the people involved to the nature of the problem itself—that is, what led up to the conflict.

3. *Focus on interests, not positions.*

Opponents should refrain from bargaining over positions and focus on interests, looking beyond their position to the personal goals and needs that have to be served for each of the participants.

4. *Invent options for mutual gain.*

One of the many incorrect assumptions that we make about conflict is that there is only room for one winner. This is not always true; if conflict is handled properly, conflicts can actually be beneficial to everyone involved. Therefore, opponents are encouraged to work hard to invent options for mutual gain.

5. *Insist on using objective criteria.*

In negotiation it is important to begin by setting the mutually agreed-upon rules within which to communicate about potential solutions. Establishing shared criteria for evaluating proposals is part of the process. If this is not done, in the heat of an intense conflict, opponents may impose subjective criteria (personal or private standards) when evaluating proposed solutions.

6. *Develop the best alternative.*

A good way to protect yourself in a negotiation is to have already developed an acceptable alternative to what you think might be the most desirable negotiated agreement. This type of alternative refers to knowing ahead of time exactly what your "bottom line" will be to resolve the conflict.

7. *Coping with resistance to negotiation.*

   In cases when your opponent "stonewalls" all attempts to negotiate conflict, the Harvard Group suggests several restatements of the earlier guidelines:

   a. Never attack the position that the resistant opponents are advocating. Look beyond the positions to the personal values and interests that are motivating the individual on the issue. Then deal directly with what is driving them to be resistant.

   b. Try to minimize the time spent defending your ideas during conflict, and solicit criticism and counsel from your opponent.

   c. Ask questions and pause for answers.

8. *Handling dirty tricks.*

   The Harvard group concluded their approach to negotiating conflicts by recommending ways to handle the large variety of dirty tricks that opponents often play on each other. These include such things as deception, using phony facts, invoking ambiguous authority, creating stress, and making personal attacks, to name a few. They recommend three steps to follow when an opponent appears to be employing a dirty trick:

   a. Recognize the tactic.

   b. Raise the issue explicitly.

   c. Question the tactic's legitimacy and desirability—negotiate over it.

V. Chapter review.

CHAPTER 12
OVERCOMING SHYNESS AND APPREHENSION

LEARNING OBJECTIVES

After studying the chapter, the student should be able to:

- Define and explain the term *communication apprehension.*

- Explain the circular relationships between communication apprehension and shyness.

- Differentiate between communication apprehension as a personality trait and as a temporary condition.

- Identify and discuss the common contextual sources of anxiety (unfamiliarity, novelty or formality, subordinate rank, conspicuousness or excessive attention, evaluation, and repeated failures).

- Explain the relationship among socialization, learning, and communication apprehension.

- Differentiate between social learning theory and reinforcement theory as an explanation for the development of communication apprehension.

- Explain the *resiliency factor.*

- Explain and discuss the consequences of inconsistency (learned helplessness and the no-win situation).

- Compare and contrast the perceptions of high and low communication apprehensives in the classroom, in interpersonal encounters, at work and in career choices.

- Define and discuss the term *stage fright.* Include in your discussion the influence of the context and the speaker's personality on stage fright.

- Discuss the three treatment programs available to reduce communication apprehension (systematic desensitization, cognitive restructuring, and skills training).

- Identify and discuss the four steps involved in cognitive restructuring.

- Explain why the skills training approach may in fact increase anxiety for some individuals.

EXTENDED CHAPTER OUTLINE

This chapter focuses on the condition of communication apprehension, its causes, its consequences, and how to cope with it.

I.   Communication apprehension as a common reaction.

Communication apprehension refers to *fear or anxiety associated with either real or anticipated communication encounters.* Note this definition does not suggest that we have to be actually communicating at the time to feel fear or anxiety; we can dread having to communicate even when we think we *might* have to speak. In other words, anxiety about communicating is a condition that can occur either prior to or during any particular encounter.

Some specialists regard communication apprehension as a special kind of shyness, but it is not true that all shy individuals experience communication apprehension. Looking at the population as a whole, about 40% report being shy, while only a little over 20% experience a significant degree of communication apprehension. A circular link between shyness and apprehension exists. It may begin with a person being shy, which creates anxiety, which reduces communication skills, resulting in increased shyness, and so on. This circular link may manifest itself in many ways.

To understand further the nature of communication apprehension, we need to differentiate between two rather different categories of people in which the condition is present: The first is *apprehensive individuals* who, regardless of the situation, almost always feel anxious about relating to others. The second is people who have had *apprehensive experiences* that have incited fears about communicating.

A. Apprehension as a personality trait.

Apprehensive individuals who fear communicating with almost anyone in any kind of situation have *trait-like* communication apprehension. More specifically, trait-like communication apprehension is defined as: *a relatively stable and predictable pattern of behavior that we observe in an individual that is presumably due to a characteristic of his or her personality.* Overall, persons with high trait-like communication apprehension avoid communication encounters; those low in the trait seek them out. While people who are high or low in communication apprehension represent the ends of the continuum, most of us can be categorized as *moderately* apprehensive. This "in-between" category experiences apprehension only when a particular situation arouses discomfort.

B. The influence of apprehensive experiences.

Many people experience temporary communication apprehension. The situation that triggers the apprehension varies greatly. When our communication capacity is temporarily reduced, we become like those who fear communication as a function of a personality trait. Like them, we will avoid apprehension-producing experiences.

II.   Causes of communication apprehension.

A. Common contextual sources of anxiety.

As suggested earlier, certain contexts as well as certain individuals, can lead us to be apprehensive. Researchers have identified a number of contextual factors that heighten our apprehension and affect our ability to communicate effectively:

1. *Communicating with unfamiliar or dissimilar others.* It is always easier to talk to people we know as opposed to those who are unfamiliar to us.

2. *Novel or formal situations.* These occasions tend to trigger communication apprehension because they are filled with uncertainty. The factor of unpredictability raises apprehension.

3. *Subordinate rank.* Certain kinds of situations are coupled with clear understandings of one's lower status compared to the status of others present. This kind of social relationship may cause anxiety.

4. *Conspicuousness and excessive attention.* Any context in which you become the center of attention can induce communication apprehension.

5. *Undergoing evaluation.* The idea that we're being assessed heightens our apprehension about what we say or do.

6. *Repeated failure.* Memories of previous failures in identical or similar situations are a common source of apprehension.

B. How we learn to be characteristically apprehensive.

One thing we know about people who are apprehensive is that they tend to distort their interpretations of the contextual factors discussed previously. That is, those high in apprehension sometimes perceive a situation to be *more* novel or formal, or they feel *very* conspicuous, and are convinced that *everyone* present notices a mistake they make and is laughing at them.

1. *Long-term socialization of the apprehensive person.* Socialization is defined as a "long-term process of communication whereby a human acquires a personality and becomes a functioning member of society. As discussed earlier, communication apprehension can be a personality trait—a product of long-term socialization.

2. *Socialization includes learning.* The importance of noting the dependency of communication apprehension on the socialization process is that it includes *learning*.

3. *The importance of learning.* A positive feature of focusing narrowly on the learning part of the socialization process is that it offers hope for changing people who have acquired excessive apprehension as a personality trait. With systematic training, apprehensive individuals may be able to *unlearn* some of the negative beliefs and *change* troublesome meanings that promote communication anxiety.

4. *Learning to fear by observing others.* This idea is also known as *social learning theory* or *observational learning theory.* Developed originally by Albert Bandura, social learning theory explains how individuals can learn, not by performing actions themselves, but by observing how other people have coped with problems that confronted them. Essentially, social learning theory explains that we begin learning to be high or low in communication apprehension by observing the behavior and reactions of people who are important as "models" in our lives.

   The key to this "modeling" approach is trying out the observed behaviors when we observe that those serving as models are *rewarded* for particular kinds of behavior. Learning specialists refer broadly to the consequences of such rewarding experiences as "reinforcement," which can be defined as an increase in the probability of engaging in the learned behavior. On the other hand, if adopting the modeled behavior results in a bad or punishing experience, it is unlikely we will make it a permanent part of our repertoire.

5. *Learning as a consequence of reward and punishment.* Although social learning theory is an attractive explanation, it fails to explain why one individual raised in a particular set of circumstances acquires a communication apprehension trait while another, reared in exactly those same circumstances, does not. Therefore, an alternative explanation to social learning theory is *reinforcement theory.* According to this theory, individuals "try out" a number of behaviors; if the consequence of these initial trials is positive or rewarding (reinforcing), then the behavior is adopted, to be repeated over and over again. Should the consequence be punishing, the behavior is likely to be dropped and replaced with some other response.

   Basically, advocates of reinforcement theory claim that people high in communication apprehension have been punished for their communication, whereas those low in apprehension have been rewarded.

6. *The resiliency factor.* This is the propensity of human beings to be flexible in their learning histories, and not be rigidly shaped by a few negative consequences of their actions. Individuals high in apprehension are not "resilient." For them, success is not expected; such individuals have learned to expect failure or punishment when they talk. A history of punishment for talking prompts those high in apprehension to *avoid* communication encounters.

7. *The consequences of inconsistency.* Irregular or inconsistent consequences of behaving in a certain way over time can induce a condition or personal *anomie—a feeling of anxiety or distress arising from confusion concerning the social expectations of others.* In the present discussion of communication apprehension, if we cannot accurately make reliable predictions about what will happen to us—whether we will be rewarded or punished when we attempt to communicate—it is very likely that we will develop fears and anxieties about it and stop attempting to do so altogether.

   Another source of anxiety is the "no-win" situation. For instance, we may find ourselves always saying the wrong thing. This no-win situation, like the repeated failures condition, is likely to make us feel very apprehensive in later encounters. Should this experience happen frequently in other contexts and with other individuals, we can see how *learned helplessness* would occur. Learned helplessness is defined as *a feeling of inadequacy and stress arising from an inability to communicate in a predictable way with a person who is completely inconsistent in his or her responses to messages.*

III. Consequences of high and low communication apprehension.

   Hundreds of research studies demonstrate that individuals high and low in communication apprehension (CA) are *evaluated* quite differently by other people in many ways. Generally, those who are low are evaluated positively for many kinds of behavior, whereas individuals who are high are regarded negatively in a variety of ways. These assessments can have long-term consequences for those individuals in a variety of contexts.

   A. Evaluations in the classroom.

   Extensive research shows that teachers perceive low CA's to be better students. Moreover, teachers call on low CA's more often, provide prompts and hints to assist their responses, initiate conversations with them much more often, and give them extra help or attention. High CA's are often perceived as detached, indifferent, and apathetic toward school.

   B. Assessments in interpersonal encounters.

   In general, interpersonal opportunities are much greater for individuals who are low in communication apprehension. They seem approachable and fun to be with. They give the appearance of being good listeners in conversations with others; they ask and answer questions; they are high in nonverbal immediacy; and they are generally personable. On the other hand, those high in communication apprehension are perceived as disinterested, uncaring, and unfriendly due to their communication avoidance.

   C. The reactions of people at work.

   Typically, people with low communication apprehension choose positions that require them to interact regularly with others, whereas high CA's select opportunities that avoid such communication encounters. Those high in communication apprehension are likely to select majors/careers in accounting, computer science, pharmacy, and engineering. Low CA's are likely to pick such areas as speech communication, theater, journalism, advertising, and public relations.

   Research indicates that employers during job interviews perceive low CA's as sociable, competent, responsible, and having leadership potential. Employers generally perceive high CA's as uncommunicative, restrained, aloof, and tense.

   D. Influences on careers.

   When it comes to promotions at work, those low in apprehension are promoted significantly more often than those who are fearful and nervous about communicating. Job satisfaction is also related to communication apprehension. Low CA's report more satisfaction with their work than do high CA's.

IV. Dealing with stage fright.

One of the most common and frustrating forms of communication apprehension is stage fright. Stage fright is defined as *a special category of the more general condition of communication apprehension that specifically focuses on anxiety about a public performance or speech before a group or an audience.* Moderate apprehension is not all negative because it helps people to channel their stage fright productively.

A. The contributions of the context.

Like all other aspects of communication, stage fright is in part a product of the context in which the activity takes place. That is, public speaking takes place in a physical place, a social setting, and among persons in particular social relationships. Each of these factors can contribute to the development of temporary communication apprehension. That is, it is the performance before unfamiliar others, on a formal occasion, that makes us feel conspicuous in such a way that everyone seems to be evaluating us.

B. What the speaker brings to the problem.

Sometimes stage fright is not so much a product of the context as it is the personality of the speaker. Persons chronically high in apprehension are truly terrified of public speaking situations, and they often need help in overcoming this problem. In contrast, easy talkers typically enjoy public speaking courses and, despite mild and normal stage fright, learn to perform quite well. For those with low and moderate levels of apprehension, stage fright can be controlled. Furthermore, a certain amount of stage fright generates motivation.

V. Reducing communication apprehension.

A number of treatment programs are available to manage communication apprehension. Those programs with the highest known success rate include systematic desensitization (SD), cognitive restructuring, and skills training.

A. Systematic desensitization.

The SD method reduces communication apprehension through gradual muscle relaxation techniques. We all become tense and tighten our muscles whenever we feel anxious—it is an involuntary response. SD works on the principle that if an alternative response, such as relaxation, can be substituted for the tension and stress, we will be able to cope with the situation—so relax.

B. Cognitive restructuring.

This approach requires changing or modifying beliefs about the particular communication event and substituting positive self-statements for negative ones. When cognitive restructuring is applied to communication apprehension, four major steps are involved:

1. *Introduction.* The first step for the trainer is to explain that apprehension toward public speaking is *learned* and that anything that has been learned can be unlearned and replaced with new ideas and behavior.

2. *Identify negative self-statements.* This step involves the identification of derogatory statements anxious people say to themselves before, during, and after a presentation event. Each of these statements is then analyzed for errors in logic or overgeneralization.

3. *Coping statements.* In this step, individuals learn a new set of alternative statements to be substituted for the previous negative statements.

4. *Practice.* The final step of cognitive restructuring requires that individuals practice their new coping statements.

C. Skills training.

Skills training assumes that apprehension stems from poor communication ability. Those who favor this explanation argue that a primary cause of fear of communicating is a *deficit in skills*. Training programs based on this assumption are designed to teach appropriate and effective communication skills.

   1. *Courses on skills.* Training people in specific skills has long been the strategy of choice in the field of speech communication as an academic subject. Off campus, businesses encourage their employees to enroll in communication skills training programs.

   2. *Limitations of the skills approach.*

      In essence, skills training sometimes reduces apprehension and sometimes does not. In fact, for those with chronically high communication apprehension, skills training can make them more anxious.

   3. An evaluation of all these methods reveals that a combination of *all three* is more effective than any single treatment alone.

VI. Chapter review.

CHAPTER 13
PREPARING THE CONTENT

LEARNING OBJECTIVES

After studying the chapter, the student should be able to:

- Discuss the steps for getting started with preparing the speech content.

- Identify and explain the three purposes for speaking.

- Determine what questions need to be raised when analyzing an audience.

- Discuss how to research a topic by finding supporting materials.

- Identify and discuss the three criteria for selecting evidence.

- Identify the basic format for an informative speech.

- Discuss what should be included in each part of an informative speech.

- Discuss the variety of organizational patterns available to organize the body of a speech (spatial, temporal, causal, problem/solution, and topical).

- Identify the two functions that need to be served in the *conclusion* of an informative speech.

- Describe in detail the basic components of an outline of an informative speech.

- Discuss the six rules for increasing effectiveness.

- Explain why a persuasive speech needs a different format than an informative speech for maximum effectiveness.

- Explain Monroe's Motivated Sequence. Include in your discussion the five steps involved.

- Describe how outlining a persuasive speech differs from outlining an informative speech.

- Discuss each of the seven strategies for persuading others.

EXTENDED CHAPTER OUTLINE

The focus of this chapter is the steps required to identify and put together the content of an effective speech.

I. Three steps for getting started.
  A. Choose the topic.
     Topics are not inherently boring, but speakers can be. If possible, speakers should select topics they already know something about; and once a general subject is selected, they must narrow it down and focus on one specific issue. Narrowing the topic prevents speakers from wandering aimlessly and helps them to focus on specific information they want to share with the audience.

B. Determine the purpose.

The next step in getting started is to consider what effect we want from our audience. The purposes for speaking are generally to entertain, to inform, and to persuade. The purpose should be capable of being stated in specific terms and limited to one simple declarative sentence.

C. Analyze the audience.

The linear and transactions models of human communication point out that every receiver (audience member) listens to a speaker with her or his personal framework for perceptions and interpretations. This means that each member of the audience will have a personal list of topics and ideas that seem more (or less) important, interesting, tasteful, amusing, and so forth. Therefore, we need to consider the audience when choosing topics. A speaker needs to ask several questions:

1. Who are these people?

2. Why are they here?

3. In what will they be interested?

4. What do they already know about the topic?

Obtaining information about the audience can help in selecting a topic. One practical basis for making assumptions about an audience is to ascertain their *demographics*, such as sex, age, marital status, social economic status, level of education, and so on. A more elaborate procedure for audience analysis could be a questionnaire to determine in greater detail the audience's motivation and feelings. In any case, obtaining information about the audience's background, beliefs, and attitudes will increase understanding of their expectations about the speech and the occasion.

II. How to research the topic to find supporting materials.

A. Rely on personal knowledge and experience.

Many students/speakers simply ignore themselves as potential resources for material. However, whenever possible, speakers should rely on their own experiences. Failure to do so may imply to audiences that the speaker doesn't understand the realities of the topic being presented. Audiences are more likely to empathize with, and eventually agree with, a speaker who demonstrates some personal connection with the issues. Consequently, speakers shouldn't be afraid to rely on themselves for important reference material.

B. Make use of what others know.

Not only can speakers use their own past experiences for developing speeches, they can ask various kinds of experts and professionals for their opinions, interpretations, and recommendations. Interviews with experts are one type of research we may choose to use as evidence. Many instructors or business professionals are often willing to talk and share information. Furthermore, library research is a helpful source of information.

C. Criteria for selecting evidence.

1. The most crucial criterion for judging the acceptability of material is *objectivity of the source*. Above all else, sources of acts and opinions should be unbiased.

2. The second criterion is that sources of evidence should be *competent* or credible in a given area.

3. The third criterion focuses on *ethical* standards. Whenever we include supporting material in a speech, we need to make careful judgments of the appropriateness and truthfulness of the sources of the facts and opinions we use.

III. Organizing a speech to inform.

The speaker is given only one chance to explain, and the audience has one chance to learn. It is a tough assignment for both, so it is important to organize such a presentation into a basic format that will maximize its effectiveness.

A. A basic format for informing.

Every speech designed to inform relies on the same basic plan. All informative speeches have an *introduction*, a *body*, and a *conclusion*. In other words, the organizational structure of an informative speech always begins with opening and introductory statements, followed by the main points and supporting materials, and always reaches conclusions that include a summary. That is, first, tell them what you're going to tell them; then tell them; and finally, tell them what you've told them!

1. *The introduction.* The introduction to a speech should be viewed as the preview of what's to come. A good introduction begins with a relevant attention-gaining opener. There are many ways to capture attention. One might open a speech with a dramatic story, a humorous anecdote, a famous quotation, a startling statement, a demonstration, a vivid illustration, or an emotional account. Ideally, the attention gainer should be relevant to the topic of the speech.

Once we have the audience's attention, we need to move to our central theme and provide an overview of what we are going to say—provide a road map. In other words, once the speaker has presented the attention-gaining opener, stated the central ideas or purpose, and listed the main points, he or she is ready to move on to the body of the speech.

2. *The body.* The body of a speech can usually focus on no more than two or three main points. Too many points may cause "information overload" to the audience. Too much information, organized around too many points, usually results in confusion and incoherence. Therefore, the speaker needs to be selective in the main points to be addressed.

In organizing the body of a speech, the speaker needs to arrange the main points in logical order. A variety of organizational patterns are available for this purpose:

a. Spatial patterns are used when location or geographic information is being discussed: for example, the location of the heart in one's body (anatomy) or descriptions of a favorite scenic route.

b. Temporal orders are used when a time sequence or chronology is demanded: for example, how to follow a recipe, such as one for Texas chili.

c. Causal sequence identifies how a particular effect or outcome is a direct consequence of one or more causes: for example, the reasons for grade inflation.

d. Problem/solution formats are used when a problem is identified and a solution is offered: for example, unruly teens and community programs.

e. Topical patterns are used when a topic is divided into two or more subtopics: for example, how and what colors communicate.

3. *The conclusion.* The conclusion serves two functions:

a. It succinctly spells out the main points. That is, the conclusion repeats in a concise manner what the speaker just told the audience.

b. It "signs off," leaving the audience wanting more. This step signals to the audience that the speaker has reached the end of the presentation.

B. Outlining the informative speech.

A detailed outline is mandatory. Every outline for an informative speech begins with a *purpose statement*. Immediately following the purpose statement, the introduction, body, and conclusion are major headings, labeled as roman numerals I, II, and III. All main points under each major heading are further classified as A, B, and C and subpoints as arabic numbers 1, 2, and 3. Finally, all outlines end with a reference list or bibliography that documents all the sources the speaker used in his or her speech. (See text example, pages 380–381.)

Generally speaking, the outline provides a clear "road map" to follow when it's time to deliver the information to the audience.

C. Six rules for increasing effectiveness.

1. *Rule 1: Keep it simple.* This is the famous KISS rule (keep it simple, stupid). The fewer points the speech presents, the more likely the audience will learn them. Every aspect of our presentations, explanations, and definitions should be brief and easy to understand.

2. *Rule 2: Keep it concrete.* Avoid abstract explanations. The more abstract the issues are and the more theoretical the explanations, the less likely the audience will comprehend the message.

3. *Rule 3: Be repetitive and redundant.* Repetition refers to explaining something exactly the same way over and over again. Redundancy involves explaining something more than once, but in a slightly different way each time. Repetition is essential for lists of simple, but important concepts (ABC's). Redundancy helps the audience remember more complex ideas and arguments.

4. *Rule 4: Elicit active responses.* One way to increase understanding and retention is to stimulate the audience to *do something* in an open and public way. A solid base of research shows that active responses greatly enhance both learning and commitment. Asking the audience to respond verbally, raise their hands, or vote are just a few examples.

5. *Rule 5: Use familiar and relevant examples.* Audiences need a framework to learn and recall information efficiently and effectively. This approach links old ideas with new information through the use of examples and illustrations that are familiar and meaningful.

6. *Rule 6: Use transitions and signposts.* Let the audience constantly know when you're leaving an old point and moving on to a new one. Transitions are statements that link together prior issues or points with the next ones. Signposts are simple words or phrases that signal organization. Both serve to alert the audience to change or movement. Transitions and signposts help the audience to visualize the speech outline and to follow the presentation with little or no effort.

IV. Organizing a speech to persuade.

The same three-part format used for the informative speech could be used to structure a persuasive speech. However, if a speaker wants to achieve maximum possible effect, another approach is needed. Why? People tend to become resistant if the speaker openly reveals his or her intent to persuade. A second reason why a format organized around an introduction, body, and conclusion is inappropriate for a persuasive speech is that it fails to "set up" the audience for the change. That is, it is important to get the audience to *want* to change. In order to get them to change, a speaker must first speak to their needs, wants, and desires.

A. A basic persuasion format: Monroe's Motivated Sequence.

Monroe's Motivated Sequence is a plan for organizing a speech that identifies people's needs, wants, or concerns. Once those are specified, the speaker then tries to satisfy or fulfill them in some way. Consequently, the speaker gives the audience a solution, and they visualize their future with the solution. Finally, the speaker tells them how to go about obtaining that solution. Monroe's Motivated Sequence consists of five separate steps:

1. *Step 1: Gain the audience's attention.*
    Once again, some kind of attention-gaining opener is needed (as discussed earlier).

2. *Step 2: Identify unfulfilled needs.*

    This second step is crucial for successful persuasion. The speaker must clearly establish in the mind of the audience that they have a problem which is not being met. The solution should not be mentioned.

3. *Step 3: Imply satisfaction by offering a solution.*

    In this step, the speaker must show how the audience's needs can be satisfied. This is done by stating the solution, explaining how it works, relating it back to each of the needs identified earlier in Step 2, and meeting any potential *objections*.

4. *Step 4: Visualize what satisfaction will mean.*

    After the solution is offered and the audience's objections are met, the speaker needs to intensify the audience's desire for the solution by getting each of them to visualize what their lives will be like once they adopt the solution (or how bleak life would be without the proposed solution), or both.

5. *Step 5: Define specific actions.*

    It may seem like the speech is over, but now comes the most important part. In the final step, the speaker should tell the audience specifically and concretely what they should do to secure the product and the benefits of the solution.

B. Outlining the persuasive speech.

After the five steps of Monroe's Motivated Sequence have been carefully considered, the next step in designing a persuasive speech is to develop the outline. The rules for outlining are the same as for the informative speech, except that the format follows Monroe's Motivated Sequence, starting with a specific purpose statement, attention-gainer, needs, satisfaction, visualization, and action steps, and ends with references or bibliography.

C. Seven strategies for persuading.

What follows is a list of seven practical strategies that have been derived from a large body of theory and research on persuasion. These strategies consider both attempts by speakers to influence and efforts by audiences to resist that influence.

1. *Strategy 1: Conceal the intent to persuade.* People are repelled generally whenever someone tries to pitch them a line or hustle a product.

2. *Strategy 2: Don't ask for too much.* This is the issue of "discrepancy." Simply put, it means that the speaker's message should not be overly demanding—should not be too far from what it is realistic to ask in the way of change. Consequently, speakers should expect and ask for only gradual, minor progress toward the changes they want. Otherwise, the well-known *boomerang* effect will result (backfires).

3. *Strategy 3: Avoid inflammatory words and phrases.* Unfortunate choices of words or phrases can backfire. That is, the speaker should avoid terms that others find offensive, such as sexist or racist ones.

4. *Strategy 4: Keep objections to a minimum.* The number of audience objections dealt with, and the time spent on them, should be limited (in Step 3 [satisfaction step] of MMS). At most, only a couple of objections should be raised. If too much attention is devoted to them, as opposed to advantages, the audience is more likely to be influenced by the objections.

5. *Strategy 5: Use a two-sided message with refutation.* Two-sided messages give both sides of an argument a "fair" hearing. Two-sided messages *with refutation* give both sides and refute or deny the validity or worth of the opposing side. One-sided messages give only the speaker's position on the issue and ignore the opponent's argument. Of the three message-sided options, audiences are most influenced when the speaker discusses both sides. What happens is that if the speaker takes the time to discuss both sides, the audience will believe in his or her credibility, intelligence, and objectivity.

6. *Strategy 6: Inoculate against counterarguments.* Occasionally, a speaker may want to inoculate or immunize the audience by providing refutation.

7. *Strategy 7: Use fear appeals.* High fear appeals are more likely to influence people than either moderate or low amounts of fear.

V. Chapter review.

CHAPTER 14
SPEAKING BEFORE A GROUP

LEARNING OBJECTIVES

After studying the chapter, the student should be able to:

- Compare and contrast public speaking versus conversations. Include in your discussion the three important issues of *planned spontaneity,* recognition of *feedback,* and *audience adaption.*

- Compare and contrast the four modes of delivery (manuscript, memorized, impromptu, and extemporaneous).

- Discuss the advantages and disadvantages of each of the four modes of delivery.

- Discuss the importance of *credibility* to public speaking.

- Identify and discuss the five dimensions of *credibility.*

- Describe the five ways speakers can enhance their perceived competence and credibility.

- Discuss how speakers can enhance their initial impressions while performing a speech.

- Identify and discuss the seven strategies a speaker can use to keep the plot (middle) from "sagging."

- Summarize the functions of the conclusion (famous final scene).

- Review and discuss the *immediacy principle* in regard to public speaking.

EXTENDED CHAPTER OUTLINE

This chapter focuses on the delivery of a speech. A second lesson to be drawn from this chapter is the importance of long-range objectives. That is, speakers need to plan ahead, organize their efforts carefully, and proceed with their presentation step-by-step.

I.   Public speaking as extended conversation.

In order to understand what the contemporary study of public speaking does and does not emphasize, it will be useful to contrast it with what it was like at the beginning of the century. Then, teachers of "elocution," as the art of oratory was called, required students to rehearse their speeches with special attention given to the voice, speech sounds, and pronunciation. These early recommendations and drill procedures were designed to minimize annoying, nervous distractions that speakers often exhibit when they are tense. In contrast, today we teach public speaking as if it were an extension of *normal, everyday conversation.* With this in mind, we need to discuss how you can transform daily interactions into practiced, polished public speaking events. Therefore, we will look at three important issues—*planned spontaneity,* recognizing and interpreting *feedback,* and role-taking for the purpose of *audience adaptation.*

A. Planned spontaneity.

In order to seem as though you are relaxed and spontaneous before an entire audience, you have to *plan* for it—prepare for it—ahead of time. Such advice may appear to be incongruent, but if you want to appear to be casual, relaxed, and unrehearsed before a group, you have to organize your message well, commit your main ideas and subpoints to memory, and practice looking like the whole thing is simple.

B. Recognizing and responding to feedback.

We elicit and receive a lot of feedback during our normal, everyday conversation with others. We watch their facial expressions and entire body movements in an effort to understand how well or poorly they are interpreting what we are transmitting. Obviously, the public speaking context does not allow for such open exchange of feedback. Most of the feedback received by public speakers takes the form of nonverbal communication. That is, in limited but visible ways, audience members express agreement or disagreement, and understanding or confusion, during a speaker's delivery. The only way a speaker can effectively capture and interpret the more subtle nonverbal signals from the audience is to look for them. That is, speakers need to be able to identify when their audience members are confused, bored, surprised, excited, thoughtful, and/or convinced. Without that kind of feedback, it's difficult to know if you are communicating accurately. Finally, speakers should attempt to acknowledge or recognize their audience members by smiling or nodding at them, asking them their names, or holding their eye contact for a moment.

C. Adapting to the audience through collective role-taking.

In conversations we engage in role-taking in order to adapt what we are communicating to receivers. Role-taking and adaptation to feedback are not the same as in one-on-one situations. Nevertheless, presenting a speech to an audience does involve *collective* counterparts of these same processes. The nonverbal cues coming from the audience as a whole tell us whether they are interested or bored, alert or lethargic. Seasoned speakers can easily determine whether an audience does or does not understand an explanation.

II. Selecting a mode of delivery.

A. Reading from a manuscript.

The manuscript mode of delivery is the most popular presentational method among beginning speakers. It is based on writing out the entire speech in advance and reading it word-for-word to the audience. The manuscript mode of delivery has the advantage of completeness and precision. However, there are a number of drawbacks associated with this approach. First, reading from a manuscript makes it difficult to approximate a natural, normal conversation between the speaker and the audience. Second, trying to read word-for-word makes it difficult to recognize or respond to feedback. Third, attempts to gesture or move away from the podium are inhibited and awkward when you're holding on to a manuscript.

B. Delivering a memorized speech.

The memorized mode of delivery is the second most popular method for novice speakers. This mode of presenting a speech is based on a procedure that requires writing out the speech beforehand and practicing it over and over again until the entire text is committed to rote memory. The principle advantage memorizing has over reading a manuscript is that it allows the speaker to use gestures, to look at the audience, and to move around rather than remain behind a podium. The biggest disadvantage to the memorized mode is that most of us will forget something. Because of this fear of "forgetting," many speakers move rapidly through their lines and talk in a monotone voice. Like the manuscript speech, a memorized speech lacks spontaneity, audience adaption, and feedback interpretation.

C. Impromptu delivery.

The third type of delivery is impromptu. This is a speech that is delivered on the spot, with little or no lead time or formal preparation beforehand. This mode of delivery is the most difficult for speakers due to the lack of time to prepare a well-organized presentation.

D. Extemporaneous speaking.

Most students in public speaking courses are required to deliver their speeches extemporaneously. This refers to making use of a well-organized, well-rehearsed speech outline, but not a complete text (or manuscript). In other words, instead of writing out the entire speech in advance and reading or reciting it word-for-word, the extemporaneous speaker uses only an outline or notes as a reminder of major points and issues. Furthermore, rehearsing a speech from an outline produces a slightly different version every time it is practiced aloud. Yet it covers the same points in the same sequence and incorporates the same essential meanings. This provides a far less formal style of delivery, more closely approximating normal conversation. Because this mode of delivery allows the speaker to gesture frequently and openly, elicit and maintain eye contact with the audience, and move freely around the stage (or audience), it is most preferred by audience members. In short, the extemporaneous style allows the speaker to accommodate, adapt, and adjust to real people in the audience as he or she moves along through the outline.

III. Five ways to establish credibility.

Regardless of the mode of delivery that is used, how the audience perceives you as a speaker will have a good deal to do with your potential effectiveness. The interpretations they construct concerning your personal characteristics will determine whether they let you inform, persuade, or entertain them. Therefore, what is critical in delivering a speech is that the audience needs to find you highly *credible* if they are going to believe and be influenced by what you tell them. As a reminder, source credibility refers to how much the audience feels that speaker is *believable*. So one of the real challenges facing every speaker is to create an attribution of credibility from the majority of people in the audience. Therefore, the five separate factors that may enhance or significantly reduce credibility need to be discussed.

A. Demonstrating competence.

The most important dimension of credibility for public speaking is perceived competence. Perceived competence has very little to do with intelligence; it has more to do with how much valid knowledge the speaker is perceived to command about the issue under discussion.

To be perceived as competent, you must first study and research as much about your subject as you can. Many speakers simplify their speeches in an attempt to make the material more interesting or entertaining. This oversimplification can distort the audience's perception about the speaker's competence. Therefore, the following guidelines are suggested to avoid this situation.

1. *Use jargon.* To be seen as competent, do not completely avoid the use of jargon. Use it, but use it sparingly. Even when defining something technical, make it sound jargonistic, but also make it clear.

2. *Include oral footnotes.* Orally footnoting, that is, citing evidence in your speech, can increase your perceived competence and thereby your credibility. Use your evidence to support and verify your assertions. Use your references as testimony to show that other experts agree with your conclusions.

3. *Admit your ignorance.* It is very important to admit ignorance when you simply don't know something. If an audience member asks you a question and you don't know the answer, admit it. Audiences are very perceptive, and they can spot an evasion when they see one. The minute you try to sidestep the question, stonewall, or make up data, they are likely to see right through you. If this happens, your entire presentation is discredited. If you admit that you don't know the answer to a question, it can be very helpful to add, "I'll find out for you and get back to you as soon as I can." Another technique is to turn the question to the audience for their opinion or for their input and support. This communicates to them that you give them credit, too. An interesting side effect can occur when you occasionally admit to not knowing everything: Admitting to a lack of expertise in one specific area can often increase perceptions of your competence in other areas.

4. *Appearing to be competent.* To make people believe that you are competent you have to "look" the part. Audiences are more likely to be impressed with a well-dressed and well-groomed public speaker than one who is not.

5. *Arrange a socially validating introduction.* Even the most prestigious speaker needs a well-organized introduction that testifies to his or her competence. Therefore, a speaker should find someone to introduce her or him. The audience is more likely to accept socially validated expertise than self-proclaimed credentials.

B. Generate trust.

Audiences appreciate speakers who seem "trustworthy"—that is, good, decent, and honest. Within the public speaking context, we demand our speakers to be consistently honest and sincere with us.

C. Exhibit composure.

A speaker who appears calm, cool, and collected before a large audience is clearly admired by others. Responding to a crisis with apparent confidence and control increases speaker credibility. Conversely, if the speaker is unable to control his or her fears and anxieties, the audience is likely to disregard what the individual has to say. You can appear self-assured by coming prepared—know your material and rehearse your presentation. A good speaker practices looking relaxed and confident.

D. Communicate sociability.

Audiences greatly prefer speakers who appear to be friendly and warm. When an audience finds the speaker likable, they are more willing to listen and to give him or her the benefit of the doubt. Communicating sociability to a group requires that you rely heavily on nonverbal immediacy.

E. Display extroversion.

A personality characteristic somewhat similar to sociability is extroversion. It refers to the degree to which someone is "outgoing," that is, people-oriented, talkative, and gregarious. Conversely, shy individuals, those who are highly apprehensive about communicating, are generally believed to be *introverted.* People tend to assign low credibility to introverts because they are quiet. On the other hand, extroverts talk a lot—they reveal a great deal about themselves. Rather than assume incompetence (as with introverts), we give them the opportunity to demonstrate their credibility.

IV. Performing the speech: Beginnings, middles, and endings.

A. Act I: Managing initial impressions.

Performing the actual speech requires advertising the event and providing an introduction that builds speaker credibility. It is necessary to pay careful attention to physical appearance, level of composure, eye behavior, and opening lines.

B. Act II: Strategies to keep the plot from "sagging."

In the middle stage, where the plot might begin to "sag," there is a need to stimulate the audience attention and comprehension.

1. *Make the plot more interesting.* The content of your speech should be interesting and relevant to the needs and interests of the audience.

2. *Use redundancy and repetition.* Both redundancy and repetition contribute significantly to audience levels of attention and retention. Sometimes we forget that audiences are exposed to the words of the speech only one time. Consequently, a speaker must build into the message both redundancy and repetition. They help the audience keep track of and remember salient points and conclusions.

3. *Signal transitions and signposts.* Transitions and signposts steer the audience in the direction you're heading so that they can anticipate what is coming. Transitions provide the audience with a sense of smoothness and continuity between the parts of your presentation. Signposts serve a different purpose. They are used to signal issue changes so that the audience knows what is coming. They act like oral paragraph headings within the text of your speech. The most commonly used signposts are numerical: first, second, and third. Other signposts include familiar words or phrases such as "next," "at last," "finally," "in conclusion," and "following."

4. *Manage vocalics effectively.* The surest way to elicit and maintain an audience's attention is by adding variety to the way you use your voice. Audiences prefer the speaker to vary speech volume, rate, and pitch. Silence or pause time is another strategy that can be used to maintain audience attention.

5. *Stimulate interest with oculesics.* Eye contact acts as a powerful stimulus for eliciting audience involvement in a presentation. The more you look at your audience while you talk, the more likely your audience will stay interested and attentive.

6. *Employ gestures and actions to hold attention.*

   A nonverbal form that can function to either distract or enhance a presentation is gestures. When a speaker uses "adaptors," such as adjusting and readjusting glasses, the audience assumes the speaker is nervous and unprepared. However, when the same speaker uses gestures that are "illustrators," intentionally designed to emphasize or demonstrate what is being said, the audience perceives the speaker to be decisive and committed. Finally, a speaker's overall body movement can make a difference in how attentive or bored an audience will be. Using a direct, face-to-face body posture suggests active interaction and a sense of inclusion or belonging to the group.

7. *Learn to handle hecklers.* The best advice is to simply ignore the hecklers. By responding to their outcries and criticisms, you will end up giving them credibility and their message substance. If necessary, other nonverbal behaviors of dismissal may be applied—that is, gradually walking over in the direction of the hecklers while continuing to talk. If physically possible, put your hand on the back of a heckler's chair—however, do not give the person eye contact.

C. Act III: The famous final scene.

Besides summarizing the main points of your speech, the conclusion should leave the audience wanting more. In order to achieve that goal, you need to conclude with what is called a "gee whiz" ending. In other words, ideally you want your speech to be memorable. That is, your final scene should be as dramatic as you can make it.

V. Enhancing immediacy.

The immediacy principle provides a way of pulling together many of the guidelines and suggestions presented in this chapter. Effective speakers should make every effort to close the physical and psychological distance that always characterizes speakers and their audiences. Both verbal and nonverbal behaviors can contribute a great deal toward narrowing the communication gap.

VI. Chapter review.

CHAPTER 15
PUBLIC SPEAKING: POLISHING AND FINE-TUNING

LEARNING OBJECTIVES

After studying the chapter, the student should be able to:

- Describe five general ways a speaker can make language more interesting.

- Explain how concrete images and the use of similes and metaphors can create strong images.

- Discuss what is a *soundbite* and how it may be orchestrated to elicit an audience.

- Suggest how a speaker can effectively manage audience applause.

- Discuss three common rhetorical styles that have proved to be useful in public speaking situations (dramatic, animated, and humorous).

- Discuss some of the pitfalls or cautions to keep in mind when choosing to use humor in a speech.

- Discuss some of the positive effects of using humor.

EXTENDED CHAPTER OUTLINE

This chapter focuses on those strategies that can help transform a speech from one that is basic and mechanically correct to a polished and refined speech. Several strategies for making one's language more interesting, orchestrating the audience's response, and developing one's own rhetorical style will be addressed.

I.   Five strategies for making your language more interesting.

To achieve lasting impressions one must use colorful and appropriate language—words and phrases that create mental and emotional pictures for our audience.

A. Use imagery imaginatively.

Imagery involves the uses of carefully chosen words and phrases that appeal to our senses of touch, taste, sound, sight, and smell. This must be done to create concrete, realistic impressions about what we are saying. Therefore, it is important to select your words carefully so as to arouse concrete pictures in the heads of those to whom you are speaking.

1. *The value of concrete images.* Vivid images are most easily aroused with the use of *concrete* language. Imagery aroused with concrete language helps your audience both attend to and perceive your message with greater enthusiasm and accuracy than would be the case with an abstract message. In essence, concrete images can help your audience "see" your point.

In addition to drawing sensory pictures through concrete language, two rhetorical devices commonly used in literature to create images are the *simile* and the *metaphor*.

2. *Evoking images with similes.* Similes create images through the use of an "expressed" analogy. The audience usually knows when a simile is being used because it is made explicit by prefacing the comparison with the word "like" or "as." Mundane similes in common use are "slept like a baby" and "sly as a fox." Speakers should avoid using mundane similes in their presentations and instead seek to create profound and unique similes.

3. *Using metaphors to create strong images.* Metaphors develop a picture by "implied" analogy. Many times similes can be converted into metaphors by omitting the comparative "like" or "as" and, instead, labeling the object or event with another dissimilar label. In this way, the metaphor implies and creates a stronger image than does the simile. For example, instead of saying one is tired as a dog, a speaker may choose to say he is "dog-tired." However, like similes, metaphors should be unique, such as Reverend Jesse Jackson's metaphor to describe the poor and unfortunate children of an impoverished area of Los Angeles called Watts: "Their grapes of hope, have become raisins of despair."

B. Strive for simplicity.

Sometimes it's the simple words and the simple ideas that have the most impact on an audience. When simple language follows from complex thought, the contrast is so great that audiences are likely to catch hold to the idea quickly. For example, consider George Bush's "Read my lips: No new taxes!" In other words, clear, modest, and uncomplicated language can communicate forceful, powerful thought.

C. Employ intense and animated language to add excitement.

Many times we find that the difference between a dull speech and an exciting listening experience is in the speaker's use of intense and animated language. This may be achieved by switching from talking in a passive voice to an active voice and by adding descriptive adjectives.

D. Maintain rhythm for emphasis.

Truly great speeches have a rhythm all their own. The recurrences of specific sounds, words, or phrases meet the audience's need for regularity, predictability, and familiarity. Rhythm enhances the pleasure and heightens the sense of emotion toward the speaker and the message. A favorite device often used by skilled orators is the *repetition* of key words or phrases, such as Dr. Martin Luther King's "I have a dream." The repetitive device is often useful because the audience will remember words or phrases they hear over and over. In addition, rephrasing with similar, redundant words or word series can add "pulse" or cadence to an otherwise ordinary presentation.

Generally, then, rephrasing and restating key phrases and words all help to build the rhythm of the speech. In such ways, rhythm excites, triggers suspense, and compels the audience to anticipate. Besides eliciting attention, rhythmic speech subtly stimulates the audience to focus, to learn, and to remember central ideas in your presentation.

II. Orchestrating audience response.

While imagery, simplicity, intense or animated language, and rhythm all contribute to making good speeches better, consideration should be given to the strategy of manipulating audience reaction throughout the presentation. There will be moments during your speech when you will want your audience to openly show their concern, express their anger, or back your points by clapping.

A. Developing and using soundbites.

The expression *soundbite* is really a metaphor for a brief passage, such as a sentence or two, taken from a press release or presentation so as to be reprinted or taped for later news reports. Soundbites usually represent some major idea expressed by the speaker, such as Clint Eastwood's (Dirty Harry) statement from *Sudden Impact*: "Go ahead—make my day!" Keep in mind, soundbites can help or hurt a speaker. Avoiding those that will hurt, and planning for those that will help, is an important step in polishing any speech. Using the five language strategies mentioned earlier can help in creating soundbites. Once you have created a soundbite into your speech, you need to provide sufficient warning for your audience to get ready to receive it. This can be achieved by the use of the pregnant pause, followed by direct eye contact and a change in the volume of your voice. Then, of course, allow your audience enough time to digest what you told them (let them applaud, etc.).

B. Managing applause.

Making use of soundbites is only one strategy to ensure audience reactions. You also want to invite or encourage your audience to respond by applauding during your presentation. Keep in mind, most audience members like to be actively involved, rather than being passive. Therefore, we have to *plan* for audience support and responsive applause. As discussed in the chapter on nonverbal communication, pausing and giving eye contact are important turn-yielding cues in normal, everyday conversations. Similarly, the public speaking context requires the speaker to signal nonverbally to the audience that it is their turn. A long and purposeful pause accompanied by eye contact from the speaker alerts the audience that they are expected to react. The natural reaction is to applaud.

III. Developing your own rhetorical style.

Rhetorical or communication style can be defined as *the overall qualitative way in which a speaker communicates, using verbal language patterns and nonverbal cues.* There are actually several styles a speaker may choose to use: attentive style, open style, friendly style, contentious style, relaxed style, and so on. However, in this section, we discuss only three common rhetorical styles that have proved to be useful in public speaking situations. The three are *dramatic, animated,* and *humorous* styles.

A. The dramatic style.

Dramatic speakers are generally humorous, but need not be funny to be dramatic. They are performers who treat the public speaking event as if they were "on stage" and "center front." Dramatic speakers know how to build tension when they tell a story, they often use colorful words or metaphors, they exaggerate for emphasis, and they often vary their vocalics to hold attention and create effects.

B. The animated style.

Animated speakers often exaggerate their nonverbal behaviors by gesturing broadly, smiling frequently, pacing purposefully, nodding knowingly, and raising and lowering their eyebrows. In brief, animated speakers show every *emotion* they are feeling. Dramatic speakers are often animated, using a lot of energy when they communicate.

C. The humorous style.

Humor is in the eye of the beholder. That is, what the speaker finds funny may not be funny by the audience. Research by Melanie and Steve Booth-Butterfield indicates that anybody can be humorous—assuming they have the opportunity to prepare their humor ahead of time. This is comforting, because the implication for public speaking situations is that we *all* can inject at least some preplanned humor into our speeches. It is essential to *practice* telling your story or joke. However, there are several cautions to keep in mind when using humor:

1. We know there is a humor threshold for every joke, story, and anecdote. Worn-out sayings are likely to initiate groans rather than laughter.
2. Speakers can try to be *too* funny. It is suggested that public speakers who choose the humorous style should be careful to use only moderate amounts of humor.
3. Your decision to use humor must depend, in part, on the topic and occasion. For example, speeches on drunk driving or AIDS do not usually elicit humor.

D. In spite of these potential pitfalls, we know that humor affects people in a number of positive ways. Research on humor indicates that speakers can build affect with their audience. That is, audiences like speakers who use humor more than speakers who do not. Audiences perceive humorous speakers as more friendly, competent, and intelligent than nonhumorous speakers.

IV. Chapter review.

CHAPTER 13
COMMUNICATING IN A MULTICULTURAL SOCIETY

LEARNING OBJECTIVES

After studying the chapter, the student should be able to:

- Understand and discuss the cultural diversity of American society.

- Discuss the sources or origins of our cultural diversity in America.

- Explain the "melting pot" policy of rapid assimilation.

- Distinguish among the concepts of general or "mainstream" culture, specialized cultures, and co-cultures.

- Define and discuss *ethnocentrism*.

- Determine the influence of culture on human communication.

- Define and explain *intercultural communication*.

- Explain intercultural communication in terms of the linear and simultaneous transactions models of human communication described in Chapter 1.

- Discuss each of the principles of intercultural communication suggested by the simultaneous transactions model of human communication.

- Understand and discuss communication patterns within distinctive co-cultures.

- Discuss the problems associated with communicating in English as a second language.

- Explain the variations in verbal and nonverbal styles of African-Americans, Mexican-Americans, Asian-Americans, Native Americans, and females and males.

- Compare and contrast *individualistic* and *collectivistic* cultural orientations.

- Define success in co-cultural communication.

- List and apply the guidelines for becoming a multicultural communicator.

EXTENDED CHAPTER OUTLINE

This chapter discusses what is involved when people from different cultures attempt to communicate with each other. Emphasizing multiculturalism in the United States, it clarifies what constitutes effective and ineffective intercultural communication.

I.   America as a culturally diverse society.

We interact daily with people from a variety of different cultural backgrounds. Our nation is built on, and continues to expand because of, the immigration of different races, ethnic groups, and nationalities. This diversity brings with it a special set of communication problems.

A. Sources of our cultural diversity.

Native Americans arrived here about 15,000 years ago. African-Americans arrived in 1619. The rest of us are the products of more recent movements. Specifically, more than 3 million Irish Catholics arrived between 1840 and 1890. Jewish immigration has produced approximately 5.6 million. Between 1880 and 1930, more than 5 million Italians arrived. More than a third of a million Poles arrived in the 19th century. The more than 10 million people of Mexican ancestry arrived after World War II. Immigration of the more than 3 million Asians began around 1850. Recent migrations are from Cuba, Haiti, and other Latin American nations.

B. The "melting pot" policy of rapid assimilation.

To cope with the immense migration of people, the United States committed to a *melting pot* policy. Schools were used to transform immigrant children from "foreigners" to "Americans." In this way, the nation attempted to *eradicate the differences* between people. The goal was to ensure a common language and a general American culture.

While the policy achieved its major goals, it failed in other respects. Cultural differences were never really eradicated. In some communities, people from one "old country" or another kept alive many traditions and feelings of identity. Even people who are several generations removed feel the influences of their cultural roots.

C. Contemporary cultural pluralism.

Our nation now espouses a policy of *cultural pluralism*. This means that we tolerate our differences, maintaining a strong sense of diversity, while remaining a unified nation committed to democratic ideals. As a nation we represent a more mature stage of our development in what is a multicultural society.

D. Types of cultures.

Culture is an "umbrella" term covering many varieties.

1. *General or "mainstream" culture*. It is the basic culture that enables us to co-exist within a larger society and relate to each other in predictable ways. It consists of the most common language, the basic social institutions, the material artifacts and technologies in use, and the dominant values.

2. *Specialized cultures*. "Specialized" cultures are distinguished by unique ways of talking, thinking, and behaving that characterize particular groups, such as factory workers, the armed forces, or prison inmates. Each has distinctive beliefs, attitudes, and norms.

3. *Co-cultures*. A co-culture has a language configuration and other cultural features of a people of similar racial or ethnic origin, including any unique structures of meaning for which they have conventions, distinctive customs, and shared beliefs that make them different from others. In some cases, they include unique diets, clothing styles, religious practices, or other unique traits and characteristics.

E. The problem of ethnocentrism: The iron grip of culture.

Ethnocentrism is the tendency for people to regard themselves and their way of life as the best and to look down on the ways of others. People everywhere like to think of their group as the "insiders" and others as "outsiders," who are not quite as acceptable. Insight into our own tendencies toward ethnocentrism can aid in understanding or even accepting people who by our own standards seem odd or even wrong.

II. The influence of culture on communication.

Culture and communication are inseparable. According to anthropologist Edward T. Hall, culture *is* communication and communication *is* culture. The way we communicate, what we believe, what we say, the language system we use, the gestures we employ, are all a function of the culture we acquire. How we relate nonverbally to others is learned from the culture in which we grow up. How we dress, our use of time, the odors we savor, the distances we use to interact with others, and when, where, and to whom we maintain eye contact all are dictated by culture.

A. Intercultural communication defined.

Intercultural communication involves an exchange of messages that takes place when people of different general, specialized, or co-cultures interact under conditions where the interfacing cultures are different enough to influence or change the process in some significant way. The criterion for classifying an exchange as intercultural is that it takes place "between people whose cultural perceptions and symbol systems are distinct enough to alter the communication event."

Given these features, we can define intercultural communication using concepts of communication discussed in Chapter 1. Intercultural communication is *a process of transmitting and interpreting messages between culturally distinct people, in which communicators may encode, perceive, decode, and interpret aspects of reality using conventions of meaning unique to their particular group.*

This definition describes people of different specialized and co-cultures who are seeking to communicate with each other. When they do so, their respective backgrounds are likely to modify the process with corresponding reductions in accuracy.

B. A model of intercultural communication.

A linear model of intercultural communication includes the following steps:

1. *Deciding on the message.* Decisions as to what messages need to be transmitted are likely to be influenced by the sender's specialized and co-cultural participations.

2. *Encoding the intended meanings.* This stage is influenced by the memory structure of the sender and the language patterns prevailing in his or her specialized and co-cultures. These can introduce connotative meanings that may not be shared by the receiver.

3. *Transmitting the message.* This stage is influenced by verbal communication habits, accents, or nonverbal behavior used in the specialized and co-cultures of the sender.

4. *Receiving the message.* This stage is influenced by the habits of perception of the receiver that are derived from specialized and co-cultural identities.

5. *Decoding and interpreting the message.* This stage is influenced by the schemata and other structures of meanings, beliefs, attitudes, and values of the receiver that are derived from her or his cultural backgrounds.

The above stages are consistent with the simultaneous transactions model, which incorporates the linear model and adds the influences of prior communication, role-taking, feedback, physical surroundings, sociocultural situation, and social relationships. But whether linear or transactional, the co-cultural extension of these models identifies those stages of human communication where *all* of the cultures in which the communicators are involved make a difference in the verbal and nonverbal message features they exchange.

C. Principles of intercultural communication.

Five principles are suggested from the models:

1. *We know that a person can belong to several specialized and co-cultures and that the number of such affiliations varies among individuals.* You may define your identity as a student, a business executive, and a Vietnam War veteran.

2. *Being a participant in a specific culture is both self and other defined.* Others may refuse to recognize your identification with a particular culture. They may also wrongly act as though you are a part of others. That is, you may perceive yourself as an independent politically, but others may regard you as a liberal Democrat.

3. *Any given specific culture can emerge to dominate a person's perceptions sufficiently to influence or alter a message exchange.* The dominance of a particular culture depends on the context and the parties involved. For example, "being a man" may not be one of your dominant identities during most of your interactions. However, there are occasions and individuals who can trigger that identification. If that happens, being a man can substantially change an interaction.

4. *The greater the number of similar cultures individuals bring to a conversation, the higher the potential for fidelity of communication.* We would expect others who share our background and cultural experiences to think like we do, behave like we do, and more important, to construct meanings like we do. If this is the case, people can communicate more accurately.

5. *The greater the number of overlapping cultures individuals can bring to a conversation, the greater their feelings of attraction and comfort while communicating.* For example, discovering that another student in one of your courses grew up in your own home town, is of the same religion, and has parents who immigrated from the same country as yours, increases your attraction toward that person significantly.

III. Communication patterns within distinctive co-cultures.

We have become sensitive about our cultural identities and resent any implication that one co-culture is better than another. We must motivate ourselves not only to learn about other people's co-cultures but also to respect and adapt to their differences in communication. Two important cautions to consider when contemplating co-cultural communication styles are:

First, don't assume that because a person represents a given co-culture, he or she will assume all of its characteristics. In other words, the danger of identifying patterns of unique co-cultural characteristics is the very human tendency of stereotyping all individuals who affiliate with that co-culture.

Second, we need to keep in mind our almost inescapable tendency to be ethnocentric. That is, we must work hard against our tendency to prejudge others—prejudgment is the foundation of prejudice.

A. When English is a second language.

Individuals for whom English is a second language are faced with the task of interacting in a language that is difficult for them. Moving in and out of two language communities requires that they discriminate between two co-cultures in their reflexive and oftentimes unconscious, nonverbal behaviors as well. Therefore, to expect individuals to recognize and then modify their own behaviors when interacting in different co-cultures is problematic.

B. Variations in verbal and nonverbal styles.

The largest category of people in the United States—nearly 207.7 million—is the *white majority*. Importantly, they exist among many co-cultures, and thus this majority offers a comparison category with which various co-cultures can be contrasted.

1. *African-Americans.* African-Americans are the largest co-culture in the United States. Like all other co-cultures, their verbal and nonverbal behaviors are unique. Compared to African-Americans, whites tend to be restrained, modest, and subdued in their normal conversations. As a result, they are likely to be perceived as cold and distant. African-Americans sometimes use the phrase "acting white" to refer to a person who appears unemotional and undemonstrative. In communication contexts among whites, however, African-Americans are often perceived as being loud, as laughing too heartily, even acting out of control.

2. *Mexican-Americans.* Compared to the general culture, Mexican-Americans tend to show a great deal of expression. To the Mexican-American, a person's manner of expression is often more important than what a person says. Mexican-Americans value elegant speech—phrasing messages in ways that others outside their co-culture might label as "flowery." To the majority, with more subtle styles, the Mexican-American sometimes appears flamboyant or dramatic. Socializing is very important to typical Mexican-Americans. They like to talk, visit, and establish an amiable climate of conversation.

3. *Asian-Americans.* The term "Asian-Americans" includes Chinese, Japanese, Korean, and people from Singapore, Thailand, Vietnam, and other countries of Asian origin. These co-cultures are not alike. Thus, whenever we draw a conclusion about "Asian-Americans," we must not assume that *all* will communicate in the same way. In a general sense, however, Asian-Americans *do* tend to share certain unique communication patterns.

   One tendency among Asian-Americans is that they represent a "collectivistic," as opposed to the dominant "individualistic," orientation toward work and family. Asian-Americans are likely to value collaboration, conformity, loyalty, and acceptance, acquiescence, or even deference to authority. These differences influence how Asian-Americans interact verbally and nonverbally. Communicators who participate in the Japanese co-culture may hesitate to voice their opinions or express what they truly think, simply because it is customary to show deference to persons of authority, higher status, or greater age.

4. *Native Americans.* Native Americans are also collectivistic in their orientations. Native Americans often consider personal competitiveness an undesirable characteristic, preferring instead cooperation and harmony. American Indians learn to avoid sustained and direct eye contact. Both the Hopi and Navajo define direct eye contact as offensive. Moreover, staring can be interpreted as a form of aggression. The Hopi also tend to be restrained in their nonverbal facial expressiveness as well. Compared to non-Indians, they are less dramatic and animated in the way they normally communicate with others.

5. *Females and males.* There are a number of major differences between the verbal communication styles of men and women. Women are more likely than men to insert *intensifiers* into their speech. Instead of saying, "That's pretty" or "I'm tired," women are more likely to say, "That's *so* pretty" or "I'm *awfully* tired." Women also use more *qualifiers*, like "maybe" or "perhaps" or "This may be trivial to ask, but . . ." Women further rely on verbal fillers to fill in silent, awkward moments: "okay," "well," "sure," and "you know." Women use *tag questions* two to three times more than men do: "It's a beautiful day, *isn't it?*" or "don't you agree?" or "don't you think so, too?"

   Moreover, men speak more loudly than women, at a lower pitch, and with less tonal variation. Women use more facial expressions than men; women initiate and return smiles more often; they also rely on more eye contact to communicate. Men usually sit with their legs apart and seem to "expand" when they sit on a chair, whereas women hold their knees together and seem to "contract." In addition, men use more sweeping hand and arm gestures and tap their feet more than women do.

IV. Successful co-cultural communication.

We need to be realistic about how successful our co-cultural communication can be in any given situation or context. If we set unrealistic expectations, we add to the barriers and thus limit our degree of success or further ensure our failure.

A. Defining success in co-cultural communication.

Successful co-cultural communication is most realistically defined along a continuum, ranging from complete failure to complete success. At the failure end, communication with people of different cultures typically results in total alienation or estrangement. At the success end of our continuum, the results of co-cultural communication mutually achieve a heightened appreciation of the cultural differences between the communicators. We feel positive about ourselves and about others.

Highly successful co-cultural communication, then, can be defined as *an exchange of messages in which all of the individuals in an encounter are satisfied with the process and consequences.*

B. Guidelines for becoming a multicultural communicator.

Most of us will never experience completely successful co-cultural communication. Whether our co-cultural encounters result in relative success or not depends on our approach. By approach we do not mean a single strategy. Rather, we advocate a combination of guidelines for maximizing co-cultural communication.

The following list describes several guidelines for maximizing success in co-cultural communication. In combination, these guidelines can be used effectively by a person who wants to *become* a truly multicultural individual—a more effective communicator in a socially diverse society.

1. *Recognize that every human being has emotions, needs, and feelings that are every bit as sensitive as your own.*
2. *Try to understand the rules and norms of the culture or cultures of any person with whom you communicate.*
3. *Respect the customs and traditions of others.*
4. *Listen actively when someone from another culture is talking to you.*
5. *Learn to cope with uncertainty of encountering people of different cultures.*
6. *Understand and appreciate your own culture.*
7. *Avoid stereotyping people who are different from us.*
8. *Be aware of your own ethnocentrism.*

V. Chapter review.

CHAPTER 14
UNDERSTANDING MASS COMMUNICATION

LEARNING OBJECTIVES

After studying the chapter, the student should be able to:

- Define and understand the idea of *media dependency* in modern society.

- Recognize and understand three *broad questions* around which the chapter is organized: (1) how our media have been shaped by our society; (2) how they operate; and (3) the kinds of influences they have on individuals and society.

- Discuss in overview the ancient cultural heritage that now enables human beings to communicate with *written symbols* and by using the technology of the *printing press.*

- Understand the history of *books* as a mass medium in the American colonies and in their later development in the contemporary United States.

- Summarize the early history, later development and current status of *newspapers* in American society.

- Gain an overview of the history and current status of *magazines* as a mass medium in American society.

- Learn the general background, development, and current status of the *motion picture* industry in the United States.

- Discuss briefly the history and development of both *radio* and *television* as broadcast media in the United States.

- Be able to define and explain each of the five stages in the *mass communication process.*

- Explain why the mass communication process more closely follows a *linear* rather than a *transactional* model of communication.

- Identify and describe briefly the major components of a *social systems model,* and explain their links to each other and how they form a relationship between society, the media, and their audiences.

- Understand and be able to discuss why early media researchers subscribed to a *magic bullet theory* of media effects.

- Explain when and why theories of *minimal and selective influences* replaced the magic bullet theory.

- Name and explain the three major factors that determine a person's selective exposure to and influences from a particular media presentation (individual psychological differences, social category memberships, and social relationships).

- Explain briefly the *adoption of innovation* process and its relationship to mass communication.

- Define and discuss the five propositions of the *accumulation theory* of long-term influences on individuals, society, and culture.

- Explain two kinds of *socialization theories* of long-term influences of the mass media (modeling theory and social expectations theory).

EXTENDED CHAPTER OUTLINE

This chapter summarizes the historical development of each of our major mass media, showing how features of the society influenced their development. It analyzes the mass communication process through the use of both a linear model of mass communication and a social systems model of the relationship among media, various agencies and groups that influence them, and the audience.

I.   Mass communication in American society.

Mass communication is a ubiquitous aspect of modern life. Our mass media are the major source of our popular culture. Mass communication plays a central role in our economic system, the political process, plus individual and family entertainment. Without the content and presentations that the media offer, our society could not function in its present form. Thus, there is a strong relationship of dependency between the mass media and their audiences and society as a whole.

A. Each of our media shares a common cultural heritage that accumulated over many centuries through contributions of people from all parts of the world. Such factors as writing, printing, photography, and electronic technologies provide the basis for our contemporary media and those that will develop in the future.

B. Each of our media has a unique history. Each was influenced by a number of features of the American society, and its form was developed over many decades. Each is also influenced by the nature of all other media.

1. Books are our most serious medium, and for a variety of reasons they are likely to remain with us in their present form into the foreseeable future.

2. Newspapers were once the only source of news beyond word-of-mouth for most people. In recent decades, newspaper readership per capita has declined significantly and patterns of consolidated ownership have developed. However, newspapers are still a major mass medium and will continue to be so in the decades ahead.

3. Magazines were once a general medium, reaching large national audiences. Since the arrival of TV they have become a medium for specialized audiences. They are an effective advertising medium for many products.

4. Movies shown in theaters are reaching fewer and fewer people, but the use of film has greatly expanded with the development of cable TV and VCRs. As an industry, movie-making will probably expand during the decades ahead.

5. Radio and television share a common early technology. TV almost eclipsed radio when it swept into the society during the decade of the 50s. Today, it is our most-used medium to which people turn for entertainment and news.

II. The mass communication process.

Mass communication can be conceptualized as a linear process (using a variation of the linear model from Chapter 1). In that framework, it is based on point-to-multipoint transmission, but it uses all of the features of human verbal and nonverbal communication discussed in earlier chapters. However, the factors of simultaneous feedback and role-taking do not operate as in interpersonal communication. Mass communication can also be conceptualized within a social systems model, which identifies each of the components of American society that influence the media and are in turn influenced by them. The key factor whose contribution stabilizes the system is media content in relatively low cultural taste but which has wide appeal.

III. The case for limited and selective effects.

During the 19th century and the first third of the 20th, the media were regarded as very powerful. A "magic bullet" theory predominated thinking about media effects. Messages were thought to reach every eye and ear and to be interpreted more-or-less uniformly. The influences of media content were thought to be direct, uniform, and powerful. An accumulation of research between the late 1920s and the beginning of the 1970s challenged that view, and the magic bullet theory was replaced by theories of selective and limited influence. The research of the time showed that people attended to the media very selectively on the basis of three basic factors: their individual differences in interest, ability and taste; the social categories of which they were members (age, gender, social class, etc.); and their relationships with other people. These factors often influenced what content to which audiences chose to listen, read about, or view. Finally, these same factors also influenced what meanings each person reconstructed from the media messages to which he or she attended.

The bottom line from 60 years of experiments, surveys, and other forms of research is that people attend to the media selectively and they are not strongly influenced (in beliefs, attitudes, or behavior) by any particular program or presentation to which they are exposed.

IV. The case for powerful and long-term effects.

While the research methods (mainly experiments and one-time surveys) used to study the effects of mass communication have generally failed to reveal media of great power, it may be because they have focused almost exclusively on short-term exposure to particular media messages (e.g., a specific film, radio program, or television presentation). The methodology of such research is ill-equipped to identify and assess truly long-term influences of mass communication. Nevertheless, such long-term influence can be identified by careful historical observation of the relationship between specific forms of media content and public behavior toward the issues portrayed in that content.

A. Examples of ways in which the media have shaped interpretations of reality over an extended period, and thereby played a key role in changing people's interpretations of events, can be seen in the case of Watergate, the civil rights movement, the Vietnam War, and the reduction of smoking in American society over a number of years.

B. The media have influenced people's interpretations of these events (and many others) by presenting similar messages and points of view persistently and consistently. Furthermore, the fact that the same messages and interpretations were encountered in each of the major media created a corroboration effect for the versions of reality being presented.

C. A theoretical formulation that appears to describe and explain such long-term and relatively powerful effects (removing a president, changing patterns of race relations, abandoning a war, and reducing the number of Americans who smoke) is called *accumulation theory*. Its essential idea is that the media play a necessary (but not sufficient) role in bringing about change by modifying people's beliefs and attitudes through an accumulation of minimal changes over time.

D. Another long-term influence of the media that can result in significant changes in people's behavior is described by *adoption of innovation theory*, in which populations take up some new form of technology or behavior over a period of time after first being exposed to the innovation via media.

E. Finally, *socialization theories* can account for long-term changes in individuals as they are exposed to media portrayals of action and ideas. One version is *modeling theory,* in which people adopt actions or ideas they see portrayed by media and make them parts of their own behavioral repertoires. Another is *social expectations theory,* in which people learn the norms, roles, ranks, and controls of groups (to which they may never belong) by encountering them via portrayals in the media. In either case, the persons involved can be influenced in significant ways.

V. Chapter review.

CHAPTER 15
CONDUCTING COMMUNICATION RESEARCH

LEARNING OBJECTIVES

After studying the chapter, the student should be able to:

- Define and understand what is meant by *research.*

- Understand and discuss the basic assumptions (*postulates*) to which scientific researchers in all fields are committed.

- Explain the manner in which research reports published in journals are *screened.*

- Define and explain the meaning of the term *variable.*

- Distinguish between *independent* and *dependent* variables.

- Discuss the difference between research whose goal is *description* and *theory development.*

- Distinguish between a *theory* and a *hypothesis.*

- Define and explain the meaning of the term *data.*

- Discuss the various types of publications that make up what researchers in a given area refer to as the *literature.*

- Distinguish between and cite the advantages and disadvantages of *quantitative* versus *qualitative* observation.

- Explain the *Hawthorne effect.*

- Explain the difference between *reactive* and *nonreactive* observation procedures.

- Discuss the meaning of the term *participant observation.*

- Distinguish between data *processing*, data *entry*, and data *analysis.*

- Explain the difference between *generalization* and *overgeneralization.*

- Define and explain the meaning of *replication* (of a study).

- Explain the basic logical strategy of an *experiment.*

- Distinguish between a *small-group* experiment, a *field* experiment, and a *quasi*-experiment.

- Explain the major steps in conducting a *survey.*

- Discuss the basic principle of selecting a *representative sample.*

- Understand and explain the concept of *sampling frame.*

- Discuss the advantages and disadvantages of conducting a survey with *face-to-face* interviews, *telephone* interviews, or a *mail-back* questionnaire.

- Explain the procedures used in a (qualitative) *field observation study*.

- Explain the nature, advantages, and disadvantages of four distinct *levels* of measurement.

- Define and explain the difference between *validity* and *reliability* (of measures).

- Discuss the major issues in the *ethics* of research, including *truth in findings, protection of subjects,* and *deception.*

EXTENDED CHAPTER OUTLINE

This chapter discusses the assumptions made by communication scholars about how and why they conduct research. We review the steps, logical strategies, procedures, techniques, and ethical considerations that make up the scientific research process. These, taken together, are called the "methodology" of communication research. The use of that methodology rests on three basic assumptions about the nature of reality, causal relationships between variables, and the integrity of the scientific process.

I. The postulates of the research perspective.

All researchers assume that whatever aspect of reality (e.g., communication behavior) they are studying follows orderly laws that can be discovered through research. They assume that the conditions they investigate have causes that can be identified through research. Furthermore, they assume that the process of conducting and reporting research takes place within a set of controls. These are sufficiently strong that they limit the degree of misrepresentation of findings or errors caused by sloppy procedures to a point that scientific reports are generally trustworthy.

II. General steps in a research project.

Six basic steps are involved in planning, conducting, and reporting the results of a research project. While each step involves many options from which to select, these general steps apply to virtually any research project, regardless of the specific topic or subject under investigation.

A. Specifying the research goals.

The first step is to make clear the objectives of the research project. This means not only describing the general objectives but also identifying the independent and dependent variables and the anticipated way that they will be related (e.g., a correlated versus causal relationship). It also means formulating and stating the hypotheses that will be tested with the data to be gathered.

B. Reviewing prior research reports.

Step 2 is to conduct a thorough review of the reports on similar research so as to find out what is already known about the topic under investigation. Such a review entails searching relevant computerized databases (of the "literature") for scholarly research reports related to the topic that have already been published. These may be in the form of journal articles, convention reports, dissertations, government documents, books, and monographs.

C. Making the necessary observations.

Empirical observations, that is, sensory discriminations, are basic to all research. Through such observation (which can be accomplished in many ways) data are assembled. The term *data* means "information known as fact," which implies that the observations must be recorded as symbols so as to make them available for inspection by other researchers.

D. Data processing, entry, and analysis.

Data processing means transforming recorded observations into numerical form. These can then be entered into a computer so that data analysis (usually based on some form of statistical procedure) can be performed. The end result usually consists of statistical indexes or coefficients from which conclusions can be drawn as to whether it is likely that chance produced them or that the variables under study are related in systematic ways.

E. Reporting the results.

To meet the criteria of science, research must be reported so as to make it *public*. This usually means submitting a research report to a journal, where it can undergo a rigorous (blind) scrutiny by a panel of experts. Many candidate reports are rejected by such judges if they do not meet accepted standards. Those that are accepted become part of the accumulating literature on the topic under investigation.

III. Formal research designs.

A research design is a detailed plan that indicates very specifically how each of the steps in a research project will be carried out. Among the designs frequently used in communication research are the experiment, survey, field or observational study, and content analysis. Each has many forms.

A. Experiments.

The logic of the experiment was formulated centuries ago. In communication research, observations are made on a number of human subjects, some of whom are designated as a "control" group and others as the "experimental" group. The experimental group receives a "treatment" deliberately introduced by the experimenter. The control group does not, or it experiences a neutral condition. Measurements of the dependent variable (thought to be influenced by the treatment) are made before and after on each group. If the experimental group changes and the control group does not, the treatment had an influence. There are a great variety of experiments. Some are performed on small groups; others involve large groups. Quasi-experiments are those whose conditions are arranged by natural events.

B. Surveys.

This design is an extension of the ancient idea of the census. However, only a representative portion of people are studied rather than all members of a population. The first step is to pick a sample so that it truly reflects the characteristics of the population. There are a number of alternative ways to do this, but the basic principle is to ensure that every member of the population has an equal chance of being selected as a member of the sample. Those selected are then contacted for observation. This may be by direct face-to-face interviews, by telephone, or with a questionnaire sent through the mail. Each procedure has advantages and limitations.

C. Field observational studies.

This research design is based on participant observation. The researcher takes part in the activities of the group under study and makes careful observation of its activities. He or she develops an intimate familiarity with the communication patterns under study. The qualitative observations are organized into disciplined abstractions that set forth the most typical patterns of verbal and nonverbal communication that take place among group members.

D. Content analysis.

Content analysis designs focus on the message. They seek to identify categories of key words, themes, depictions of a particular social role, or actions that are relevant to the goals of the research. Once these units have been identified and counted, they can be subjected to statistical or other kinds of analyses. Studies of message content can tell the researcher what the message contains. Such studies cannot tell what the intentions of the communicator were or what effect the message may have on receivers.

IV. Measuring variables.

Measurement is a process of converting the observer's subjective sensory experiences into numerical symbols that can be counted, added, subtracted, multiplied, and divided. It is not possible to conduct empirical research without measurement in some form. Even qualitative research is based on determining whether some attribute or pattern is present or absent in the communication activities under study. That is a binary (present or absent) measurement situation.

Four distinct levels of measurement are common in communication research. These are nominal measurement, ordinal ranking, interval measurement, and ratio measurement.

A. Nominal measures.

This elementary form of measurement is essentially a classification procedure. It is based on the presence or absence of some quality of an entity that permits it to be identified as a member of a particular category. It is not based on the entity having a greater or lesser amount of some quality. Typical categories in communication research are gender, political affiliation, race or ethnicity, and so on.

B. Ordinal measures.

Ordinal measures are what are commonly called ranks. That is, entities are judged to be in first place, second place, third place, and so on down to last place, on the basis of some quality that they possess. Such ranked positions do not have equal distances between them, and they have no true zero origin. Therefore, they cannot be added, subtracted, or otherwise manipulated mathematically. While this is a limitation, ordinal measures are widely used to indicate relative position in an array.

C. Interval measures.

Interval measures do have equal distance between units, so they provide numbers that can be added and subtracted. While they lack a known zero point along a scale, they are widely used in the measurement of such variables as attitudes and many communication-related variables.

D. Ratio measures.

This is both the most familiar and most sophisticated level of measurement. It is so commonly used that most people are familiar with it and it seems simple. Ratio measures have a true zero, and they have equal distances between units. Family income is an example. One can have zero income, and the difference between $1,000 and $2,000 is the same as between $4,000 and $5,000. This permits the numbers obtained by ratio measurement to be used in all mathematical manipulations.

E. Judging the quality of measurement.

There are two major considerations in assessing the quality of measurement. First, does the procedure used actually measure what it is intended or is purported to measure? Second, does the procedure provide consistent results?

1. Validity.

    The most common use for the term *validity* is to indicate the degree to which a procedure actually assesses what it purports to measure. For example, does a scale of communication apprehension actually measure that quality in a person, or does it assess something different?

    (Note that the term *internal validity* is used in a different way to indicate whether an experiment actually reproduces the natural process that it is designed to simulate. In addition, the term *external validity* refers to the degree to which the findings obtained in an experiment actually apply to the natural processes outside the laboratory setting.)

2. Reliability.

    This term is commonly used to indicate the degree to which a procedure yields consistent results when used repeatedly to assess the same people.

    (Note that a measure can have low validity but high reliability. It cannot have high validity if it has low reliability.)

V. Ethical issues in communication research.

Researchers have long been concerned about maintaining the scientific integrity of research reports. However, they have become increasingly sensitive about the way that participants in experiments, or other research designs, are treated. The deepest concerns came from medical research where human beings were sometimes treated in harmful ways, but psychological stress can result from experiments where deception or other duplicitous techniques are used. There are three major areas of ethical concerns in communication research.

A. Truth in findings.

Hoaxes are rare in scientific work, and communication research has been fortunate in this respect. If they do occur, they are cruel. They undermine public confidence in the integrity of research, and they mislead other investigators.

B. Assessing risks versus benefits.

Research projects must be evaluated carefully before they are actually conducted so as to assess the benefits to advancing knowledge that they represent. Against that, potential risks to persons who participate must also be carefully assessed. If the risk of harm is high and the benefits low, it may be that the research should not be conducted.

C. Protection of subjects.

Researchers must safeguard the privacy of participants in their research and maintain confidentiality about the performance of any person in an experiment or other form of investigation.

VI. Chapter review.

PART III

EXAMINATION QUESTIONS

CHAPTER 1
THE COMMUNICATION PROCESS: AN OVERVIEW

MULTIPLE CHOICE

1. The linear model of communication involved five distinct stages. Which of the following is NOT one of those stages? (p. 14)
   A. Deciding on the message
   B. Encoding the intended meanings
   C. Transmitting the message
   *D. Comparing the message with stored meanings
   E. Decoding or interpreting the message

2. In which stage of the linear communication model does the source search her or his memory for specific words or gestures and their associated meanings that can be put together in a pattern that will describe the desired facts, ideas, and images? (p. 14)
   A. Encoding the intended message
   B. Transmitting the message
   C. Decoding the message
   D. Receiving the message
   *E. Deciding on the message

3. A subjective response that individuals learn to make, either to objects, events, or situations that they experience through their senses, is called: (p. 16)
   A. Communication
   B. Perceptions
   *C. Meanings
   D. Symbols
   E. Information

4. Imprinted records of experiences registered in the brain by electrochemical activities of its nerve cells are termed: (p. 16)
   *A. Traces
   B. Schemata
   C. Symbols
   D. Paths
   E. Memories

5. A pattern or configuration of traces of meaning that have been put together in an organized way and recorded in a person's mental storage system is called a: (p. 16)
   A. Trace
   *B. Schema
   C. Symbol
   D. Cluster
   E. Signal

6. When a sender assesses the likelihood that a receiver will be able to interpret the intentions and meanings of a particular message, the sender is engaging in: (p. 18)
   A. Encoding
   B. Decoding
   *C. Role-taking
   D. Interpreting
   E. Meanings

7. Seeing, hearing, or feeling something (with the senses) and then identifying what it is within the interpretations learned from your own language and culture is the definition of: (p. 19)
   *A. Perceptions
   B. Meanings
   C. Communication
   D. Role-taking
   E. Feedback

8. The linear model of communication can be transformed into an interactive model by adding what component? (p. 20)
   A. Traces
   B. Decoding
   *C. Feedback
   D. Role-taking
   E. Context

9. The simultaneous transactions model of communication can be summed up in six basic propositions. Which of the following statements is NOT a proposition? (p. 22)
   A. Communicating parties simultaneously engage in role-taking and feedback.
   B. Communicating parties are simultaneously influenced by the social situation within which their communication takes place.
   C. Communicating parties are simultaneously influenced by their prior communicative interactions.
   *D. Communicating parties simultaneously analyze the act of communication.
   E. Communicating parties are simultaneously influenced by the social relationships that exist between them.

10. A way in which a message intended and transmitted by a source can be assessed for accuracy against the message received and interpreted by a receiver is the definition of: (p. 27)
    *A. The index of fidelity
    B. Accurate communication
    C. Distorted communication
    D. Comparative communication
    E. Feedback

11. Social scientists who attempt to understand human communication by looking at animal communication as well are employing which of the following perspectives? (p. 10)
    A. Universal
    B. Contemporary
    *C. Comparative
    D. Comprehensive
    E. International

12. Words, grammatical rules, and syntax structures work together to form: (p. 14)
    *A. Symbols
    B. Signs
    C. Sets of experiences
    D. Signals
    E. Meanings

13. The concept of meaning is central to the encoding process. What something actually means to someone, however, is difficult to define. The primary reason why meaning is so difficult to understand is that it is _____ behavior: (p. 14)
    A. Objective
    *B. Subjective
    C. Figurative
    D. Detached
    E. Denotative

14. _____ is a kind of "reading of the mind." The source mentally places himself or herself in the shoes of another person to determine the best way to communicate the intended meanings so that the receiver can interpret them. (p. 18)
    A. Feedback
    B. Encoding
    *C. Role-taking
    D. Sympathy
    E. Receptiveness

15. The nature of relationships such as those between spouses, friends, acquaintances, or supervisors and subordinates at work can strongly influence: (pp. 24–25)
    *A. What is communicated
    B. Traces and paths
    C. Subsequent communication
    D. Satisfaction with communication
    E. Length of communication

TRUE OR FALSE

16. Human communication can be thought of as a process during which a source initiates a message using conventionalized symbols, nonverbal signs, and contextual cues to express meanings by transmitting information in such a way that similar or parallel understandings are constructed by an intended other.
    Ans: T   Page: 11

17. Once communication messages are understood by the receiver, they are reversible.
    Ans: F   Page: 14

18. Meanings are subjective responses that individuals learn.
    Ans: T   Page: 15

19. The encoding process is unbelievably fast and automated.
    Ans: T   Page: 18

20. The physical surroundings where communication takes place have little influence on how a message is understood.
    Ans: F   Pages: 23–24

21. Relationships such as those between spouses, friends, acquaintances, or strangers can strongly influence both the content of messages and the way in which they are transmitted and received.
    Ans: T   Page: 24

22. Accurate communication means that all of the intended meanings of the sending individual are reconstructed by the receiver so that they match.
    Ans: T   Page: 25

23. An outcome in which meanings intended by the source become compounded with or displaced by other meanings constructed by the receiver is the definition of incomplete communication.
    Ans: F   Pages: 25–27

24. Complete and accurate communication occurs only if the total combination of traits and schematic configurations of meanings intended and developed by a source is identical to the total combination constructed and experienced by a receiver.
    Ans: T   Pages: 25–27

25. Adequate fidelity in communication occurs only when the sender understands the goals that he or she wants to achieve and the characteristics of the receiver that make accurate communication likely.
    Ans: T   Pages: 25–27

ESSAYS

26. Discuss how speech and language distinguish humans from animals.
27. Discuss why effective communication skills are even more important today than in the past.
28. List and discuss the components of the definition of human communication, including process, symbols, nonverbal signs, contextual cues, and meanings.
29. Understand and discuss the connection between accurate and distorted communication.
30. Explain the index of fidelity and how we can live with limited accuracy in our lives.

CHAPTER 2
VERBAL COMMUNICATION

MULTIPLE CHOICE

1. The concept which developed from evolutionary theory that animals can be arranged along a kind of scale in terms of the complexity of their bodily structures and organization is known as the: (p. 36)
   A. Interspecies measure
   *B. Phylogenetic continuum
   C. Comparative perspective
   D. Darwin's theory
   E. Evolution continuum

2. Insects are good examples of animals that communicate effectively to one another to find food, protect themselves from danger, and provide for reproduction. Insect communication is largely based on _____ and is not dependent on learning. (p. 37)
   A. Instincts
   B. Interspecies behavior patterns
   *C. Inherited behavior systems
   D. Genetics
   E. Pheromones

3. The chemical secretions used by insects and other animals to mark trails, territory, or readiness for mating are termed: (p. 37)
   *A. Pheromones
   B. Animal secretions
   C. Phylogenetic residue
   D. Natural signs
   E. Species odors

4. Adaptive behavior patterns that are inherited, unlearned, and universal in a species are often called: (p. 39)
   A. Signals
   B. Natural signs
   *C. Instincts
   D. Genetic abilities
   E. Inherited skills

5. An event or events that animals learn to associate with and use to anticipate subsequent events, including coexistence with other animals, are known as: (p. 39)
   A. Symbolic language
   B. Instinctual communication
   C. Learned signals
   D. Biological patterns
   *E. Natural signs

6. The study of the relationships among events, words, and the meanings we construct is called: (p. 49)
   *A. Semantics
   B. Symbolics
   C. Syntax
   D. Natural signs
   E. Personal meanings

7. Verbal labels help us to standardize meanings for aspects of reality to enable us to have similar internal meanings. These labels are also called: (p. 49)
   A. Signs
   *B. Symbols
   C. Signals
   D. Parallel meanings
   E. Concepts

8. _____ are made-up remembered aspects of things, events, or situations that exist outside ourselves. (p. 50)
   A. Attributes
   B. Traces
   *C. Meanings
   D. Experiences
   E. Schemata

9. A set or configuration of attributes by which any particular instance of a whole class of similar objects or events can be recognized is a _____: (p. 51)
   A. Trace
   B. Schema
   C. Meaning
   *D. Concept
   E. Perception

10. The process of making sense or attaching meaning to some aspect of reality is known as: (p. 51)
    A. Meaning
    B. Concept
    C. Scheme
    D. Symbol
    *E. Perception

11. When the process of labeling a new concept does not follow some rigid or systematic rule, we call this the principle of: (pp. 53–55)
    *A. Arbitrary selection
    B. Conventions
    C. Meaning
    D. Systematic labeling
    E. Symbolic reality

12. The diagram showing that meaning, symbol, and referent constitute a kind of system, with each element linked by a convention, is referred to as the: (p. 57)
    A. Perception process
    B. Phylogenetic continuum
    C. Redundancy model
    *D. Meaning triangle
    E. Comparative perspective

13. Personal or unshared meanings that an individual uniquely associates with a referent because of past experiences refers to what kind of meanings? (p. 58)
    A. Denotative
    B. Experiential
    *C. Connotative
    D. Traditional
    E. Individualistic

14. The structural aspect of language which refers to the rules for ordering words into sentences or phrases in such a way that their meanings are clear is called: (p. 60)
    A. Vocabulary
    B. Grammar
    C. Redundancy
    D. Conventional patterns
    *E. Syntax

15. One of the features of English, and many other languages, is that a message often contains a lot of words that are not actually needed for understanding. This feature of language is known as: (p. 60)
    A. Repetition
    *B. Redundancy
    C. Consistency
    D. Denotation
    E. Connotation

TRUE OR FALSE

16. Communication abilities are all learned.
    Ans: F   Page: 35

17. The comparative perspective involves the assessment of the different capacities and behavioral characteristics of various species.
    Ans: T   Page: 35

18. For human beings, our most acute sense is sight, which is used to detect nonverbal cues.
    Ans: T   Page: 38

19. The communication patterns among species high on the phylogenetic continuum are limited by inherited capacities and techniques and are based mainly on learning to respond to complex natural signs.
    Ans: T   Page: 40

20. The signs that animals use are arbitrarily selected and their meanings are shared by conventions.
    Ans: F   Page: 40

21. There are clear scientific grounds to conclude that whales are equal to human beings in intelligence.
    Ans: F   Page: 43

22. The home-rearing experiments with Gua and Vicki allowed for clear recognition that the reason the chimpanzees had difficulty in speaking was because of their vocal physiology.
    Ans: T   Page: 44

23. The absence of a language environment in early life has little consequence to a developing infant.
    Ans: F   Page: 47

24. The cases of "Anna" and "Isabelle" demonstrated that humans, unlike animals, are not limited in their development of communication skills by their inherited capacities.
    Ans: F   Pages: 47–49

25. By "knowing reality," we mean acquiring internal and subjective experiences, images, or understandings.
    Ans: T   Page: 49

26. Learning leaves traces—that is, elements of meaning that we associate with an external object and with a label for the object.
    Ans: T   Page: 50

27. Words can be regarded as concepts.
    Ans: T   Page: 51

28. Whereas concepts refer to abstractions, like "democracy" and "trends," schemata refer to categories of concrete objects or events, like "television set" and "cosmetics."
    Ans: F   Pages: 51–52

29. Signs are socially agreed-upon labels that we use to arouse meanings for concepts stored in schemata within our memory system.
    Ans: F   Page: 53

30. When concepts are formed, the process of labeling them does not follow some rigid or systematic rule.
    Ans: T   Page: 55

31. A convention is a rule that people of a given language community agree to follow.
    Ans: T   Page: 55

32. Connotative meanings are standardized meanings for concepts.
    Ans: F   Page: 58

33. Grammar is the building block of language.
    Ans: F   Page: 59

34. Syntax refers to the rules for ordering words in a sentence or any expression in such a way that their meaning is clear.
    Ans: T   Page: 60

35. Communication is a simple process, requiring very little effort for mutual understanding.
    Ans: F   Page: 60

ESSAYS

36. Discuss how communication based on inherited behavior systems differs from communication learned through signs and symbols.
37. Discuss the implication of animal studies with regard to language and communication.
38. Discuss how meanings are acquired.
39. Explain the meaning triangle and its relevance to communication.
40. List and discuss three conclusions that you can draw from your study of language and communication for both humans and animals.

CHAPTER 3
NONVERBAL COMMUNICATION

MULTIPLE CHOICE

1. The deliberate or unintentional use of objects, actions, sounds, time, and space so as to arouse meanings in others is the definition of: (p. 69)
   A. Human communication
   *B. Nonverbal communication
   C. Body communication
   D. Verbal communication
   E. Nonverbal immediacy

2. Which of the following is NOT a function of nonverbal communication commonly used with our verbal messages? (p. 70)
   A. Complementing
   B. Regulating
   C. Substituting
   *D. Supporting
   E. Contradicting

3. The use of nonverbal actions, such as rolling our eyes or shrugging our shoulders, helps to frame our verbalizations. Framing is included within which function of nonverbal communication? (p. 70)
   A. Regulating
   B. Contradicting
   C. Turn-taking
   D. Substituting
   *E. Complementing

4. The informal "rules of order" that control the flow of speech among people are known as which of the following nonverbal functions? (p. 71)
   A. Complementing
   B. Substituting
   *C. Regulating
   D. Contradicting
   E. Reinforcing

5. People commonly use nonverbal gestures or facial expressions rather than words when trying to communicate such emotions as dismay, disgust, frustration, hostility, or love. These nonverbal actions serve which of the following functions? (p. 72)
   A. Complementing
   B. Regulating
   C. Contradicting
   D. Reinforcement
   *E. Substituting

6. Sarcasm is a type of communication that serves which nonverbal function? (p. 73)
   *A. Contradicting
   B. Substituting
   C. Reinforcement
   D. Complementing
   E. Regulating

7. Driving a BMW or writing with a Mont Blanc pen communicates personal and social information about ourselves. Objects or things that communicate are called: (p. 74)
   *A. Artifacts
   B. Symbols
   C. Possessions
   D. Resources
   E. Social system

8. Which of the following is NOT a communication function of clothing? (pp. 76–79)
   A. Communicating status and power
   B. Dressing to be socially acceptable
   C. Communicating sexual attractiveness
   *D. Dressing to keep warm or protect us from the environment
   E. A way to show our inner feelings

9. The study of body movements, including gestures, posture, and facial expression, is termed: (pp. 81–82)
   *A. Kinesics
   B. Vocalics
   C. Oculesics
   D. Proxemics
   E. Haptics

10. Gestures that have specific conventions of meanings in our culture, such as using our thumb to "hitch" a ride, are known as: (pp. 72, 82)
    A. Illustrators
    B. Adaptors
    *C. Emblems
    D. Proxemics
    E. Affect displays

11. Gestures that are unintentional, including hand, arm, leg, or other bodily movements, and which are used to reduce stress or relieve boredom are called: (p. 82)
    A. Emblems
    B. Illustrators
    C. Affect displays
    *D. Adaptors
    E. Regulators

12. The study of eye contact and pupil dilation is called: (p. 83)
    A. Vocalics
    *B. Oculesics
    C. Haptics
    D. Kinesics
    E. Eye behavior

13. The study of the meanings communicated by space and distance is called: (p. 84)
    A. Kinesics
    B. Haptics
    *C. Proxemics
    D. Territory
    E. Oculesics

14. Fixed or semifixed space that we claim or stake out as our own is called: (p. 84)
    A. Personal space
    *B. Territoriality
    C. Ownership
    D. Interpersonal zones
    E. Encroachment

15. The interpersonal distance zone that ranges from 4 to 8 feet, which we usually reserve for business associates or acquaintances, is called: (p. 84)
    A. Intimate
    B. Casual-personal
    *C. Socio-consultative
    D. Public
    E. Professional

16. The study of touch as a means of nonverbal communication is called: (p. 87)
    *A. Haptics
    B. Proxemics
    C. Kinesics
    D. Encroachment
    E. Chronemics

17. The study of the way in which people use time to transmit nonverbal messages is called: (p. 89)
    A. Haptics
    B. Kinesics
    C. Oculesics
    D. Proxemics
    *E. Chronemics

18. Individuals differ in their tolerance for early or late time schedules, as related to their biological clock. Individuals who work best at night are known as: (p. 89)
    A. Sparrows
    B. Pigeons
    *C. Owls
    D. Sprowls
    E. Vampires

19. In terms of psychological time orientations, Chinese and Native Americans are examples of _____ societies. (p. 90)
    A. Present-oriented
    *B. Past-oriented
    C. Late-oriented
    D. Future-oriented
    E. Punctual

20. The use of nonverbal signals and actions that promote physical and psychological closeness with others is referred to by communication specialists as: (p. 90)
    A. Liking
    *B. Immediacy behaviors
    C. Affinity-seeking
    D. Symbolic interactions
    E. Biological predispositions

TRUE OR FALSE

21. Nonverbal communication reveals true feelings and intentions.
    Ans. F   Page: 69

22. Nonverbal gestures that have direct verbal translations which are widely understood are known as illustrators.
    Ans: F   Page: 72

23. The relationship between verbal and nonverbal communication is primarily one of symbiosis.
    Ans: T   Page: 73

24. In our culture, one's height carries little nonverbal meaning overall.
    Ans: F   Page: 74

25. The body itself transmits messages that others interpret as our central personal qualities.
    Ans: T   Page: 74

26. Artifacts communicate to others where we belong in the social class system, the financial resources we command, and our background as reflected in tastes, hobbies, and interests.
    Ans: T   Page: 76

27. Stretching your arms over your head to emphasize your level of fatigue is an example of an emblem.
    Ans: F   Page: 82

28. Research on accents demonstrates a clear link between regional and ethnic accent and level of intelligence.
    Ans: F   Pages: 82–83

29. Negative emotions, such as sadness or anger, are much more likely to be identified accurately from vocalic cues alone than are positive ones (happiness or relief).
    Ans: T   Page: 83

30. People use their eyes to indicate their degree of interest, openness, and even arousal as they communicate.
    Ans: T   Page: 83

31. When a person fails to look at us directly "in the eye," we can be fairly certain that she/he is trying to deceive us.
    Ans: F   Page: 83

32. The immediate zone or "bubble" we carry with us during our daily interactions with others is known as personal space.
    Ans: T   Page: 84

33. Females tend to interact at closer distances with other females than do males with other males.
    Ans: T   Page: 84

34. Americans here in the United States represent a contact-oriented society.
    Ans: F   Page: 85

35. Fight responses are more common when invasions occur within primary or exclusive territory.
    Ans: T   Page: 85

36. Touch-avoiders are those people who feel uncomfortable touching or being touched by others.
    Ans: T   Page: 89

37. Time intervals are often imprecise and misinterpreted.
    Ans: T   Page: 89

38. The nonverbal immediacy principle states that people approach things and others they like or prefer and avoid things/others they don't like or don't prefer.
    Ans: T   Page: 91

39. One potential problem with nonverbal immediacy is that it often results in less communication with others.
    Ans: F   Page: 92

40. When people engage in immediacy behaviors of approach, they are often perceived by others to be more popular, well liked, responsive, and sensitive.
    Ans: T   Page: 92

ESSAYS

41. Discuss the relationship between verbal and nonverbal communication.
42. Explain how the body is used as a communication device.
43. Explain how eye contact can communicate both positive and negative feelings toward others.
44. Discuss the effects of touch deprivation on humans.
45. Define nonverbal immediacy and identify those nonverbal behaviors that lead to perceived nonverbal immediacy. What are two advantages and two disadvantages of using immediacy behaviors?

CHAPTER 4

LISTENING AS COMMUNICATION

MULTIPLE CHOICE

1. An active form of behavior in which individuals attempt to maximize their attention to, and comprehension of, what is being communicated to them through the use of words, actions, and things by one or more people in their immediate environment is the definition of: (p. 102)
   A. Communication
   B. Hearing
   *C. Listening ✓
   D. Comprehension
   E. Context

2. Which of the following is NOT a purpose listening serves in our lives? (pp. 102–103)
   A. Acquiring needed information
   B. Evaluating and screening messages
   C. Recreation
   *D. Discrimination
   E. Social efficacy ✓

3. When we listen to our stereo or television, or attend a concert, we are engaging in which of the following listening purposes? (p. 104)
   A. Screening
   *B. Recreation
   C. Acquiring needed information
   D. Social efficacy
   E. Relaxation ✓

4. The active reception of messages to maximize attention to, and comprehension of, what is being communicated is termed which type of listening? (p. 105)
   A. Passive
   B. Habitual
   *C. Active ✓
   D. Discriminative
   E. Recreational

5. The concept that refers to various ways in which both senders and receivers independently modify how they think and behave toward each other is: (p. 106)
   A. Assimilation
   B. Accommodation ✓
   C. Habitual behavior transformation
   D. Observable actions
   *E. Adaptation

6. Active attempts to adapt can produce a number of positive outcomes for a listener within a communication encounter. Which of the following is NOT a positive outcome discussed in the text? (p. 107)
   A. Increased message attention
   B. Improved message comprehension
   C. Maintained message attention
   D. Improved communication accuracy
   *E. Increased source credibility

7. The process based on simultaneous role-taking and feedback by senders and receivers is known as: (p. 108)
   A. Feedback
   *B. Sender/receiver reciprocity
   C. Mutual adaptation
   D. Sender/receiver similarity
   E. Role-taking adjustment

8. Which of the following is NOT one of the four common misconceptions made by poor listeners? (p. 112)
   *A. Listening is a complex activity.
   B. Listening is easy.
   C. Listening is just a matter of intelligence.
   D. Listening requires no planning.
   E. Improving our reading ability will improve our listening ability.

9. Which of the following barriers to effective listening includes noise interference? (p. 113)
   A. Personal problems
   *B. Physical condition
   C. Prejudices
   D. Physical attractiveness
   E. Psychological intentions

10. Sickness, exhaustion, and overindulgence of food or drink are examples of which type of listening barrier? (p. 113)
    A. Personal prejudices
    B. Physical conditions
    C. Connotative meanings
    *D. Personal problems
    E. Noise interference

11. Personal, subjective, and unshared interpretations we have for verbal and nonverbal symbols and signs are known as: (p. 116)
    A. Selective perceptions
    *B. Connotative meanings
    C. Active listening
    D. Denotative meanings
    E. Personal prejudices

12. Those personal attributes and individual differences that help or hinder our capacity to receive and interpret messages accurately are called: (p. 117)
   *A. Receiver eccentricities
   B. Receiver personalities
   C. Social skills
   D. Sender ethnocentrism
   E. Sender/receiver reciprocity

13. Which of the following is NOT a step required for effective listening? (p. 118)
   A. Controlling concentration
   B. Showing alertness and interest
   C. Suspending judgment about message and source
   D. Preparing ourselves to listen
   *E. Avoid searching actively for meanings

14. The activity or step that can help us plan to be more effective listeners which calls for us to minimize any tendency we might have to make premature judgments about either the source or the message is termed: (p. 119)
   A. Controlling concentration
   *B. Suspending judgments
   C. Showing alertness
   D. Keeping active while listening
   E. Receiver eccentricities

TRUE OR FALSE

15. Comprehension depends immediately and directly on the existence of parallel meaning experiences, which can accurately be produced only by effective listening behavior.
   Ans: T   Page: 102

16. Listening serves at least three primary purposes in our lives. We listen to acquire information, to screen information, and to develop new relationships.
   Ans: F   Pages: 102–103

17. Social efficacy means being competent as a social person, that is, being able to form, manage and maintain all kinds of social relationships in an effective manner.
   Ans: T   Page: 105

18. Passive listening requires little or no effort by the receiver. Passiveness stems from boredom, hunger, disinterest, and apathy.
   Ans: T   Page: 105

19. Listening is an internal process that cannot be observed.
   Ans: T   Page: 106

20. A necessary condition for effective listening is being perceived and classified by others as a good listener.
   Ans: T   Page: 106

21. Effective listening is a simple activity that requires little effort.
   Ans: F   Page: 112

22. All smart people listen well, it is just a matter of intelligence.
    Ans: F   Page: 113

23. The large amount of listening we do every day will automatically make us good listeners by the time we are adults.
    Ans: F   Page: 113

24. By improving our reading ability, we will also improve our ability to listen.
    Ans: F   Page: 113

ESSAY

25. Discuss the five responsibilities of senders and the five responsibilities of receivers in the listening process.
26. Discuss what is meant by sender/receiver similarity.
27. Identify and discuss the four broad categories of barriers to effective listening.
28. Explain why planning is so important to effective listening.
29. Identify and describe the seven-part plan than can help improve one's competence in listening.

CHAPTER 5
COMMUNICATING INTERPERSONALLY

MULTIPLE CHOICE

1. The feature of the simultaneous transactions model of communication that includes the "stage" or context in which human interactions take place is called the: (p. 130)
   A. Social setting
   *B. Physical setting
   C. Social situation
   D. Social relationships
   E. Psychological situation

2. Norms, roles, and rankings are all enforced by: (p. 131)
   A. Division of labor
   B. The context
   *C. Controls
   D. Persuasion
   E. Participant rank

3. The process of transmitting messages between two people through the use of language and actions that are intended by the source is the definition of: (p. 132)
   A. Nonverbal communication
   *B. Interpersonal communication
   C. Human communication
   D. Group dynamics
   E. Organizational communication

4. The process by which people try to move their relationship from an impersonal to a personal basis is called: (p. 132)
   *A. Engagement
   B. Initiation
   C. Management
   D. Withdrawal
   E. Disengagement

5. Interpersonal communication can be discussed within the context of two major background features: The first is that interpersonal communication takes place in the dyad. The second major feature of interpersonal communication is that as the individuals involved come to know one another better, . . . : (p. 133)
   *A. Their relationship moves from impersonal to personal
   B. Their relationship moves from physical attraction to social attraction
   C. The more intimate their discussions become
   D. Their relationship moves from undesirable to desirable
   E. The less likely the two will engage in self-disclosure

6. Which of the following is NOT a key characteristic of interpersonal communication? (pp. 133–135)
   A. Interpersonal communication begins with the self.
   B. Interpersonal communication is fully transactional.
   C. Interpersonal communicators share physical proximity.
   *D. Interpersonal communication is reversible. ✓
   E. Interpersonal communication is shaped by social roles.

7. The central and unique characteristics of an individual that set him or her off from others are called a(n): (p. 134)
   *A. Persona
   B. Self ✓
   C. Personality
   D. Image
   E. Belief

8. Which of the following is NOT a reason for engaging in a lasting interpersonal relationship? (p. 136)
   A. Constructing a positive self-image
   B. Coping with daily problems
   C. Maintaining a positive self-image
   D. Maximizing rewards and minimizing punishments
   *E. Satisfying the needs of others

9. Supplying emotional support to others when they are feeling anxious or afraid, or even depressed, is known as the: (p. 137)
   A. Cost/benefit ratio
   B. Principle of utility
   *C. Cushioning function
   D. Principle of utilitarianism
   E. Pragmatic function

10. The idea that we choose to engage in those behaviors that maximize pleasure and avoid those that result in pain is known as the: (p. 137)
   A. Principle of utilitarianism
   B. Self-fulfilling prophecy
   *C. Principle of utility
   D. Cushioning function
   E. Principle of immediacy

11. Highly standardized and predictable conversations that occur in the first critical moments are called: (p. 139)
   *A. Stereotypic
   B. Packaging
   C. Nondisclosing
   D. Safe
   E. Factual

12. Revealing personal and private information to a person we've never met before or expect to encounter again is called: (p. 139)
    A. Self-disclosure
    B. Small talk
    C. Stereotypic conversation
   *D. The stranger on the plane phenomenon ↙
    E. Audition for friendship experience

13. Which of the following is NOT one of the six skills of small talk? (pp. 141–144)
   *A. Avoiding direct eye contact
    B. Using first names
    C. Accentuating the positive
    D. Drawing out the other person
    E. Keeping the conversation light

14. According to the _____, we implicitly count up the history of rewards received from interacting with the other person, weigh that against the history of costs, and make an estimate of the worth of that relationship to us. (p. 144)
    A. Cost/benefit ratio
   *B. Exchange theory
    C. Principle of delayed gratification
    D. Principle of utility
    E. Reservoir principle

15. The idea that we sometimes put up with a great amount of costs as long as we can also predict that significant rewards will follow is called the principle of: (p. 145)
    A. Utility
    B. Cost/reward comparison
    C. Exchange
    D. Chance
   *E. Delayed gratification

16. A characteristic of participants in close relationships is their use of _____, such as special words or nonverbal gestures and meanings for situation that others may not quite understand, recognize, or know about. (p. 147)
    A. Self-disclosure
   *B. Intimate idioms
    C. Secret tests
    D. Labels
    E. Public dialogue

17. Reducing the use of the pronoun "we" or "us," and reverting back to the individualistic "you" and "I," is a sign of saying goodbye. This particular process is called: (p. 149)
    A. Physical distancing
   *B. Disassociation
    C. Psychological distancing
    D. Difference emphasizing
    E. Disengagement

18. The termination strategy that can be called the "don't call me, I'll call you" approach is: (p. 150)
    A. Ending on a positive note
    B. Machiavellianism
    C. Open confrontation
    D. Fading away
    *E. Avoidance

19. Which of the following disengagement strategies might others find "socially appropriate"? (p. 150)
    A. Machiavellianism
    B. Open confrontation
    C. Avoidance
    *D. Ending on a positive note
    E. Withdrawal

20. Mary wants to end her relationship with Michael. Somehow she is able to convince him that he wants to end the relationship—that it's in his own best interest. Mary's strategy is termed: (pp. 150–151)
    *A. Machiavellianism
    B. Open confrontation
    C. Avoidance
    D. Withdrawal
    E. Ending on a positive note

TRUE OR FALSE

21. Individuals engage in interpersonal communication with other individuals so they can accomplish goals in social situations that they could not have achieved by individual action alone.
    Ans: T   Page: 137

22. The transactions model of communication specifies that senders and receivers are simultaneously influenced by their physical surroundings, the social situation in which they are pursuing various goals, and the social relationships that influence the interactions between them.
    Ans: T   Page: 132

23. In the systematic study of interpersonal communication, researchers recognize that interpersonal affiliations are static.
    Ans: F   Page: 132

24. The communication strategies people use to maintain valued interpersonal ties is known as engagement.
    Ans: F   Page: 132

25. The term *self* can be defined as our personal conception of who we are, what we are, and where we are in the social order.
    Ans: T   Page: 133

26. Interpersonal communication takes place with two individuals engaging in face-to-face interaction.
    Ans: T   Page: 134

27. Interpersonal communication is both repeatable and reversible.
    Ans: F   Page: 135

28. Interpersonal communication is the foundation on which intimate human bonds are built.
    Ans: T   Page: 136

29. One of the most important reasons for entering into relationships with others, then, is that we learn more about how others perceive and feel about us.
    Ans: T   Pages: 136–137

30. Initial conversations with others tend to center on personal and private topics to quickly advance the relationship from the awkward small-talk stage.
    Ans: F   Page: 139

31. Auditioning for friendship involves looking over one another in an effort to determine whether or not a relationship is worth establishing.
    Ans: T   Page: 140

32. Small talk serves as an "interpersonal pacifier."
    Ans: T   Page: 140

33. During the small-talk stage, actual conversations between new acquaintances is an exchange of very basic biographical data.
    Ans: T   Page: 141

34. Revealing something about our family or friends that affects us only indirectly is a process of testing the water.
    Ans: T   Page: 145

35. Avoiding confrontation works well in terminating both unwanted friendships and marriages.
    Ans: F   Page: 150

ESSAYS

36. Discuss the causes of relational disengagement.
37. Describe the six images or personas involved in any communication transaction.
38. Identify and discuss the reasons for engaging in interpersonal communication.
39. Describe the critical first moments of engagement.
40. Why is small talk important to engagement? Identify and discuss the six skills of small talk.

CHAPTER 6
COMMUNICATING IN SMALL GROUPS

MULTIPLE CHOICE

1. The type of small group that includes both the human family and peer groups of close friends is known as a(n): (p. 161)
   A. Peer group
   *B. Intimate group
   C. Coalition
   D. Task-oriented group
   E. Secondary group

2. People who participate in a(n) _____ group do so to get something done through group participation, to achieve some goal they have mutually set as an objective. (p. 162)
   A. Intimate
   B. Primary
   C. Secondary
   *D. Task-oriented
   E. Goal-conscious

3. Therapy groups, encounter groups, consciousness-raising groups, and sensitivity training groups are examples of which of the following types of groups? (p. 162)
   A. Discussion
   *B. Experiential
   C. Decision-making
   D. Intimate
   E. Social

4. Which term refers to the long-term process of communication within which deliberate or indirect lessons are internalized, enabling the person to become a unique human being, a functioning member of society, and a participant in the general culture? (p. 164)
   A. Personality
   B. Enculturation
   *C. Socialization
   D. Role-taking
   E. Norms

5. An individual's more or less enduring organization of meanings, motivations, emotional patterns, orientations, skills, and other attributes that make that person different in psychological make-up from others is termed: (p. 164)
   A. Socialization
   B. Enculturation
   C. Social understandings
   *D. Personality
   E. Social rank

6. A small group of friends who get together socially and find themselves discussing some sort of problem that seems to be troubling all of them are involved in a: (p. 166)
  *A. Private, informal, and casual discussion
  B. Private, informal, but deliberate discussion
  C. Private and formal discussion group
  D. Public and formal discussion group
  E. Public, informal, but deliberate discussion

7. A discussion group that usually has regular meetings over a lengthy period of time and a clear organization with an intellectual leader who coordinates the discussion of students is called a: (p. 167)
  A. Forum
  B. Round table
  C. Symposium
  D. Panel
  *E. Seminar

8. Which of the following groups is widely used for assisting people who have personal problems? (p. 167)
  *A. Therapy
  B. Encounter
  C. Assertiveness
  D. Consciousness-raising
  E. Peer

9. In the _____ group, participants present positions, exchange views, and gain insight into a topic of mutual concern, such as environmental issues. (p. 168)
  A. Assertiveness
  B. Therapy
  C. Encounter
  *D. Consciousness-raising
  E. Experiential

10. Which of the following is NOT a category of judgments commonly made in decision-making groups? (pp. 169–171)
  A. Evaluating performance
  B. Allocating scarce resources
  *C. Determining group memberships and roles
  D. Formulating policies
  E. Weighing facts to reach the truth

11. The stage in which conflict starts to emerge in small-group development is: (p. 172)
  A. Forming
  *B. Storming
  C. Conforming
  D. Norming
  E. Performing

12. Participants at this stage of group development have examined the various solutions and have finally reached a consensus about how to best solve the problem: (p. 172)
    A. Forming
    B. Norming
    C. Storming
    *D. Performing
    E. Accomplishing
13. General rules that each group member is expected to follow concerning what issues, topics, and modes of transmission are acceptable within the group are called communication: (p. 173)
    *A. Norms
    B. Roles
    C. Rankings
    D. Orders
    E. Patterns
14. The rules that define communication patterns based on authority, power, and privilege within a group are called: (pp. 174–175)
    A. Norms
    B. Roles
    *C. Rankings
    D. Leadership
    E. Social controls
15. The rules for communicating in small groups are maintained through messages that provide "sanctions" for compliance and deviance. These rules are known as: (p. 175)
    A. Norms
    B. Social rankings
    C. Maintenance patterns
    *D. Subtle social controls
    E. Socialization
16. The style of leadership that solely determines policies and steps to implement them and gets the most done in the shortest amount of time is known as: (p. 176)
    A. Director
    B. Democratic
    *C. Authoritarian
    D. Laissez-faire
    E. Productive
17. The style of leadership that builds cohesiveness and group involvement is: (p. 176)
    A. Authoritarian
    *B. Democratic
    C. Team builder
    D. Facilitator
    E. Laissez-faire

18. The set of factors in every kind of group, large or small, intimate or formal, that moves the participants to maintain their membership and to perform the activities required of them is termed group _____. (p. 181)
  *A. Cohesiveness
   B. Hierarchy
   C. Disorganization
   D. Social ranking
   E. Togetherness

19. The type of cohesion based on bonds of affection generated within the group is: (p. 181)
  *A. Sentiment-based
   B. Reward-based
   C. Assignment-based
   D. Friendship-based
   E. Legitimate

20. _____ confusion refers to a situation in which shared understandings are inadequate, ineffective, or unclear about who should transmit what kind of messages to whom. (p. 182)
   A. Normative
   B. Rank
   C. Topic
  *D. Role
   E. Cohesion

TRUE OR FALSE

21. A group consists of five or more people who repeatedly interact together, regulating their conduct and communication within some set of rules that they mutually recognize and follow.
    Ans: F   Page: 160

22. The optimal size for discussions and getting decisions made in a small group with all members participating fully is between 10 and 12 members.
    Ans: F   Pages: 160–161

23. Three subcategories of task-oriented groups have been identified. They are: discussion, self-improvement, and decision-making.
    Ans: T   Page: 162

24. A panel is a private discussion group in which participants discuss diverse views on topics of special interest.
    Ans: F   Page: 162

25. Discussion groups that are organized for the purpose of identifying and coping with difficulties experienced in daily life are called encounter groups.
    Ans: T   Page: 168

26. Deciding what is true is the function of a jury in the American court system.
    Ans: T   Page: 170

27. Social relationships between members of a group are controlled and defined by the group's rules of communication.
    Ans: T   Page: 171

28. Forming, storming, conforming, and performing are the four stages of small-group development.
   Ans: F   Page: 171

29. The group development stage in which communication rules and roles become stabilized is the conforming stage.
   Ans: F   Page: 172

30. Cohesiveness tends to be greatest in the democratic group because the experience results in greater member satisfaction.
   Ans: T   Page: 177

31. The trait theory of leadership states that the reason some people become leaders and others do not is related to the personal characteristics of the individual.
   Ans: T   Page: 177

32. Formal communication is defined as controlled communication between parties who are allowed or required by the group's coded rules to transmit particular kinds of messages to specific receivers using designated rules.
   Ans: T   Page: 180

33. Reward-based cohesion is based on bonds of affection generated within the group.
   Ans: F   Page: 181

34. Assignment-based cohesion is a condition binding a person to a group based on a willingness to work with others to accomplish goals because that has been defined as one's duty.
   Ans: T   Page: 182

35. Group disorganization often stems from "bad communication processes" rather than from "bad people."
   Ans: T   Page: 183

ESSAYS

36. Discuss the similarities and the differences in communication between intimate and task-oriented groups.

37. Discuss the various types of socialization that occur because of communication in groups.

38. Discuss how our role-taking skills and the ability to interpret feedback improve through our communication in peer groups.

39. List and explain the communication goals in task-oriented groups.

40. Explain how the communication that occurs in therapy and encounter groups helps people to improve themselves.

CHAPTER 7

COMMUNICATING WITHIN ORGANIZATIONS

MULTIPLE CHOICE

1. The transmission of messages through both formal and informal channels of a relatively large deliberately designed group, resulting in the construction of meanings that have influences on its members, both as individuals and on the group as a whole, is the definition of: (p. 191)
   A. External communication
   B. Group dynamics
   *C. Organizational communication
   D. Social institution
   E. Internal communication

2. The _____ institution is organized around the need to understand and try to influence the supernatural. (p. 192)
   A. Government
   B. Economic
   C. Family
   *D. Religious
   E. Science

3. The _____ institution evolved to handle the production and distribution of goods and services. (p. 192)
   *A. Economic
   B. Government
   C. Religious
   D. Medical
   E. Family

4. A deliberately designed plan of the goals, norms, roles, ranks, and controls in an organization is the technical meaning of: (p. 193)
   A. Organization
   *B. Bureaucracy
   C. Scientific management
   D. Leadership
   E. Formal communication

5. According to Weber, which of the following is NOT a principle or factor that every bureaucratic organization should have? (pp. 194–195)
   A. Hierarchy of power
   B. Fixed rules
   C. "Universalistic" system of sanctions
   D. Division of labor
   *E. Participative decision-making

6. Piece-work is an example of _____, in which earnings for a worker were determined by the number of units the individual produced in a given time period. (p. 197)
   *A. The wage-incentive system
   B. Quality control
   C. Scientific management
   D. Bureaucracy
   E. The Hawthorne effect

7. Taylor's "time and motion" studies involving systematic observation of how workers actually performed led to the era of: (p. 197)
   *A. Scientific management   A
   B. Bureaucracy
   C. Universal principles of management
   D. Humanism
   E. Wage-incentive management

8. Which of the following is NOT an outcome of the Hawthorne studies? (pp. 201–204)
   A. Increased work efficiency was found to be related to perceived attention and concern.
   B. Through the process of informal communication, people develop important peer groups.
   C. Job satisfaction is related to high work performance.
   D. Workers need more "time out" or "breaks" to be more efficient at their jobs. D
   *E. Work output is related to the level of lighting—the more light the more work.

9. Small discussion groups composed of individuals from a particular unit in an organization whose members all face the same production task are called _____. They meet with their supervisor to find ways in which their assembly work can be done more efficiently and at a higher level of excellence. (p. 206)
   *A. Quality-control circles A
   B. Wage-incentive units
   C. Social institutions
   D. Organizational subcultures
   E. Subordinates

10. Which of the following is NOT a type of message that flows upward? (p. 207)
    *A. Specific orders and instructions
    B. Routine operational messages
    C. Reports on problems   C
    D. Feedback about the completion of tasks
    E. Assessment of experts

11. Messages that flow upward may become distorted for a number of reasons. When messages are couched or phrased in terms that are familiar within the organization's special argot or jargon, this is a problem of distortion called: (p. 209)
    A. Idealization
    B. Jargon   B
    *C. Standardization
    D. Synthesis
    E. Simplification

12. When a subordinate leaves out certain details and modifies messages so as to cast her/his own behavior in the best possible light, upward messages may become distorted. This form of upward distortion is called: (p. 209)
   A. Synthesis
   B. Simplification
   *C. Idealization
   D. Condensed
   E. Standardization

13. Messages coming down the line can undergo characteristic changes. For example, individuals receiving formal messages from supervisors can fail to interpret messages correctly because they may not read or hear the entire message. This failure is due to: (p. 209)
   A. Poor listening
   *B. Selective exposure
   C. Selective perception
   D. Vocabulary differences
   E. Simplification

14. A complex social pathway in a network of intimate groups is known as the _____. This type of message bypasses the formal communication channels and travels through social ties among people. (p. 211)
   A. Chain of command
   B. Rumors
   *C. Grapevine
   D. Informal network
   E. Socializing

15. The kinds of messages carried on the grapevine can be generally classified into four groups. Which of the following is NOT one of those types of messages? (p. 211)
   A. Rumors
   B. Gossip
   C. Speculation
   D. Interpretations
   *E. Criticism

16. When a person learns "firsthand" of some information and then passes on a message about it by word-of-mouth to another, and then that person passes on a new version of it to another, there is a chance that distortion may occur. This process of distortion is known as the: (p. 211)
   A. Compounding pattern
   *B. Embedding pattern
   C. Rumor mill
   D. Interpretation pattern
   E. Grapevine

17. During informal communication, the content of a message may become distorted as it moves along a chain of tellers and retellers. Many times the original richness and details of a message are shortened and organized around its more central or "salient" details. This form of distortion is termed: (p. 212)
   A. Compounding pattern
   B. Assimilation
   C. Leveling
   *D. Sharpening
   E. Selective exposure

18. Some messages transmitted along the grapevine gain additional details and interpretations that were never part of the original message. This pattern of distortion in word-of-mouth networks has been identified as which pattern type? (p. 212)
    *A. Compounding
    B. Embedding
    C. Assimilation
    D. Leveling
    E. Sharpening

19. The total pattern of all the shared beliefs, sentiments, attitudes, values, rules, special languages, and everything else that is produced and shared by the members of an organization is known as organizational: (p. 213)
    A. Climate
    B. Cohesion
    C. Communication
    *D. Culture
    E. Chart

20. The type of organizational cohesion that is based on the complex division of labor that produces a strong pattern of dependencies among individuals and units within an organization is known as _____-based cohesion. (p. 214)
    A. Sentiment
    B. Reward
    *C. Dependency
    D. Assignment
    E. Personal

TRUE OR FALSE

21. Because of the need for order, predictability, and security in social life, the social institution of government was developed.
    Ans: T   Page: 192

22. Leaders that are selected or appointed because they have technical managerial skills and are permitted to exercise power as defined by official definitions of the organization are known as traditional authority.
    Ans: F   Page: 194

23. Weber's principle of a fixed and universalistic system of sanctions states that workers should be hired, promoted, rewarded, reprimanded, or separated on the basis of competence and performance and not due to personal likes and dislikes.
    Ans: T   Page: 195

24. The idea that workers are things to be used along with machinery and exploited like raw materials is characteristic of the human relations approach to management.
    Ans: F   Page: 196

25. An organizational chart communicates in graphic terms the chain of authority and command within an organization.
    Ans: T   Page: 197

26. The focus of the classical bureaucratic theory is on the essential nature of deliberate planning in the design of communication systems in organizations.
Ans: T   Page: 200

27. As a result of the Hawthorne studies, managers began to realize the importance of lighting to increase production and decrease socializing.
Ans: F   Page: 202

28. The Hawthorne experimenters discovered that people, through the process of informal communication, develop peer groups which act as important influences on developing shared social meanings.
Ans: T   Page: 203

29. Routine operational messages are one of the types of message content that flows downward in formal communication.
Ans: F   Page: 208

30. Requests, specific orders and instructions, operating guidelines, and policy shift directives are types of messages that typically flow downward in organizations.
Ans: T   Page: 208

31. Formal messages may become distorted because they are often condensed, simplified, standardized, idealized, and synthesized.
Ans: T   Pages: 208–209

32. Perceptual defense occurs during selective perception when a receiver expects a meaning to be implied in a message.
Ans: F   Page: 210

33. Generally speaking, messages sent through the grapevine are more flexible and much faster than formal communication.
Ans: T   Page: 211

34. Rumors and gossip are typically the only kinds of messages carried by the grapevine.
Ans: F   Page: 211

35. Leveling of a message refers to a shortening of the original account, rumor, or story.
Ans: T   Page: 212

36. Sharpening is a process that distorts a communication message by reshaping it by the psychological characteristics and culturally learned habits of the person who hears it.
Ans: F   Page: 212

37. The compounding pattern of message distortion involves the adding of details and interpretations that were never part of the original message.
Ans: T   Page: 212

38. Within organizations, a subculture develops that is unique to each particular group.
Ans: T   Page: 213

39. Dependency-based cohesion is based on the division of labor that produces a strong pattern of dependencies between individuals and units within an organization, such as assembly-line work and a payroll clerk.

Ans: T   Page: 214

40. Informal communication is the basis on which dependency-based cohesion is established and maintained.

Ans: F   Page: 215

ESSAYS

41. Distinguish among the three general theories of management: human use, human relations, and human resources.
42. Distinguish between formal and informal communication flow in large organizations.
43. Compare and contrast the kinds of messages that flow upward and downward.
44. Discuss how messages that flow upward may become distorted.
45. Discuss how messages that flow downward may become distorted.
46. Explain how embedding and compounding patterns of distortion work together in the transmission of rumors through the grapevine.
47. Distinguish among the three forms of distortion that often characterize the content of a message: leveling, sharpening, and assimilation.
48. Define and explain *organizational subculture*.
49. Discuss the terms *organizational cohesion* and *dependency-based cohesion*. How are they related?
50. Define *organizational communication*.

CHAPTER 8

COMMUNICATING WITH MEDIA

MULTIPLE CHOICE

1. Which of the following is NOT an advantage of writing a letter as a communication medium? (pp. 229–230)
   A. Letters are truly portable.
   B. A good letter requires intellectual ability.
   *C. A letter provides a hard copy that can be filed, saved, or reread later.
   D. It can be composed at the writer's own convenience.
   E. Privacy is ensured by the U.S. Postal Service.

2. A written document widely used in organizational communication for the purpose of transmitting significant messages between members of an organization is termed: (p. 231)
   A. Letter
   B. Briefing
   *C. Memorandum
   D. Form
   E. Vita

3. Which of the following is NOT a telephone norm for business calls? (pp. 233–234)
   A. Business calls should be restricted to business hours.
   B. Avoid letting a telephone call take priority over other forms of communication.
   C. Identify yourself when calling.
   D. Callers should consult their watches before calling.
   *E. If you want to chat, ask if the receiver has time.

4. A telephone-based system in which a network of users rely on a central computer-operated answering machine is called a(n): (p. 234)
   A. Answering machine
   B. Fax
   *C. Voice-mail network
   D. Telephone
   E. Memorandum

5. A telecommunication system by which exact copies of a document or even a photograph can be sent via phone lines is known as a(n): (p. 234)
   *A. Facsimile
   B. Telephone
   C. Xerox
   D. Answering machine
   E. Computer network

6. BITNET and INTERNET are examples of what type of networks? (p. 238)
   *A. Large-scale
   B. Local area
   C. On-line
   D. Electronic
   E. Telephone

7. Which of the following statements is a disadvantage of electronic-mail? (p. 240)
   A. E-mail maintains its own archive or file for new and old messages.
   B. E-mail can save labor costs.
   C. E-mail is fast.
   *D. E-mail is not totally private.
   E. The receiver of e-mail can respond immediately if he/she is on-line.

8. The use of media to link spatially dispersed people for the purpose of community in ways that to some degree approximate the conditions of a face-to-face conference or meeting is referred to as: (p. 241)
   A. Networking
   *B. Teleconferencing
   C. Technology
   D. Grouping
   E. Electronic mail

9. The most limited in terms of duplicating the conditions of face-to-face exchanges is _____ conferencing: (p. 242)
   A. Video
   *B. Computer
   C. Photo
   D. Audio
   E. Telephone

10. Which type of conferencing provides the closest approximation to face-to-face communication? (p. 243)
    *A. Video
    B. Audio
    C. Computer
    D. Telephone
    E. Photo

11. In the very near future, we can expect our system of networks in the United States to become superceded by: (p. 239)
    *A. One gigantic mega-network
    B. On-line information services
    C. Electronic mail
    D. Computerized video conferencing
    E. Audio conferencing

12. BRS and Prodigy are both examples of: (p. 239)
    A. Computerized games
    *B. On-line information services
    C. Video conferencing
    D. Scientific publications
    E. Audio networks

13. The primary purpose of media is to: (p. 224)
    A. Connect people
    B. Mediate meanings
    *C. Move information
    D. Transform signals
    E. Provide stability

14. Which of the following media technologies is *least* convenient for multiple users? (p. 244)
   A. Audio conferences
   B. Fax machines
   C. E-mail
   *D. Video conferences
   E. Computer networks

15. Which of the following is NOT proper telephone etiquette? (pp. 233–234)
   A. Returning a phone call immediately
   B. Ignoring a phone that rings during a meal
   C. Identifying yourself when you call
   D. Redialing until you get through to someone
   *E. Asking someone you're talking with in the room to wait a few minutes while you take a call

TRUE OR FALSE

16. A medium is simply a device that moves information over distance so that people who are apart can communicate.
   Ans: T   Page: 224

17. The use of media can limit the accuracy of feedback while maximizing role-taking.
   Ans: F   Page: 225

18. Using a letter as a medium of communication has the distinct advantage of being portable.
   Ans: T   Pages: 229–230

19. In business correspondence, there is an absolute requirement for correct grammar, spelling, and punctuation.
   Ans: T   Page: 230

20. The telephone continues to be, and will remain, one of our most important media.
   Ans: T   Page: 232

21. One limitation of fax is that it may not be private.
   Ans: T   Page: 235

22. A local area network unites hundreds of universities and organizations in the nation into a single system.
   Ans: F   Page: 238

23. E-mail is the name given to messages sent from one computer to another by combining word-processing software.
   Ans: T   Page: 239

24. The very speed of electronic messages can create problems; like other forms of communication, e-mail is irretrievable.
   Ans: T   Page: 241

25. A conference call is an example of audio conferencing.
   Ans: T   Page: 243

26. Video conferencing allows for relatively effective role-taking, feedback, and the use of nonverbal cues.
    Ans: T   Page: 243

27. Long-distance telephone charges are the major costs of computer conferencing.
    Ans: F   Page: 241

28. A clear advantage of audio conferencing is that an audio conference can be set up with only minor lead time and less disruption to work schedules than face-to-face conferences.
    Ans: T   Page: 243

29. Video conferences are more convenient than those that are based on computer networks or audio systems.
    Ans: F   Page: 244

30. As teleconferencing becomes commonplace, the airline, hotel, and restaurant industries may begin to suffer.
    Ans: T   Page: 244

ESSAYS

31. Compare and contrast the similarities and differences between face-to-face and mediated communication.
32. Discuss the personal and social influences of news media.
33. Distinguish between letters and memorandums. Include in your discussion the advantages and disadvantages of each form of mediated communication.
34. Discuss the importance of the telephone for communication. Include in your discussion suggestions for business and personal telephone etiquette.
35. Compare and contrast computer conferencing, audio conferencing, and video conferencing.

CHAPTER 9

PRESENTING ONESELF EFFECTIVELY

MULTIPLE CHOICE

1. The process by which a person comes to know and to think about other persons, their characteristics, qualities, and inner states is called: (p. 254)
   A. Personality
   *B. Person perception
   C. Stereotyping
   D. Predisposition
   E. Attributions

2. The work by Solomon Asch on impression formation demonstrated that subjects quickly form elaborate impressions of others after receiving only limited information about the individual. This process is referred to as the principle of: (pp. 254–256)
   A. First impressions
   B. The salient characteristics
   *C. Rapid impression formation
   D. Labeling
   E. Implicit personality

3. Terms such as "former mental patient" or "juvenile delinquent" can have a dramatic and negative influence on the impressions people form about others. This idea that one critical piece of information about a person can communicate a powerful message is referred to as the principle of: (p. 256)
   A. Implicit personality
   B. Rapid impression formation
   C. Impression management
   *D. Labeling
   E. Personality development

4. _____ refers to a pattern of psychological attributes that makes each individual human being different and unique. (p. 257)
   *A. Personality
   B. Salient characteristics
   C. Attributions
   D. Impression formation
   E. Labeling theory

5. Which of the following is NOT a common difficulty discussed in the text when meeting people? (pp. 258–259)
   A. Finding things in common with strangers
   B. Not knowing how to say things appropriately
   C. Feeling self-conscious
   D. Adjusting to language difficulties
   *E. Meeting people who like you

6. There are two major reasons why preselection of qualities can create positive impressions. The first is that everyone has many positive qualities. What is a second reason? (p. 263)
   A. It is important to minimize potentially negative influences.
   *B. Most people tend to like other people.
   C. First impressions tend to be lasting.
   D. Most people like others who are outgoing and sociable.
   E. Everyone wants to make a good impression.

7. The selection and assignment to another individual various personal qualities, conditions, or dispositions that we believe are the causes of or the influences on some aspect of that person's behavior is the definition of: (p. 265)
   A. Personality
   *B. Attribution
   C. Stereotype
   D. Perception
   E. Preliminary game plan

8. Attitudes, values, and motivations are examples of what type of attributions? (p. 265)
   A. External
   B. Selective
   C. Personal
   *D. Internal
   E. Social

9. Rigid and usually negative sets of assumptions about the personal and social qualities of people who are members of a particular social category are called: (p. 266)
   *A. Stereotypes
   B. Attributions
   C. Prejudices
   D. Labels
   E. Impressions

10. Informing another person about our beliefs, attitudes, values, accomplishments, status, and other personal and social characteristics is the definition of: (p. 270)
    A. Intimacy
    B. Immediacy
    C. Credibility
    D. Perception
    *E. Self-disclosure

11. A general rule designed to help us understand how people attribute either internal or external causes to our behavior—based on how consistently it's associated with one or the other over time—is called the principle of: (p. 276)
    A. Labeling
    *B. Covariance
    C. Impression management
    D. Coordination
    E. Assimilation

12. The occurrence of coalitions among pairs of people is a problem associated with: (p. 260)
   *A. Meeting one person versus several people
   B. Individual differences among people
   C. Conversational intrusions in interactions
   D. Long-term versus short-term relationships
   E. The number of people in a group interaction

13. The setting of goals in initial encounters contributes to achieving control of: (p. 263)
   A. What is communicated in an encounter
   *B. Early impressions in encounters
   C. The number of people in an encounter
   D. Where people encounter each other
   E. Prejudicial responses in encounters

14. The universal tendency to _____ is at the heart of impression formation. (p. 263)
   A. Label
   B. Be ethnocentric
   *C. Selectively perceive
   D. Attribute
   E. Be judgmental

15. A practical technique for assessing how and why people will probably respond to what we say about ourselves is to observe behavior that indicates unique: (p. 266)
   A. Physical characteristics
   B. Cultural characteristics
   C. Regionally derived characteristics
   *D. Psychological characteristics
   E. Family characteristics

TRUE OR FALSE

16. There is little doubt that we feel more comfortable—physically, emotionally, and intellectually—meeting people in familiar than unfamiliar places.
   Ans: T   Page: 261

17. A single bit of information about an individual, particularly a salient characteristic, can significantly alter our individual impressions.
   Ans: T   Page: 256

18. The reason we form impressions of another person, constructing our interpretations of their "implicit" personality, is that we are trying to predict in our own minds how they will behave toward us and others.
   Ans: T   Page: 257

19. People construct a well-organized pattern of what they think is important about someone on the basis of very few facts.
   Ans: T   Page: 257

20. *Where* we meet people has little influence on the outcome of an interaction.
   Ans: F   Page: 261

21. Goal clarification helps identify what it is people need to believe about you.
    Ans: T   Page: 262

22. The depth of self-disclosure refers to the amount of personal information we communicate.
    Ans: F   Page: 270

23. Self-disclosure that is other than what is obvious, likely to be misinterpreted, or too intense and revealing for strangers is both undesirable and risky.
    Ans: T   Page: 270

24. Attributions concerning our behavior are a function of three factors: distinctiveness of our behavior, its consistency over time, and the success of our communication goal.
    Ans: F   Page: 276

25. Changing embedded impressions that people already have of a person is very difficult.
    Ans: T   Page: 276

ESSAYS

26. Discuss how contextual issues of *where* people meet can influence initial encounters.
27. Discuss the importance of planning and goal clarification on self-presentation.
28. Discuss the significance of *selective perception* on self-presentation.
29. Distinguish among the three kinds of messages that create opportunities for self-disclosure (greetings, small talk, and the main topic).
30. Discuss the principle of covariance.
31. Discuss how one may construct new realities.

CHAPTER 10
INFLUENCING OTHERS

MULTIPLE CHOICE

1. The view of the persuasion process where a sender *causes* a change in the receiver by using clever words, arguments, and appeals is known as the _____ interpretation (p. 288)
   A. Transactional
   *B. Magic-bullet
   C. Two-way
   D. Simultaneous
   E. Interactional

2. A communication transaction in which a source constructs and transmits messages designed to influence a receiving person's constructions of meaning in ways that will lead to change in the receiver's beliefs, attitudes, or behavior is the definition of: (p. 289)
   A. Communication
   B. Credibility
   C. Meaning
   D. Compliance
   *E. Persuasion   E

3. Compelling someone to do something, or restraining them from acting in some way, by threatening them with consequences that they find unacceptable is the definition of: (p. 290)
   A. Expectations
   B. Punishment
   C. Compliance
   *D. Coercion   D
   E. Negative reinforcement

4. Perceiving, interpreting, remembering, and recalling are part of cognitive: (p. 292)
   A. Reorganization
   *B. Processing   B
   C. Functions
   D. Restructuring
   E. Grouping

5. A kind of "statement of truth" that an individual accepts about some object, situation, or event is the definition of: (p. 294)
   A. Attitudes
   B. Meanings
   *C. Beliefs   C
   D. Values
   E. Expectations

6. The statement "the world is round" is an example of a(n): (p. 294)
   A. Value
   B. Fact
   C. Testimony
   D. Attitude
   *E. Belief

7. A relatively enduring organization of affective beliefs about some broad object that increases the probability that an individual will respond to the object in a manner consistent with those beliefs is the definition of: (p. 296)
   *A. Attitude
   B. Sociocultural condition
   C. Value
   D. Personal view
   E. Persuasion

8. Which of the following is NOT a critical factor in understanding the relationship between attitudes and the probability of consistent behavior? (p. 297)
   A. Topic importance
   B. Social pressures
   C. Physical constraints
   D. Action constraints
   *E. Nonsocial constraints

9. In Stanley Milgram's experiment on obedience, subjects were ordered to administer dangerous levels of electric shock to other individuals. A few subjects chose not to comply with the orders. Refusing to go along provides an example of _____ resistance: (p. 303)
   *A. Constructive
   B. Reactive
   C. Destructive
   D. Passive
   E. Compliance

10. Yielding publicly or observably to an influence attempt, without actually accepting the change privately, is termed: (p. 304)
    A. Identification
    B. Resistance
    C. Faking
    *D. Compliance
    E. Internalization

11. Yielding to others based on one's wish to gain satisfaction as being "like" some individual or group that we want to imitate, or that we admire, is termed: (p. 304)
    A. Compliance
    *B. Identification
    C. Influence
    D. Internalization
    E. Imitation

12. A type of yielding to influence that we do because it is personally rewarding or useful is termed: (p. 304)
   A. Compliance
   B. Identification
   C. Persuasion
   *D. Internalization 𝔇
   E. Satisfaction

13. How believable a person perceives a message source to be is termed: (p. 307)
   *A. Credibility
   B. Utility
   C. Trustworthiness 𝒞
   D. Acceptance
   E. Immediacy

14. The dimension of credibility that refers to how likable and friendly a source is perceived is called: (p. 307)
   A. Extroversion
   B. Competence
   C. Trustworthiness
   D. Composure
   *E. Sociability 𝔈

15. How knowledgeable a source is perceived to be in a given context area is known as the _____ dimension of credibility. (p. 307)
   *A. Competence 𝗄
   B. Trustworthiness
   C. Extroversion
   D. Composure
   E. Sociability

TRUE OR FALSE

16. Persuasion is a transactional process that requires two-way communication.
   Ans: T   Page: 289

17. The process of sociocultural persuasion is based on social expectation, in which norms, roles, ranks, and social controls play a part in clarifying what is acceptable and what is deviant behavior.
   Ans: T   Page: 290

18. The psychodynamic strategy rests on the assumption that the route to achieving cognitive changes lies in achieving behavioral change.
   Ans: F   Page: 292

19. The psychodynamic strategy of shaping or altering beliefs focuses on factual truth statements.
   Ans: F   Page: 294

20. Beliefs are guides to action.
   Ans: T   Page: 295

21. Attitudes are inherited from our parents.
    Ans: F   Page: 296

22. There is a direct association between attitudes and behavior in most real-life situations.
    Ans: F   Page: 296

23. As human beings, we are universally resistant to change.
    Ans: T   Page: 299

24. Psychological reactance occurs when a person is motivated to comply with a persuasive message.
    Ans: F   Page: 299

25. There are essentially two types of resistance—good and bad.
    Ans: F   Pages: 302–303

26. Destructive resistance is essentially misbehavior.
    Ans: T   Page: 303

27. To develop an effective strategy to reduce resistance, it is important to understand whether, from the standpoint of the person, it is seen as constructive.
    Ans: T   Page: 303

28. Identification lasts only as long as the influence source is present.
    Ans: F   Page: 304

29. Women are significantly more susceptible to persuasion than men.
    Ans: F   Page: 305

30. People who are characterized as aggressive, well informed, and efficient are just as likely to be persuaded as people who are dependent, obliging, and unstable.
    Ans: F   Page: 305

31. Two-sided message strategies that refute the other's position are more effective than other types of messages.
    Ans: T   Page: 306

32. Research has demonstrated that the primacy-recency effect has very little effect on influence.
    Ans: T   Page: 306

33. Moderate fear appeals are more effective than high and low fear appeals.
    Ans: F   Page: 306

34. Behavior-alteration techniques can be categorized into two general types—effective and ineffective.
    Ans: F   Page: 306

35. Signals of nonverbal immediacy are an effective form of persuasive communication.
    Ans: T   Page: 306

ESSAYS

36. Explain how people can be persuaded to conform to *social expectations*.
37. Explain how *cognitive reorganization* can be used to achieve behavioral change.
38. Explain how shaping or altering *beliefs* can influence change.
39. Discuss the relationship between attitudes and behavior.
40. Explain Brehm's theory of psychological reactance.
41. Distinguish between destructive and constructive resistance.
42. Compare and contrast among the three types of yielding (compliance, identification, and internalization).
43. Explain the concept of receiver susceptibility.
44. Discuss the five features of effective messages (sidedness, message ordering, fear appeals, behavior-alteration techniques, and nonverbal cues).
45. Identify and discuss the five dimensions of source credibility.

CHAPTER 11
COPING WITH CONFLICT

MULTIPLE CHOICE

1. A dispute in which different values result in claims to rewards or resources that are in limited supply, and where the main objective of the people engaged in the process is to either neutralize or eliminate the prospects of their opponent to win what is at stake is the definition of: (p. 317)
   A. Competition
   B. Goal attainment
   C. Hostility
   *D. Conflict
   E. Disagreement

2. Disputes between members of a family over an inheritance are an example of what type of conflict? (p. 319)
   A. Family
   *B. Unproductive
   C. Constructive
   D. Intense
   E. Productive

3. Conflicts common to almost all professions and business environments in which problem-solution discussions are the norm are characteristic of which type of conflict? (p. 320)
   *A. Constructive
   B. Counterproductive
   C. Destructive
   D. Back-biting
   E. Competitive

4. The manner in which an individual is likely to behave when anticipating or engaging in a confrontation is known as: (p. 321)
   A. Personality
   B. Competitiveness
   *C. Conflict style
   D. Assertiveness
   E. Confrontational nature

5. According to Kilmann and Thomas, our personal style of handling conflict is based on our need to meet two interconnected yet competing objectives: One of these is our *concern for self;* the other is: (p. 321)
   *A. Our concern for our opponent
   B. A belief in ourselves
   C. How we respond to stress
   D. Our individual skills in argumentation
   E. Our own need for approval

6. A strategy for handling conflicts in which people narrowly view all conflicts as win-lose events characterizes which conflict style? (p. 323)
   *A. Competitive
   B. Collaborative
   C. Compromising
   D. Avoidance
   E. Accommodation

7. A strategy for handling conflicts in which people work jointly or willingly in cooperation with their opponent is characteristic of individuals with which of the following conflict styles? (p. 324)
   A. Competitive
   *B. Collaborative
   C. Avoidance
   D. Accommodation
   E. Compromising

8. A strategy for handling conflict in which participants reach agreement by making mutual concessions is known as: (p. 324)
   A. Accommodation
   B. Collaborative
   C. Avoidance
   D. Competitive
   *E. Compromising

9. A strategy for handling conflicts in which a potential participant chooses not to be a part of the confrontation and instead chooses to stay away from situations where disagreements and disputes are likely to occur describes which conflict style? (p. 324)
   A. Competitive
   B. Collaborative
   C. Compromising
   *D. Avoidance
   E. Accommodation

10. A strategy for handling conflicts in which people "give in" to their opponents is characteristic of which conflict style? (pp. 324–325)
    A. Avoidance
    B. Collaborative
    *C. Accommodation
    D. Compromising
    E. Competitive

11. The process of communicating proposed solutions back and forth between opponents for the purpose of reaching a joint agreement and thus resolving a conflict is the definition of: (pp. 328–329)
    A. Conflict
    B. Competition
    C. Bargaining
    *D. Negotiation
    E. Mutual consensus

12. The suggestion that people should not explain or justify the different positions they hold on an issue follows which "principled negotiation" directive? (p. 330)
    A. Separate the people from the problem.
    *B. Don't bargain over positions.
    C. Invent options for mutual gain.
    D. Insist on using objective criteria.
    E. Focus on interests, not positions.

13. The Harvard system of "principled negotiation" stresses firmly the need to get the participants to look beyond personal characteristics and suspected motives of the people involved and examine the nature of the problem itself. This principle can be represented by which of the following directives? (p. 330)
    A. Cope with resistance to negotiation.
    B. Develop the best alternative.
    *C. Separate the people from the problem.
    D. Focus on interests, not positions.
    E. Invent options for mutual gain.

14. Countering the assumption that there is room for only one winner is best represented by which of the following "principled negotiation" directives? (p. 331)
    A. Don't bargain over positions.
    B. Separate the people from the problem.
    C. Insist on using objective criteria.
    *D. Invent options for mutual gain.
    E. Develop the best alternative.

15. Asking questions and pausing for answers is one way of overcoming "stonewalling" attempts by your opponent. This suggestion is part of which "principled negotiation" guideline? (p. 332)
    A. Handle dirty tricks.
    B. Develop the best alternative.
    *C. Cope with resistance to negotiation.
    D. Bargain over positions.
    E. Elicit feedback for mutual gain.

TRUE OR FALSE

16. Conflict is both widespread and a normal part of social life.
    Ans: T   Page: 315

17. Conflicts generally occur only between people who dislike each other.
    Ans: F   Page: 316

18. As a people, we exhibit a *culturally approved readiness* toward engaging in conflict.
    Ans: T   Page: 316

19. Conflict may range from trivial disagreements to devastating clashes that become brutal and destructive.
    Ans: T   Page: 315

20. In the United States, Americans have a cultural tendency to avoid conflict and competitive situations as a way of life.
    Ans: F   Page: 316

21. Conflicts are inherently negative and adverse.
    Ans: F   Page: 318

22. Conflicts are followed by unproductive, negative, or even destructive outcomes when we enter the process with negative attitudes or hostile feelings toward our opponent.
    Ans: T   Page: 319

23. In general, what occurs between people during the early stages of a conflict will often dictate what happens later in the encounter as well as the ultimate consequence.
    Ans: T   Page: 319

24. Individuals likely to de-escalate a conflict and cause it to have productive outcomes often show signs of stress.
    Ans: F   Page: 319

25. Individuals generally use one type of conflict style across almost all situations.
    Ans: F   Page: 325

26. While communication skills enable us to show aggression and hostility toward each other, it is precisely the same skills that provide the foundation for peaceful resolution of conflicts.
    Ans: T   Page: 325

27. Problems of meaning are at the heart of virtually all conflicts.
    Ans: T   Pages: 325–326

28. A high index of fidelity is likely to characterize messages transmitted and interpreted by senders and receivers who are in the process of conflict development.
    Ans: F   Page: 326

29. Problems in the construction of meaning and low accuracy work together as central causal factors in producing and intensifying controversies.
    Ans: T   Page: 326

30. The social situation and the social relationship in which people are involved play an important part in the generation or escalation of conflict.
    Ans: T   Page: 326

31. Without communication there is no negotiation.
    Ans: T   Page: 329

32. Looking beyond one's position on an issue and to the personal goals and needs that have to be served for each person involved in negotiation is known as the "don't bargain over position" guideline.
    Ans: F   Page: 330

33. Setting mutually agreed-upon rules within which to communicate about potential solutions characterizes the negotiation guideline of "focusing on goals."
    Ans: F   Page: 331

34. A good way to protect yourself in a negotiation is by having already developed an acceptable alternative to what might be the most desirable negotiated agreement.
    Ans: T   Pages: 331–332

35. Handling dirty negotiation tricks can best be accomplished by (1) recognizing the tactic; (2) raising the issue explicitly; and (3) questioning the tactic's legitimacy and desirability—negotiate over it.

Ans: T   Page: 332

ESSAYS

36. Explain how the definition of *conflict* represents an economic model of conflict.
37. Explain why conflicts are not, in and of themselves, either productive or unproductive.
38. Identify and discuss the five conflict styles.
39. Discuss the common causes of conflict.
40. Identify and discuss the method of principled negotiation. Include in your discussion five of the eight recommendations that can lead to successful negotiations and conflict resolution.

CHAPTER 12

OVERCOMING SHYNESS AND APPREHENSION

MULTIPLE CHOICE

1. The fear or anxiety associated with either real or anticipated communication encounters is the definition of: (p. 340)
    A. Speaker anxiety
    B. Stage fright
    C. Shyness
    *D. Communication apprehension
    E. Cognitive stress

2. Apprehensive individuals who fear communicating with almost anyone in any kind of situation have _____ communication apprehension. (p. 340)
    A. Temporary
    *B. Trait-like
    C. Experiential
    D. Severe
    E. Mild

3. Researchers have identified a number of contextual factors that can heighten our level of communication apprehension. The idea that it is easier to talk to people we know as opposed to those we do not know is best characterized by which of the following situational causes? (p. 343)
    A. Formal situations
    B. Undergoing evaluation
    C. Subordinate rank
    D. Repeated failures
    *E. Communication with unfamiliar others

4. Increased communication apprehension due to uncertainty, like the first day on the job, is characterized by which of the following situational causes? (p. 343)
    *A. Novel or formal situations
    B. Undergoing evaluation
    C. Subordinate rank
    D. Communicating with unfamiliar or dissimilar others
    E. Repeated failures

5. Certain kinds of situations seem to heighten our sensitivity to having lower status compared to others who are present. This type of "one-down" situation could then cause us to be apprehensive. What do we call this situational cause? (p. 343)
    A. Feelings of potential failure
    *B. Subordinate rank
    C. Fear of evaluation
    D. Uncertainty with formal situations
    E. Fear of communicating with unfamiliar others

6. More than any other aspect of public speaking, the belief that all eyes are riveted on you, scrutinizing everything about you, can induce communication apprehension. This particular cause is due to: (pp. 343–344)
   A. Novel situations
   B. Undergoing evaluation
   *C. Conspicuousness
   D. Unfamiliar others
   E. Uncertainty

7. A long-term process of communication whereby a human being acquires a personality and becomes a functioning member of society is the definition of: (p. 345)
   A. Personality
   B. Learning
   *C. Socialization
   D. Reinforcement
   E. Maturation

8. Learning to be high or low in communication apprehension by observing the behavior and reactions of people who are important to us as "models" is the basis for which of the following theories? (pp. 346–347)
   A. Reinforcement
   B. Reaction
   C. Observational
   *D. Social learning
   E. Imitation

9. Advocates of _____ theory claim that people high in communication apprehension were punished for their communication whereas those low in apprehension probably were rewarded. (p. 347)
   A. Consequence
   *B. Reinforcement
   C. Modeling
   D. Social learning
   E. Behavioral learning

10. The propensity of human beings to be flexible in their learning histories, and not be rigidly shaped by a few negative consequences of their actions, is the definition of: (pp. 348–349)
    A. Learning theory
    B. Learned helplessness
    *C. Resiliency factor
    D. Expectancy
    E. Reinforcement

11. A feeling of anxiety or distress arising from confusion concerning the social expectations of others can induce a condition of: (p. 349)
    *A. Anomie
    B. Confusion
    C. Anxiety
    D. Isolation
    E. Failure

12. In a no-win situation, a feeling of inadequacy and stress arising from an inability to communicate in a predictable way with a person who is completely inconsistent in his or her response to messages is the definition of: (p. 349)
    A. Hopelessness
    B. Anomie
    *C. Learned helplessness
    D. Situational anxiety
    E. Trait-like anxiety

13. Compared to low communication apprehensive (CA) students, high CA's: (p. 352)
    A. Receive more attention from teachers
    B. Are perceived as better students
    C. Are thought to be more intelligent
    D. Receive extra help or prompts from the teacher
    *E. Are perceived as detached and apathetic toward school

14. Compared to high communication apprehensives, low CA's: (p. 352)
    *A. Report higher levels of job satisfaction
    B. Report lower levels of job satisfaction
    C. Are promoted less often
    D. Do worse in job interviews
    E. Avoid opportunities to communicate

15. In terms of college major and career selections, individuals with low levels of communication apprehension are more likely to pick the area of: (p. 354)
    A. Accounting
    *B. Public relations
    C. Computer science
    D. Pharmacy
    E. Engineering

16. There are two potential causes of stage fright: our own personal level of communication apprehension and: (p. 354)
    *A. The anxiety-producing event itself
    B. Feelings of uncertainty
    C. Fear of audience rejection
    D. Undergoing evaluation
    E. The process of developing a speech

17. Reducing communication apprehension may be achieved by pairing muscle-relaxation techniques with anxiety-producing stimuli (communication encounters). This method of reducing communication apprehension is known as: (pp. 355–356)
    A. Relaxation treatment
    B. Skills training
    C. Muscle stretching
    D. Cognitive restructuring
    *E. Systematic desensitization

18. An approach to reducing communication apprehension by focusing on the psychological process of changing or modifying our response to a communication event is known as: (p. 356)
    A. Attitude change
    B. Systematic desensitization
    C. Mind modeling
    *D. Cognitive restructuring
    E. Skills training

19. Which of the following is NOT a step in the cognitive restructuring process? (p. 357)
    A. Introduction to the basic principles of cognitive restructuring
    *B. Measuring one's level of communication apprehension
    C. Identifying negative self-statements
    D. Learning a new set of coping statements
    E. Rehearsing or practicing new coping statements

20. The approach to reducing communication apprehension that assumes that apprehension stems from poor communication proficiency is called: (p. 358)
    *A. Skills training
    B. Systematic desensitization
    C. Communication deficiency
    D. Cognitive restructuring
    E. Anxiety-reduction techniques

TRUE OR FALSE

21. Communication apprehension is a condition experienced by individuals only when they are actually communicating.
    Ans: F   Page: 340

22. Communication apprehension is the same as shyness.
    Ans: F   Page: 340

23. Apprehensive individuals, regardless of the situation, almost always feel anxious about relating to others.
    Ans: T   Page: 340

24. A more-or-less permanent and predictable apprehension is termed *state* anxiety.
    Ans: F   Page: 340

25. In terms of communication apprehension, learning from past experiences can contribute to an overall, generalized trait of anxiety about communicating.
    Ans: T   Page: 340

26. Individuals who experience chronic apprehension tend to avoid communication encounters, whereas those with low levels of trait apprehension seek them out.
    Ans: T   Page: 341

27. A person low in communication apprehension tends to look forward to attending a party where he or she may not know anyone, whereas an individual high in this trait would tend to dread such a situation.
    Ans: T   Page: 341

28. Having some fear of communicating is normal for most people.
    Ans: T   Page: 342

29. In situations where we know that our supervisor at work, or a professor in class, is appraising us on the basis of an oral performance, we are likely to become anxious. The cause for this anxiety is due to our fear of repeated failure.
    Ans: F   Page: 344

30. People whose apprehensions are stable and trait-like tend to distort their interpretations of contextual factors; that is, they feel *very* conspicuous or perceive a situation to be *more* novel or formal than it really is.
    Ans: T   Page: 345

31. Communication apprehension is learned and therefore can be unlearned entirely.
    Ans: F   Page: 346

32. A student low in communication apprehension is more intelligent than a person high in communication apprehension.
    Ans: F   Pages: 351–352

33. In general, interpersonal opportunities are much greater for individuals who are low in communication apprehension. They seem more approachable, are more fun to be with, and give the appearance of being good listeners.
    Ans: T   Page: 352

34. All things being equal, those who communicate easily do much better in job interviews than those who are more anxious.
    Ans: T   Page: 353

35. When it comes to job satisfaction, those low in communication apprehension report being just as satisfied as those high in apprehension.
    Ans: F   Page: 353

36. Overall, people who are less permanently apprehensive about communicating appear to be less likely to succeed in academic pursuits, social relationships, and career opportunities.
    Ans: F   Page: 353

37. Even though stage fright is common for most of us, it is rare among experienced performers.
    Ans: F   Page: 353

38. Skills training, cognitive restructuring, and systematic desensitization are among the most successful methods for reducing communication anxiety.
    Ans: T   Page: 355

39. Skills training is the most effective method for reducing communication apprehension.
    Ans: F   Page: 358

40. For those with chronically high communication apprehension, skills training can make them more anxious.
    Ans: T   Page: 358

ESSAYS

41. Explain the circular relationship between communication and shyness.
42. Differentiate between communication apprehension as a personality trait and as a temporary condition.
43. Differentiate between social learning theory and reinforcement theory as explanations for the development of communication apprehension.
44. Compare and contrast the perceptions of high and low communication apprehensives in the classroom, in interpersonal encounters, at work, and in career choices.
45. Discuss the three treatment programs available to reduce communication apprehension.

CHAPTER 13
PREPARING THE CONTENT

MULTIPLE CHOICE

1. The goal to change the audience's factual beliefs in some way is the purpose of a(n) _____ speech. (p. 370)
   A. Persuasive
   B. Entertainment
   C. Impromptu
   *D. Informative
   E. Political

2. Whatever the topic, the purpose to get people to feel, think, or behave differently as a consequence of the speech is typical of a(n) _____ speech. (p. 370)
   *A. Persuasive
   B. Entertainment
   C. Impromptu
   D. Informative
   E. Behavioral

3. In order to analyze your audience, you need to address several questions. Of the questions listed below, which question is least likely to help with audience analysis? (p. 371)
   A. Who are these people?
   B. Why are these people here?
   C. In what will these people be interested?
   *D. How do we discover information about the topic?
   E. What do these people already know?

4. Several clear guidelines are available for deciding what evidence to use and what to ignore. Using a priest or minister as a source of evidence on a religious or moral belief, such as abortion, *may* violate which of the following criteria for selecting sources of evidence? (p. 376)
   *A. Objectivity of the source
   B. Competence of the source
   C. Ethical standards or truthfulness of the source
   D. Credibility of the source
   E. Moral history of the source

5. Politicians and lawyers are famous for distortion of evidence they select to arouse emotional responses to sway juries and voters. This practice violates which of the following criteria for selecting sources of evidence? (p. 377)
   A. Objectivity of the source
   B. Competence of the source
   *C. Ethical standards or truthfulness of the source
   D. Persuasiveness of claim
   E. Popularity of the source

6. The "tell 'em" part of a speech is the: (p. 377)
   A. Introduction
   *B. Body
   C. Preview
   D. Conclusion
   E. Redundancy

7. "Today I will explain why you should buy a used car, what to look for, and where you can find one." This statement satisfies which function of an introduction? (p. 378)
   A. Gain and maintain attention
   B. Relate topic to audience
   C. Relate speaker to topic
   *D. Overview of the central ideas or purpose
   E. The "tell 'em" part of a speech

8. Too much information, organized around too many points, may result in confusion and incoherence. For the audience this translates into what is known as: (p. 378)
   A. Chaos
   *B. Information overload
   C. Selective attention
   D. Poor organization
   E. Attention-maintaining

9. To convince an audience that there are dangers in consuming large quantities of alcohol, and then to offer ways to avoid these dangers, a speaker should use a _____ pattern of organization: (p. 379)
   A. Spatial
   B. Temporal
   C. Causal
   *D. Problem-solution
   E. Topical

10. When a time sequence or chronology is required, a speech pattern known as _____ should be used. An example may include a recipe for baking bread. (p. 378)
    A. Spatial
    *B. Temporal
    C. Causal
    D. Topical
    E. Problem solution

11. An informative speech on "How to Make Homemade Wine" would be organized best using a _____ pattern. (p. 378)
    A. Spatial
    B. Topical
    C. Cause-effect
    *D. Temporal
    E. Problem-solution

12. When we have two categories of information that address different, but related aspects of our particular topic, the _____ pattern of organization is recommended. (p. 379)
    A. Spatial
    B. Causal
    *C. Topical
    D. Linear
    E. Temporal

13. A speech can be arranged by demonstrating how a particular effect or outcome is a direct consequence of one or more causes. For instance, a speaker may suggest that the effect of teacher burnout in our schools is caused by two factors: teachers are teaching too many students per class, and universities are providing too few rewards. This type of speech arrangement is known as: (p. 378)
    A. Problem solution
    B. Topical
    C. Temporal
    D. Spatial
    *E. Causal

14. Which function does the sentence "In summary . . ." fulfill? (p. 379)
    A. To end the speech in an upbeat manner
    *B. To remind the audience of your main points
    C. To specify what the audience should do
    D. To provide a memorable statement
    E. To "sign off," leaving the audience wanting more

15. The more abstract the issues are and the more theoretical the explanations, the less likely the audience will comprehend the message. Which of the following rules applies to this idea of avoiding abstraction? (p. 382)
    A. Keep it simple.
    *B. Keep it concrete.
    C. Be repetitive and redundant.
    D. Elicit active responses.
    E. Use familiar and relevant examples.

16. Asking for a simple show of hands as a response to some questions is an example of which rule for increasing speaker effectiveness? (p. 383)
    A. Use transitions and signposts.
    B. Keep it simple.
    *C. Elicit active responses.
    D. Request support.
    E. Be repetitive and redundant.

17. To tell an audience that socialized medicine will work on the same principle as insurance, where many pay for the major expenses of a few, follows which rule for effectiveness? (p. 383)
    *A. Use familiar and relevant examples.
    B. Elicit active responses.
    C. Use transitions and signposts.
    D. Keep it simple.
    E. Keep it concrete.

18. "The *second* reason why Hyper University should relax the general education requirements is . . ." This statement is an example of a(n): (pp. 383–384)
    A. Transition
    *B. Signpost
    C. Figure of speech
    D. Division
    E. Organization

19. Monroe's Motivated Sequence follows which organizational pattern? (p. 384)
    *A. Problem solution
    B. Cause and effect
    C. Need consequence
    D. Temporal
    E. Topical

20. Explaining what is wrong with the status quo or identifying a problem which is not being resolved is discussed in which step of Monroe's Motivated Sequence? (p. 385)
    A. Attention
    *B. Needs
    C. Imply satisfaction
    D. Visualization
    E. Action

21. Countering potential objections is an important element in a persuasive speech. In which step of Monroe's Motivated Sequence should a speaker counter objections? (pp. 385–386)
    A. Action
    B. Introduction
    C. Visualization
    *D. Satisfaction
    E. Need

22. Statements about the future in Monroe's Motivated Sequence are discussed in which step? (p. 386)
    A. Action
    B. Need
    C. Satisfaction
    *D. Visualization
    E. Attention

23. Telling the audience specifically and concretely what they should do to secure the product and the benefits of the solution occurs within which step of Monroe's Motivated Sequence? (p. 386)
    A. Attention
    B. Satisfaction
    C. Conclusion
    *D. Action
    E. Need

24. Which of the following statements is NOT a strategy for persuading others? (pp. 390–392)
    A. Conceal the intent to persuade.
    B. Don't ask for too much.
    C. Avoid inflammatory words or phrases.
    D. Keep objections to a minimum.
    *E. Avoid fear appeals.

25. Using a two-sided message and refuting the "other" side is an attempt to help your audience be more resistant to opposing points of view. What is this resistance strategy called? (p. 392)
    A. Reactance
    *B. Inoculation
    C. Message discrepancy
    D. Comparative advantage
    E. Counterarguments

TRUE OR FALSE

26. Topics aren't boring, people are.
    Ans: T   Page: 368

27. An important lesson in topic selection is to focus first on something about which the speaker already knows.
    Ans: T   Page: 369

28. Speakers should keep their topic broad and avoid narrowing the topic.
    Ans: F   Page: 369

29. The purposes for speaking are generally to entertain, to inform, or to persuade.
    Ans: T   Page: 369

30. Purpose statements should be limited to one declarative phrase or sentence, such as "to persuade the audience that commuter marriages are often necessary and feasible."
    Ans: T   Page 371

31. One practical basis for making assumptions about an audience is to ascertain the "demographic" makeup, such as sex, age, socioeconomic status, or level of education.
    Ans: T   Page: 371

32. Relying on personal knowledge and/or experience as a source of evidence during a speech is a bad idea. The speaker is most likely to be perceived as lazy and low in credibility.
    Ans: F   Pages: 374–375

33. Every speech designed to inform has an introduction, a body, and a conclusion.
    Ans: T   Page: 377

34. The outline of a speech provides a "road map" to follow when it's time to deliver a speech to an audience.
    Ans: T   Page: 382

35. Repetition involves explaining something more than once, but in a slightly *different* way each time.
    Ans: F   Page: 382

36. Transitions are simple words or phrases that signal organization, such as "First, we will consider . . ."
    Ans: F   Page: 383

37. During a persuasive speech, a speaker should make it clear to the audience that her/his intent or objective is to persuade.
    Ans: F   Page: 390

38. According to the body of research on message discrepancy, speakers should avoid asking for too much change.
    Ans: T   Page: 390

39. The "boomerang effect" occurs when speakers ask for gradual or minor progress toward the changes they want.
    Ans: F   Page: 390

40. Speakers should avoid using inflammatory words or phrases such as "sexist," "feminist," or "chauvinist."
    Ans: T   Page: 391

ESSAYS

41. What questions need to be raised when analyzing an audience?

42. Discuss what should be included in each part of an informative speech.

43. Explain why a persuasive speech needs a different format than an informative speech for maximum effectiveness.

44. Explain Monroe's Motivated Sequence. Include in your discussion the five steps involved.

45. Discuss five of the seven strategies we can use to persuade others effectively.

CHAPTER 14

SPEAKING BEFORE A GROUP

MULTIPLE CHOICE

1. A speaker who spends a great deal of time preparing the delivery in an attempt to *look* as if she/he was speaking in a natural manner without self-consciousness is known as: (p. 400)
   A. Feedback
   *B. Planned spontaneity
   C. Audience adaptation
   D. Role-taking
   E. Casual conversation

2. A speech prepared in advance that is usually read word for word is called: (p. 402)
   A. Memorized
   *B. Manuscript
   C. Impromptu
   D. Extemporaneous
   E. Informative

3. The _____ mode of delivery requires that you write out the speech beforehand and practice it over and over again until you know it by heart. Then you present the speech without text. (p. 403)
   *A. Memorized
   B. Manuscript
   C. Impromptu
   D. Extemporaneous
   E. Persuasive

4. You have just been told to come to the boardroom and tell the unexpected vice-president the status on the project you have been asked to complete. This is an example of using a(n) _____ delivery style. (p. 404)
   *A. Impromptu
   B. Manuscript
   C. Extemporaneous
   D. Memorized
   E. Business-causal

5. The type of delivery in which the speaker uses an outline as a road map is called a(n): (p. 404)
   A. Manuscript
   *B. Extemporaneous
   C. Impromptu
   D. Memorized
   E. Conversational

6. The degree to how much the audience feels that a speaker is believable is known as: (p. 405)
   *A. Source credibility
   B. Audience adaptation
   C. Source competence
   D. Speaker expertise
   E. Audience role-taking

7. Vicki is giving a speech to the class. She cites several recent research studies and sources as evidence for her argument. Which dimension of credibility is she trying to enhance? (pp. 405–406)
   A. Composure
   B. Sociability
   C. Character
   *D. Competence
   E. Sociability

8. Which of the following statements can help a speaker to demonstrate competence? (p. 406)
   A. Use jargon.
   B. Admit your ignorance.
   C. Appear to be competent.
   D. Arrange for a validating introduction.
   *E. All of the above

9. When asked a question closely related to his topic, Joaquin did not know the answer. To maintain his credibility with the audience, Joaquin might respond: (p. 406)
   A. "Looking at that . . . uh . . . I would think the area most closely related would be . . ."
   B. "I don't think we need to concern ourselves with that."
   *C. "I don't know, but I could find out and get back to you later."
   D. "That is a very good question. Are there any other questions?"
   E. "I'm sorry, that is not the issue we are discussing."

10. A speaker who appears calm, cool, and collected before a large audience is exhibiting which dimension of credibility? (p. 409)
    A. Competence
    B. Sociability
    *C. Composure
    D. Extroversion
    E. Trustworthiness

11. The dimension of credibility that focuses on how likable a speaker is perceived to be is known as: (p. 410)
    A. Extroversion
    B. Composure
    C. Competence
    *D. Sociability
    E. Trustworthiness

12. The perceptions of physical and psychological closeness based on nonverbal cues is known as: (p. 410)
    A. Sociability
    *B. Immediacy
    C. Extroversion
    D. Nonverbal communication
    E. Source credibility

13. The degree to which someone is perceived as "outgoing," "people-oriented," and "talkative" refers to which dimension of credibility? (pp. 410–411)
    *A. Extroversion
    B. Sociability
    C. Introversion
    D. Friendliness
    E. Composure

14. To avoid mid-speech sag, several strategies can be used. Which of the following is NOT a suggestion that would avoid this "sagging middle"? (p. 415)
    A. Use redundancy and repetition.
    B. Use a variety of gestures and body movements.
    C. Use vocal variety.
    D. Maintain eye contact with audience members.
    *E. Learn to handle hecklers by responding to their outcries and criticisms.

15. Research on immediacy in interpersonal relationships demonstrates that immediacy has several outcomes. Which of the following is an outcome of perceived immediacy? (p. 417)
    *A. Increased liking
    B. Increased proximity
    C. Decreased composure
    D. Decreased feedback
    E. Increased speaker trust

TRUE OR FALSE

16. In order to seem as though you are relaxed and spontaneous before an entire audience, you have to prepare for it fully ahead of time.
    Ans: T   Page: 400

17. Most of the feedback received by public speakers takes the form of nonverbal communication.
    Ans: T   Page: 400

18. Trying to show every person that you recognize them by smiling, nodding, holding eye contact, and/or asking them their names is called "recognition strategies."
    Ans: T   Page: 401

19. Speeches should appear planned and formal, appearing distinctly different from a casual conversation.
    Ans: F   Page: 401

20. The manuscript mode has the advantage of completeness and precision.
    Ans: T   Page: 402

21. The advantage to the memorized mode is the simple fact that you can commit an entire speech to memory.
    Ans: F   Pages: 403–404

22. Like manuscript reading, the memorized mode often sounds monotonous, and fails to allow for either feedback interpretation or effective role-taking for adaptation.
    Ans: T   Page: 404

23. The extemporaneous mode of delivery prevents a speaker from adapting to audience feedback.
    Ans: F   Page: 405

24. The most important dimension of credibility for public speaking is trustworthiness.
    Ans: F   Page: 405

25. Audiences appreciate speakers who seem trustworthy; therefore, if a speaker is asked a question and he/she doesn't know the answer, then the speaker should fake an answer to appear competent.
    Ans: F   Pages: 408–409

26. Responding to a crisis with apparent confidence and control increases speaker credibility.
    Ans: T   Page: 409

27. In a public speaking situation, a speaker should at least "act like" an extrovert, whether he/she really is one or not.
    Ans: T   Page: 411

28. Silence or pause time is a strategy used before or after a phrase or line to add special meaning and emphasis to a message.
    Ans: T   Page: 414

29. One way to handle a heckler is to give him/her eye contact to communicate disinterest.
    Ans: F   Page: 415

30. Besides summarizing the main points of your speech, the conclusion should leave the audience wanting more—this is a memorable conclusion.
    Ans: T   Page: 416

ESSAYS

31. Compare and contrast public speaking with casual dyadic conversations.
32. Discuss the importance of credibility to public speaking.
33. Describe four of the five ways a speaker can enhance her/his perceived *competence*.
34. Identify and discuss five of the seven strategies a speaker can use to keep the plot (middle) from "sagging."
35. Review and discuss the *immediacy principle* as it relates to public speaking.

CHAPTER 15

PUBLIC SPEAKING: POLISHING AND FINE-TUNING

MULTIPLE CHOICE

1. The use of carefully chosen words and phrases that appeal to our senses of touch, taste, sound, sight, and smell involves the use of _____ in language, which can help to arouse concrete pictures in the minds of audience members: (p. 428)
   A. Simile
   *B. Imagery
   C. Rhythm
   D. Applause
   E. Vocalics

2. Creating images through the use of an "expressed" analogy, such as saying a person is "sly as a fox," is referred to as a(n) _____. (p. 428)
   *A. Simile
   B. Example
   C. Metaphor
   D. Proverb
   E. Folklore

3. "The floors of the New York Stock Exchange became the scene from *Nightmare on Elm Street*" is an example of a: (p. 428)
   A. Quote
   B. Simile
   C. Proverb
   *D. Metaphor
   E. Sentence

4. President Bush's statement "Read my lips: no new taxes!" follows which of the strategies for making your language more interesting? (p. 429)
   A. Evoke images with similes.
   *B. Strive for simplicity.
   C. Maintain rhythm for emphasis.
   D. Employ intense and animated language to add excitement.
   E. Use imagery imaginatively.

5. A brief passage or sentence, such as "Go ahead—make my day!" is an example of a(n): (pp. 433–434)
   A. Simile
   B. Metaphor
   *C. Soundbite
   D. Press release
   E. Analogy

6. The overall qualitative way in which a speaker communicates, using verbal language patterns and nonverbal cues, is known as rhetorical or communicator: (p. 435)
   A. Behavior
   B. Pattern
   C. Signal
   *D. Style
   E. Personality

7. Speakers who are really "performers," and treat the public speaking event as if they were "on stage," have a(n) _____ rhetorical style of communication. (p. 435)
   A. Actor
   B. Performance
   *C. Dramatic
   D. Animated
   E. Humorous

8. Energy, enthusiasm, and excitement are central characteristics of the _____ rhetorical style. These types of speakers show every emotion they are feeling. (p. 436)
   *A. Animated
   B. Humorous
   C. Exaggerated
   D. Dramatic
   E. Emotional

9. Talk-show hosts such as Arsenio Hall, Johnny Carson, and Joan Rivers have which of the following styles of communication? (p. 437)
   A. Animated
   *B. Humorous
   C. Dramatic
   D. Comedian
   E. Immediate

10. There are several cautions to keep in mind when using humor. Which of the following is NOT a pitfall when using humor? (pp. 437, 439)
    A. A humor threshold exists for every joke, story, and anecdote.
    B. Speakers can be too funny.
    C. The use of humor depends on the topic and occasion.
    *D. Humor can enhance the perception of immediacy.
    E. Informative or persuasive speakers who use more humor than their audience wants to hear are likely to be dismissed as "jokers."

11. Transforming words and phrases from the bland and routine to the unique and inspirational involves what are called: (p. 425)
    *A. Rhetorical devices
    B. Interpretive devices
    C. Immediate devices
    D. Illusionary devices
    E. Stylistic devices

12. Vivid images are most easily aroused with the use of _____ language. For example, Governor Thomas Kean employed such language: "We offer poor America not the junk food of more big government but the full meal of good private sector jobs." (p. 428)
    A. Subjective
    B. Abstract
    *C. Concrete
    D. Regional
    E. Political

13. Ronald Reagan used the principle of _____ when he claimed that "facts are stubborn things" at least five times in a speech at the Republican National Convention. (p. 429)
    A. Imagery
    *B. Simplicity
    C. Intensity
    D. Illusion
    E. Style

14. A good example of _____ language is found in a speech by Governor Thomas Kean of New Jersey denouncing the effects of pollution on our environment: "Today, our air is plagued by acid rain—our oceans and beaches are sullied by sewage and syringes—our very future is threatened by sunburn from above and poisoned water from below." (p. 432)
    A. Rhythmic
    B. Concrete
    C. Self-evident
    D. Subdued
    *E. Intense

15. The fact that audiences often perceive humorous speakers as friendly substantiates that humor is actually a component of _____. (p. 439)
    A. Animation
    B. Simplicity
    C. Composure
    *D. Immediacy
    E. Intensity

TRUE OR FALSE

16. Rephrasing and restating key phrases and words during a speech all help to build the rhythm of the speech, which in turn, helps to increase retention.

    Ans: T   Page: 433

17. Applause is not something that can be managed by a speaker; it's simply a form of audience feedback.

    Ans: F   Pages: 434–435

18. In order to activate your audience, you need to keep in mind an important principle: Audiences like to be involved.

    Ans: T   Page: 435

19. Audience support does not just happen; a speaker must plan for it.

    Ans: T   Page: 435

20. "Ask not what your country can do for you, but what you can do for your country," is an example of a simile.

    Ans: F   Page: 428

21. Animated speakers emote—and they show every emotion they are feeling.

    Ans: T   Page: 436

22. Research on humor in the classroom indicates that award-winning teachers use humor sparingly.

    Ans: F   Pages: 437, 439

23. Your decision to use humor must depend on the topic and the occasion.

    Ans: T   Page: 439

24. The use of humor by a speaker has no effect on perceived competence and intelligence. It is the actual serious content of the speech that influences those perceptions.

    Ans: F   Page: 439

25. Speakers can be too funny.

    Ans: T   Page: 437

ESSAYS

26. Describe the five general ways a speaker can make her/his language more interesting.
27. Define *sound bite*. What role do sound bites serve? How can sound bites be orchestrated to elicit an audience response?
28. Suggest how a speaker can effectively manage audience applause.
29. Discuss the three common rhetorical styles that have proved to be useful in public speaking situations. Identify ways a speaker can capitalize on each.
30. Discuss two advantages and two disadvantages of using humor in a speech.

CHAPTER 13
COMMUNICATING IN A MULTICULTURAL SOCIETY

MULTIPLE CHOICE

1. The "melting pot" policy of the United States was intended to: (p. 370)
   A. Recognize and respect individual cultural differences
   B. Welcome immigrants into our country
   C. Keep alive the traditions of each and every cultural group
   *D. Eradicate differences between people
   E. Help school children become bilingual

2. African-Americans, Mexican-Americans, Jews, and Catholics all represent which cultural variety? (p. 374)
   A. Mainstream cultures
   *B. Co-cultures
   C. Specialized cultures
   D. Intercultures
   E. Umbrella cultures

3. Membership in or identification with a specific co-culture depends on: (p. 380)
   A. Your commitment to that culture
   *B. Whether or not you and others perceive you to be a part of that culture
   C. The uniqueness of that particular cultural affiliation
   D. The number of different co-cultures you identify with
   E. Your cultural background or heritage

4. The largest co-culture in the United States is: (p. 383)
   *A. African-American
   B. Mexican-American
   C. Asian-American
   D. Native American
   E. Irish-American

5. African-Americans are likely to perceive the stereotypic white as: (p. 383)
   *A. Cold and distant
   B. Warm and friendly
   C. Emotional and demonstrative
   D. Nervous and edgy
   E. Intelligent and rich

6. Compared to whites, many African-Americans seem: (p. 384)
   *A. Immodest and boastful
   B. Stodgy and stiff
   C. Uncommunicative or hostile
   D. Attentive and interested
   E. Quiet, but self-assured

7. The U.S. policy of cultural pluralism: (p. 372)
   A. Has been replaced by our more recent policy of the "melting pot" society
   B. Recognizes that communication and culture are inseparable
   *C. Emphasizes cultural differences and diversity
   D. Supports an ethnocentric orientation toward groups
   E. Is designed to "homogenize" people from different ethnic and racial groups

8. Students at this university represent which type of cultural variety? (pp. 373–374)
   A. Mainstream
   B. Co-culture
   C. Subculture
   D. Interculture
   *E. Specialized

9. Fidelity of intercultural communication and attraction between interactants relies heavily on: (pp. 380–381)
   *A. The number of similar co-cultures the individuals share
   B. Physical appearance
   C. Our tendency to be ethnocentric with others
   D. Our affiliation with collectivistic cultures
   E. Our affiliation with individualistic cultures

10. Compared to the white majority, Mexican-Americans often appear: (p. 384)
    A. Anxious and withdrawn
    *B. Dramatic and intense
    C. Cold and reserved
    D. Intimidating
    E. Immodest or boastful

11. Of all the co-cultures we have studied, which of the following appears to be the most expressive or flamboyant in their communication style? (p. 384)
    A. African-Americans
    B. White majority
    C. Asian-Americans
    *D. Mexican-Americans
    E. Native Americans

12. Compared to the collectivistic tradition, people from individualistic cultures are more likely to value: (p. 384)
    A. The family
    B. Loyalty to friends and family
    *C. Competition
    D. Status and authority
    E. Self-restraint

13. Compared to the white majority, we find that Asian-Americans are more likely to: (p. 384)
    A. Give advice to others
    B. Self-disclose personal information
    *C. Be sensitive to the feelings of others
    D. Show their emotions
    E. Argue their position

14. Which of the following co-cultures is most like the Asian-Americans in their value orientations? (p. 385)
    A. Whites
    B. African-Americans
    C. European-Americans
    D. Mexican-Americans
    *E. Native Americans

15. Which of the following statements is more likely to be expressed by females than by males? (p. 385)
    A. "I have a headache."
    B. "I like your tie."
    C. "Do you believe in the power of the crystal?"
    *D. "I like squaw bread better than white, don't you agree?"
    E. "We should wait for Mary to join us."

TRUE OR FALSE

16. Native Americans tend to be open and expressive in their interactions with others.
    Ans: F   Page: 385

17. Maintaining eye contact is a sign of respect in the white majority culture.
    Ans: T   Page: 385

18. Unlike African-Americans, Native Americans are more likely to strive for power and personal success.
    Ans: F   Page: 385

19. When men use tag questions, they are likely to be perceived as uncertain or weak.
    Ans: F   Page: 386

20. When women use tag questions, they are likely to be perceived as polite.
    Ans: F   Page: 386

21. Women talk more than men.
    Ans: F   Pages: 386–387

22. Women are more expressive than men in their communication style.
    Ans: T   Page: 387

23. Understanding and appreciating our own co-cultural identities can help us reduce ethnocentrism toward other cultures.
    Ans: T   Page: 390

24. We are all, to some extent, ethnocentric.
    Ans: T   Page: 390

25. Uncertainty is a normal part of any co-cultural interaction.
    Ans: T   Page: 389

ESSAYS

26. In the chapter, the authors talk about "the iron grip of culture." What exactly does that mean? What are the implications of that grip on our ability to relate effectively with others living within a multicultural society?

27. Differentiate between *ethnocentrism* and *cultural relativity*. How do both of these constructs influence how we think and communicate with others?

28. Assuming a stance of cultural relativity, are there any cultural practices that we should not condone? Why or why not?

29. The authors provide you with eight communication guidelines to help us maximize our success in relating with others from different co-cultures. List and discuss four of those.

30. Compare and contrast female and male communication patterns. Why do women and men often report they have difficulty communicating with one another?

CHAPTER 14

UNDERSTANDING MASS COMMUNICATION

MULTIPLE CHOICE

1. In contemporary society, people no longer get the information they need for making decisions, or for other purposes, by word-of-mouth from family, friends, and neighbors. Instead, they must rely on mass media content, such as news, advertisements, and entertainment. This condition is called: (p. 396)
   A. Media saturation
   B. Mass communication agenda-setting
   *C. Dependency on mass media
   D. Incidental information reliance
   E. Media modeling influences

2. According to the text, our most respected medium is: (p. 400)
   *A. Books
   B. Television
   C. Computer networks
   D. Newspapers
   E. Magazines

3. The first large-circulation newspaper in the United States that was supported mainly by advertising and designed to attract ordinary citizens (as opposed to an educated and affluent elite) was the: (p. 402)
   A. *Boston Globe*
   B. *New York Times*
   C. *Philadelphia Inquirer*
   *D. *New York Sun*
   E. *New Boston Gazette*

4. The mass communication process can best be conceptualized as linear (as opposed to interactional or transactional) because: (pp. 410–411)
   A. It takes place very rapidly
   B. Mass media messages reach large and diverse audiences
   C. Media messages are formulated by professional communicators
   D. The index of fidelity is always low
   *E. Immediate feedback and role-taking are essentially missing

5. A conceptualization of the mass communication process in American society that takes into consideration the social controls and constraints within which the media function is a(n): (p. 411)
   *A. Social systems model
   B. General linear model
   C. Interactional model
   D. Simultaneous transactions model
   E. Transactional linear model

6. An explanation of the effects of exposure to mass communications based on assumptions that a media message immediately reaches virtually every member of an audience and influences everyone's ideas and conduct in powerful ways is called a(n): (p. 414)
   A. Selective power theory of media effects
   B. Classic influence theory of media effects
   *C. Magic bullet theory of media effects
   D. Baseline linear theory of media effects
   E. Exposure-influence theory of media effects

7. The theory of minimal and selective influences of the content of mass communications was based on a recognition of the part played by which of the following factors? (pp. 416–417)
   A. Individual (psychological) differences between people
   B. The social categories in which people are located
   C. The social relationships prevailing among people
   *D. All of the above
   E. None of the above

8. Looking back over 60 years of research on the process and effects of mass communication, we reach which of the following generalizations? (pp. 417, 419)
   *A. The influence of any particular exposure to a specific mass-communicated message on an individual's beliefs, attitudes, or behavior is likely to be limited at best.
   B. The mass media actually have no influence on the people who are exposed to their content.
   C. Some media messages have immediate and very powerful influences on nearly everyone. However, the majority have no influence whatsoever.
   D. Virtually any mass media message has a strong influence on people, whether they realize it or not.
   E. Media content containing violence has a powerful and immediate influence on every child who is exposed to it.

9. When viewing the process of mass communication historically, where media content has been consistent and persistent over a long period, it seems clear that: (p. 419)
   A. The media have had almost no influence on our society
   B. The media have had some minor influences on our society
   *C. The media sometimes had powerful influences on our society
   D. The media have always influenced everyone in society
   E. No conclusions can be drawn from such a historic perspective

10. Among the following, which term refers to long-term effects of mass communication? (pp. 420–425)
    A. Accumulation theory
    B. Modeling theory
    C. Social expectations theory
    D. Adoption of innovation theory
    *E. All of the above

11. Over the years, magazines have become: (p. 405)
    *A. More specialized
    B. The primary source of news information
    C. A failing industry
    D. Our most serious medium
    E. Outdated, less popular with the readers

12. Which of the following mass media effects theories would support the claim that pornography has a direct and immediate effect on violent sex crimes? (pp. 414–415)
    A. Accumulation theory
    B. Modeling theory
    *C. Magic bullet theory
    D. Social expectations theory
    E. Adoption of innovation theory

13. Which of the following mass media effects theories would support the claim that the media can alter our version of reality over time? (p. 420)
    A. Adoption of innovation theory
    B. Social expectations theory
    C. Magic bullet theory
    D. Modeling theory
    *E. Accumulation theory

14. According to the research on selective or limited influences of the media, political advertising on television is most likely to _____ already decided or committed voters. (p. 416)
    A. Convert
    B. Challenge
    C. Socialize
    *D. Reinforce
    E. Change the exposure rates of

15. The primary role the mass media play in the adoption of innovation process is: (p. 422)
    A. Trying out the innovation
    B. Evaluating the innovation
    C. Triggering interest in the innovation
    D. Getting people to repeat their purchasing behavior
    *E. Making people aware of the existence of the innovation

TRUE OR FALSE

16. The cultural heritage from which our contemporary mass media emerged got its start early in the last century with the invention of the steam-powered press.
    Ans: F   Pages: 397–399

17. The mass media include books, magazines, newspapers, film, radio and television but not the telephone, computer networks and fax machines.
    Ans: T   Page: 410

18. The number of daily newspapers read per capita in the United States has been declining for several decades.
    Ans: T   Page: 405

19. The number of full-length feature movies produced in the United States today is about twice the number that were made each year during the 1930s.
    Ans: F   Page: 406

20. The majority of radio stations to which people listen today are transmitted on the FM, as opposed to the AM, band.
    Ans: T   Page: 408

21. Television technology is advancing rapidly, and soon we will all have clearer pictures to view. This means that completely new kinds of content will dominate the medium and people's viewing tastes.

    Ans: F   Page: 409

22. Even though media research groups study audiences and their preferences closely and continuously, and make feedback information available to professional communicators, the mass communication process really cannot be viewed as interactional.

    Ans: T   Page: 411

23. Looking at our mass media as a whole, including books, magazines, newspapers, movies, radio, and television, the best term to describe the majority of their content is "educational."

    Ans: F   Page: 411

24. After several decades of research on the process and effects of mass communication, the theory that is best supported by the research evidence is the theory that describes minimal and selective influences.

    Ans: T   Page: 417

25. According to the "magic bullet" theory, audiences are influenced by the media when the content presented is both persistent and consistent over time.

    Ans: F   Page: 423

ESSAYS

26. The chapter on the process and effects of mass communication in American society is organized around three broad questions. What are these questions, and on what does each focus?

27. Explain how the process and effects of mass communication can be approached within the perspective of a linear model, and explain why such a model is more appropriate than either an interactive or simultaneous transactions alternative.

28. Explain the basic ideas of the "magic bullet" theory of the process and effects of mass communication, and indicate the status of that theory today.

29. After 60 years of research on the process and effects of mass communication, what is the "bottom line"? That is, do the findings from numerous surveys and experiments indicate that the media are powerful or limited in their influences? Explain.

30. What theory suggests that the effects of mass communication on our society may be powerful? Explain the basic ideas of that theory, and indicate from examples why it seems to have merit.

CHAPTER 15

CONDUCTING COMMUNICATION RESEARCH

MULTIPLE CHOICE

1. Researchers in all fields of science are committed to a set of very general assumptions about the nature of the subject matter they investigate and how they go about it. Those assumptions are: (p. 434)
   A. A set of beliefs that only science is worthwhile
   B. Beliefs indicating that science can study any subject matter
   *C. The postulates of the research perspective
   D. The foundation values of the statistical method
   E. A commitment to place science ahead of everything

2. The three requirements that (1) science is a public process, (2) research reports must be vigorously screened, and (3) secret research is unacceptable, all provide the foundation for the assumption of: (p. 435)
   A. Caveat emptor
   *B. Experto credite
   C. In vino veritas
   D. Diem perdidi
   E. Ex post facto

3. A variable that appears to influence another is, for research purposes, called: (p. 437)
   A. Intervening
   B. Dependent
   C. Extraneous
   *D. Independent
   E. Correlated

4. A statement that poses a tentative relationship between two variables (one that is subject to verification on the basis of observation) is called a(n): (p. 438)
   A. Postulate
   B. Theory
   C. Assumption
   D. Generalization
   *E. Hypothesis

5. The term *empirical*, as in the phrase *empirical observations*, means: (p.439)
   *A. Apprehended by the senses
   B. Statistical data
   C. Qualitative information
   D. A dependent variable
   E. Quantitative data

6. The degree to which the findings of a research project can be extended beyond the sample studied and used to interpret what happens in a larger population is indicated by the conclusion's: (p. 455)
   A. Reliability
   B. Generalization
   C. Replication
   *D. External validity
   E. Level of measurement

7. A researcher classifies the people being observed in a research project as "Democrats," "Republicans," or "Independents." Such a classification represents: (p. 451)
   A. Field observation
   B. Nonreactive participation
   *C. Nominal measurement
   D. A dependent variable
   E. Internal validity

8. In an experiment, participants are required to make use of a set of materials and a device in order to respond to the conditions posed by the independent variable. Such a situation represents: (p. 445)
   A. Direct observation
   B. Low validity
   C. An ethical problem
   *D. Demand characteristics
   E. Low reliability

9. A researcher is able to study a sample of a population both before and after a major flood in the area. She also compares a sample of people who experienced the flood with a sample of similar people who did not experience the flood. This strategy of research is found in the: (p. 446)
   *A. Quasi-experiment
   B. Field sample survey
   C. Field experiment
   D. Field observation study
   E. Replicated sample study

10. A researcher has developed a measure that gives very consistent results when used to assess a characteristic of people in a sample. This means that the measure is: (p. 455)
    A. Valid
    B. Nonreactive
    C. At the interval level
    *D. Reliable
    E. Ethical

11. Dr. Allen asked respondents, "How old are you?" Later in the interview, Allen asked, "What is the date of your birth?" This illustrates that Allen was interested in the _____ of the measurement. (p. 455)
    A. Interval measurement
    B. External validity
    C. Precision
    *D. Reliability
    E. Ordinal measurement

12. Which of the following is a nominal variable? (p. 451)
    *A. Gender (female/male)
    B. Age (under 21 years, 21–25, 26–30, 35–40)
    C. Employment status (identify actual occupation)
    D. Income (indicate exact gross earnings)
    E. Educational level (elementary, high school, college)

13. One major disadvantage of interviewing participants face-to-face is: (p. 448)
    *A. The technique is expensive
    B. People tend to lie in interviews
    C. The wrong people are always the ones who cooperate
    D. Very little relevant information can actually be obtained
    E. Potential participants may have unlisted phone numbers

14. A study in *Communication Quarterly* was entitled "The Effects of Nonverbal Involvement on Interpersonal Attraction." The dependent variable was: (p. 437)
    A. Nonverbal involvement
    *B. Interpersonal attraction
    C. The manipulation
    D. Can't tell from the title
    E. There is no dependent variable

15. According to the Hawthorne effect, people who became aware that they were being observed or studied: (p. 440)
    A. Behaved the same way they always do
    B. Became the "bad subjects"
    C. Decided to drop out of the experiment
    D. Complained to Human Subjects Committees
    *E. Became the "good subjects"

TRUE OR FALSE

16. It is not necessary to make any kind of assumption about potential causes and effects in subject matter to be studied within a scientific perspective. Instead, it is better to assume that events are random.
    Ans: F   Page: 435

17. The assumption of *experto credite* is based on a faith that researchers are honest and basically virtuous.
    Ans: F   Page: 435

18. An independent variable is one that influences another in some regular or systematic way.
    Ans: T   Page: 437

19. The term *data* refers to "information known as fact" by virtue of empirical observations that have been recorded.
    Ans: T   Page: 439

20. Completely unobtrusive and direct observation of behavior by a researcher is not difficult.
    Ans: F   Page: 440

21. A sample consists of a group of people to study who are willing to participate in a project. It really doesn't matter how they were selected.
    Ans: F   Page: 447

22. A sampling frame consists of the list of people who are finally selected through the use of a procedure which ensures that every one had an equal probability of being included.
    Ans: F   Page: 448

23. In a field observation study, the researcher becomes part of the group under study and participates in their daily lives.
    Ans: T   Page: 449

24. The most sophisticated level of measurement, in the sense that it permits all kinds of mathematical manipulations of data, is the ratio level.
    Ans: T   Pages: 451–452

25. Researchers maintain that it is always unethical, under any circumstance whatsoever, to deceive people who will participate in an experiment, even though its nature and purpose are explained afterward.
    Ans: F   Page: 457

ESSAYS

26. Briefly, what are the basic postulates of the research perspective?
27. What is meant by the term *empirical observation*?
28. What is the nature and what are the purposes of a theory?
29. What is the difference between validity and reliability in measurement? How are the two related?
30. What is meant by the term *informed consent* (in relation to people who will participate in an experiment), and why is this an important issue?

PART IV

DISCUSSION TOPICS AND ACTIVITIES

CHAPTER 1
THE COMMUNICATION PROCESS: AN OVERVIEW

1. **GETTING ACQUAINTED #1:** A traditional way of reducing tension among class members is to have each person introduce himself or herself. If you decide to use this form of ice-breaker, be sure to give students a format to use. For example, you may start by introducing yourself (including what you prefer to be called), your area of interest (communication?), any special hobbies or interests, and anything else you would like to mention (like what you do for fun, your favorite restaurant, or where you would like to travel). Be sure to allow enough time for everyone to share information about themselves. Also, students like it when you ask them questions or comment on their answers. For example, if a student mentions that he works at a department store, you may want to ask, "In what department do you work?" and so on.

2. **GETTING ACQUAINTED #2:** Another way to allow students to become familiar with each other and reduce tension is by having a "structured conversation." That is, read each question below, asking each person to answer briefly without explanation, honestly, with the first response that comes to mind. Ask a different student to respond to each new question, then go around the circle clockwise, as quickly as possible. Each student should answer every question. If you have a large class, you may want to use only some of the following questions.

   A. What is your name?

   B. Who do you think is the most important person who has ever lived?

   C. What is the best (or worst) movie you ever saw?

   D. What is the ugliest (or most beautiful) thing you know?

   E. What TV program do you most enjoy?

   F. If you could be any animal (other than human), what would it be?

   G. What is your favorite sport?

   H. What is your favorite food/drink?

   I. Who is your favorite music group/individual?

   J. How do you select your friends?

   K. What do you like most/least about yourself?

   L. What are your career goals?

   A variation on the above activity would be to have each student pair up with another individual and "interview" that person. After 20 minutes or so, you can then ask the pairs to "report" back to the group what they learned about each other.

   You might also try taking "roll" by asking each student to provide a *brief* response to a "Question of the Day."

3. **COMMUNICATION, A DAILY ACTIVITY:** Discuss with your students what role communication plays in their daily lives. Ask students to give examples of effective and ineffective communication encounters. Ask your students how important they believe communication skills are for success in relationships, at work, as consumers, and in the classroom. You may even want them to identify one communication skill they would like to improve this semester/quarter.

4. **DEFINING COMMUNICATION:** Divide the class into groups of four or five, and ask them to derive an original definition of human communication and to develop an original communication model. Ask them to compare their definition and model with the definition and model provided in the text. Discuss what similarities and differences emerged.

5. **COMMUNICATION COMPETENCE SCALE (CCS):** Ask students to complete the scale on page 8 in your text. Instructions for calculating and interpreting their scores are provided with the scale. Discuss whether or not they perceive themselves to be a competent communicator. Ask them what influenced their self-perception the most. A variation to this activity would be to assign the students to have another person evaluate their competence and for them to compare their scores.

CHAPTER 2

VERBAL COMMUNICATION

1. **HUMAN VERSUS ANIMAL COMMUNICATION:** Discuss the role of communication among animals and between individuals. For example, ask students if they have any pets. If so, ask if they "communicate" with their pets. Ask if their pets "communicate back." How do they know that communication has occurred? Do they believe animals communicate with each other? In what way? Be sure to discuss the distinction among *inherited* communication functions, those that are based on *learned* signs and signals, and those that depend on language.

2. **RANKING ANIMALS BY LANGUAGE:** Divide the class into groups of four or five. Give each group a list of animals, and have them arrange each along the *phylogenetic continuum* in terms of language and learning capacity. Animals you may want to include are apes, whales, dolphins, humans, dogs, cows, ants, birds, and fish. The point of this activity is to look at the tools of animal communication as an important basis for comparing and contrasting lower-order with higher-order animals. (See Table 2.1 on page 38 in your text) Within your discussion, you may want to have students point out which animal behaviors are inherited and which are learned.

3. **WORDS AND THEIR MEANINGS:** Have students as a class develop a list of words that have caused personal confusions due to inconsistent denotative and connotative meanings (e.g., slang words, such as "bad" or "gay"). You may want to extend this list to include words or labels that have negative meanings associated with them (e.g., "liberal," "feminist"). How can these words be modified or "relabeled" to avoid negative meanings in the future? To help get you started, you may want to refer to Table 2.2, on page 58 in the text, for a list of words that have undergone changes/redefinition.

4. **VERBAL IMMEDIACY:** Ask students to complete the Verbal Immediacy Scale on page 54 in their text. Instructions for calculating and interpreting their scores are provided with the scale. Discuss the implications of using immediate language. In short, people perceive immediate others to be warm and friendly; they find them easy to talk to and prefer spending time interacting with them. Ask students to come up with ways they can increase their personal immediacy. When might nonimmediacy be a valuable tool? How can they communicate nonimmediacy without also communicating disliking?

5. **CULTURAL IDIOMATIC EXPRESSIONS:** Another way to show differences among languages in regard to idiomatic expression is to provide a list of expressions from a particular culture or co-culture and then have your students attempt to "explain" each expression. See if they can trace the derivative of each. Try these expressions to get them started:

A. "I'm busier than a cat covered up."

B. "Way!"

C. "Not"

D. "It's raining cats and dogs."

E. "Get a life."

F. "Geez Louise"

G. "Birds of a feather"

H. "To die for"

I. "He/she's a pistol."

J. "Crocodile tears"

K. "Get a hold" of somebody

L. "Weasel word"

M. "Scaredy cat" or "chicken"

N. "Far out" or "groovy"

O. "Get down."

P. Money: "Dough" or "bread"

Q. "Crib"

R. "Hood"

S. "Gay"

CHAPTER 3

NONVERBAL COMMUNICATION

1. **TOUCH APPREHENSION MEASURE:** Ask students to complete the Touch Apprehension Measure (TAM) on page 88 in their text. Instructions for calculating and interpreting their scores are provided with the scale. Discuss with your students their feelings toward touch in general and across situations, like school, work, and play. Ask them, "To what extent do touch approachers even know they are being touched or touching others? What cultural or ethnic differences influence touch? How do children learn the unique cultural norms about where, who, and when to touch?"

2. **NAME THAT MEANING:** Divide the class into groups of five to seven people. Hand each group an envelope containing seven slips of paper. Each slip should contain one of the instructions listed below. Instruct your students to only look at the slip of paper they draw from the envelope. Each student should nonverbally signal or "act out" to the group the instructions listed on her/his own slip of paper. Students from the other groups are to "name the meaning" of each nonverbal signal.

   A. Without saying anything, nonverbally signal to the group that you are bored and uninterested in what is going on in the group.

   B. Without saying anything, signal to the group that you want the floor or a chance to speak.

   C. Signal to the group that you are angry with the group members. Do not use any words.

   D. Signal nonverbally to a particular group member (choose anyone you want) that you find him or her attractive and or interesting. Do not use words to do this.

   E. Indicate nonverbally that you are time conscious and want the group to hurry up with the assignment. Do not use any words.

   F. Ask a question for information in such a way that your vocal cues, facial expression, movements, and eyes all signal that you are in charge and want to be the boss.

   G. You see one group member as a nuisance and a threat to your status. Indicate nonverbally how you might put him/her down by using nonverbal "one-up" signals.

3. **TALKING ABOUT TIME:** We talk about time in a variety of ways. Time flies, time won't wait, time goes by, time is money, and so on. Have students brainstorm in groups and make a list of all the different ways we talk about time. Afterward, ask students to examine their list carefully and answer the following questions as a class:

   A. Given the large number of ways we talk about time in our culture, what does that communicate about our preoccupation with time?

   B. Why is time so important to us in this culture? Why is it relatively unimportant in some other cultures?

   C. How do people abuse time? What happens when people you know abuse it?

4. **ORIENTATIONS TOWARD TIME:** Below are a series of statements concerning the ways people generally think about or use time. Provide each student with the list below (or read the statements aloud), and have them indicate their response to each question, using the following scale:

(5) = Strongly agree

(4) = Agree

(3) = Neutral or undecided

(2) = Disagree

(1) = Strongly disagree

1. I am always on time for an appointment.
2. I like to come early just to make sure I won't be late.
3. I am generally one of the first to arrive at a dinner party.
4. I have trouble getting to work or school on time.
5. No matter how hard I try, I always seem to be late.
6. I do my best work in the morning.
7. I like to get up early and get my work done.
8. I have trouble staying awake after 9:00 P.M.
9. It takes me a long time to wake up and get going in the mornings.
10. I would just as soon sleep in late and start my work in the afternoons or evenings.
11. I like to plan ahead all my activities for the week.
12. I don't know what I would do without my calendar.
13. I don't understand people who don't like to make plans and schedule their activities in advance.
14. I'm spontaneous; to plan ahead of time constrains me.
15. I hate it when someone tries to pin me down to a social engagement weeks ahead of time.

SCORING: Use the scoring instructions below to help your students compute their own orientations toward time in terms of: Punctuality, Owls and Sparrows, and Preplanning. (For each of the following, scores should range from 5 to 25. If your score doesn't fall within that range, then you made a computational error.) Then, follow up with a discussion about each. (See information provided with each factor below.)

FACTOR 1: PUNCTUALITY

1. 12 + your scores from items 1, 2, and 3.
2. – your scores from items 4 and 5.

The higher the score, the more punctual you are. How much patience do you have toward those who aren't as punctual as you? What does being "on time" communicate to you? For low scorers, why do people make such a fuss when you're habitually late? How do you feel when someone arrives right on time to your home for a social event? (Are you even dressed yet?)

FACTOR 2: OWLS AND SPARROWS

1. 12 + your scores from items 6, 7, and 8.
2.   – your scores from items 9 and 10.

The higher your score, the more sparrowlike you are. Sparrows enjoy getting up early in the morning and do their best work in the early hours of the day. By afternoon, they need a nap. Owls (lower scores) much prefer afternoons and evenings to do their best work. They don't understand sparrow's preoccupation with "the early bird gets the worm." Discuss how society here in the United States rewards sparrows and punishes owls. Note how everyone must conform to a sparrow work ethic, even though a large number of us are owls.

FACTOR 3: PREPLANNING

1. 12 + your scores from items 11, 12, and 13.
2.   – your scores from items 14 and 15.

The higher your score, the more scheduled your life tends to be. In fact, you prefer mapping out your work and social activities. Not only do you keep a calendar (and carry it with you at all times), but you may even have appointments written in your book weeks or months ahead. Low scorers, on the other hand, cringe at the idea of keeping track of their work and social lives. Preplanning is a waste of time, simply because they may not "feel" like doing that activity when it does come due—and won't know until then anyway.

CHAPTER 4

LISTENING AS COMMUNICATION

1. **RECEIVER APPREHENSION TEST:** Ask your students to complete the test on page 114 in the textbook. Instructions for calculating and interpreting their scores are provided with the scale. Discuss the range of scores with your students. Begin by asking them, "In what ways can you increase your own RAT score overall? Why should you want to? How do you think your RAT score might influence learning in the classroom? Do you think receiver apprehension might be situational—as well as a trait? That is, are there certain courses, teachers, and situations that might make you more apprehensive about listening than others? Are there even individuals or situations where you may have "learned" NOT to listen well?"

2. **THE TRUTH IS STRANGER THAN FICTION:** This activity is designed to illustrate to students how messages are distorted as we pass on information from one individual to the next. Select five to seven people as participants, or ask for volunteers. Ask all but one participant to leave the room. Provide the one remaining participant with the following message. Read it aloud to him/her and the class only once. But be sure to preface your reading by telling the participant that he/she will have to remember it and repeat it later on. This way, the student will be given sufficient warning that he/she must listen well.

> Today it was reported on the 6 o'clock news on Channel 4 that a man from the Philippines, who is now a U.S. resident, is 5 months pregnant. He says he is a she; the State says he is a he; and his/her doctor says he is both. At birth, he had both reproductive organs; as an adult he decided to become fully female by getting rid of his male reproductive organs. Currently, he wishes to marry the father of his baby, but the church will not allow the marriage because his birth certificate says he is male (even though the state says he is female). Currently he is awaiting the birth of his first child. (Incidently, this is a true story!)

After the first participant hears the message one time (only once) as you read it aloud to the entire class, have the second participant step back into the room. Now have the first participant repeat the story to the second participant. Then #2 tells #3 and so on. Each person should tell the story only once so that each following person hears it only once before they are asked to repeat it. The last participant should tell the story to the class.

Have the other students keep notes about what information has been added, deleted, or distorted. Lead a short discussion with the class on message distortion and listening barriers.

3. **STORY TIME:** Read the following story to the class. Ask students to listen closely. Following the story, inform the class that you will be asking them a series of simple questions.

> At 5:00 P.M. on Friday evening at the corner of Washington and Jones streets, a man came out of a bar staggering. A second man approached the first apparently to inquire as to whether there was a problem. An argument ensued. The second man pushed the first. A crowd gathered to watch. One spectator left to get help. About 15 minutes later, a person in uniform came and tried to break up the fight between the two men. The disagreement settled down and first aid was administered to a spectator who was apparently overcome by a heart attack.

Short Answer Questions

(1) What time did the man come out of the bar?

(2) Which man had been drinking? (Key: We don't know if anyone had been drinking.)

(3) Who started the fight? Who shoved whom first?

(4) What were the two men arguing about?

(5) When did the policeman arrive? (Key: We don't know if the uniformed person was a police officer or even if the individual was male.)

(6) Who had the heart attack?

(7) How long was it before the uniformed person broke up the fight?

(8) Who administered the first aid?

(9) Where did the incident occur?

Even though you told the students that they would be "tested" on the story, many of them still had problems listening accurately. Discuss how barriers interfere with our ability to listen well. What barriers were evidenced in this case? Have students identify them.

4. **CONTROLLING OUR BIASES AND ASSUMPTIONS:** Each student should read the statements that follow and decide for himself or herself what the answers are. Next, you may want to divide the students into groups of four or five. The group should discuss each statement and arrive at a consensus.

During the group discussion, each student should paraphrase the comments of the person who just spoke before making any new comments. Everyone should agree that the paraphrase represents what was really said.

A. People under 21 should not be allowed to vote.

B. All potential parents should be required to take a parenting and child development class.

C. Grades should be eliminated in college.

D. Special-interest schools, such as single sex, religious, and racial schools, should be eliminated.

E. Aids testing should be required of all health-care professionals.

After each group is finished, have the class as a whole respond to the following discussion questions:

(1) How difficult/easy was it for you to accurately paraphrase one another? What problems did you encounter in your paraphrasing attempts?

(2) What function(s) does paraphrasing serve? In other words, why might paraphrasing be important? Under what circumstances would you recommend that participants practice this technique?

(3) Television and newspaper reporters continually paraphrase or "highlight" politicians' remarks. Based on some of your own difficulties paraphrasing others in your group activity, how accurately do you predict reporters are in their paraphrasing attempts of others? What might you recommend to reporters to ensure accuracy in reporting?

5. **SEMANTIC BARRIERS TO LISTENING:** Present the following list of words to your class. Have each student indicate their first response to each word using the following scale:

(5) = Highly favorable

(4) = Favorable

(3) = Neutral

(2) = Unfavorable

(1) = Highly unfavorable

A. welfare

B. marijuana

C. fraternity

D. Jesus

E. right to life

F. liberal

G. AIDS

H. law and order

Discuss with your students whether a person's reaction to these words would affect a listener's ability to concentrate fully on a speaker's message. What are some other words that may distract from an intended message? What other word(s) could a speaker use to replace or neutralize the words above? (You may even want to lead into a discussion of idioms and euphemisms. What functions do they serve? What kinds of people or occupations would be more likely to use euphemistic phrases or words?)

CHAPTER 5

COMMUNICATING INTERPERSONALLY

1. **SMALL TALK:** Ask your students to complete the scale on page 142 in their text. Instructions for calculating and interpreting their scores are provided with the scale. Discuss with your students what it means to be "good" or "bad" at small talk. Ask your students how they engage in small talk. How successful are they at small talk? What makes them successful (or unsuccessful)? How did they learn to engage in small talk? How does small talk differ from "big" talk? Why does big talk always seem to begin first with small talk?

2. **INTERPERSONAL ENTERTAINMENT:** Each student should select a song, television show, or recent movie that emphasizes the development and deterioration of an interpersonal relationship. Given time constraints of your class, selected portions of songs or videos may be played to illustrate each student's example. Be sure students are given a time limit (3 to 7 minutes) to present their example.

   You might begin their search by giving them some relevant examples, such as Paul Simon's "There Must Be 50 Ways to Leave Your Lover" or a special episode of a television sitcom, like "Doogie Howser, M.D.," or the movie *When Harry Met Sally*. Then follow up with the discussion questions listed below:

   A. How is the relationship depicted in this song (or movie) like "real life"?

   B. Can you discern a particular pattern or stages that people seem to go through when engaging in or disengaging from a relationship?

   C. What did the principal characters find "attractive" about each other in the first place? Or what led to the demise of the relationship?

   D. What strategies did the principal characters use to attract the other; to gain affinity? Or what strategy(ies) did the principal characters use to get out of the relationship?

   E. Why do you suppose so much of television, the movies, and the songs we hear on the radio is devoted to falling in love or falling out of love?

3. **INTERPERSONAL REFLECTIONS:** Have each student reflect on a relationship that has terminated (friendship or intimate relationship). Then ask each student to write a one- to two-page paper on why they think this relationship ended, how it ended, and how their communication changed. Finally, have the students divide up into groups of four or five to discuss their papers. Discussion should center on how each relationship ended (not so much on "why"). You may want to debrief the class by discussing Baxter's four main strategies for saying goodbye (see text) or see if students can label their own disengagement attempts.

4. **INITIAL INTERACTIONS THROUGH ROLE-PLAYING:** This activity is designed to help students become more sensitive to the ways in which one can successfully manage the initial stages of interactions. First, you will need to ask for volunteers who would be willing to role-play various situations depicting initial interactions between two people. Depending on your time limit, you may want to have three to six dyads. Each of the dyads should be given 5 to 7 minutes alone to discuss their situation. Then, in front of the class, each dyad should role-play their planned situation. Once all role-plays are finished, discussion should focus on the awkwardness of communication at the beginning of relationships and how individuals can manage that awkwardness. Have students identify *why* initial relationships are so awkward (uncertainty, novelty, etc.).

Role-Play Situations

   A. A man meeting his future mother-in-law for the first time

   B. Two roommates meeting for the first time

   C. A wife meeting her husband's "ex" for the first time

   D. A woman and a man on a blind date

   E. An employee's first meeting with his/her boss

   F. A father meeting his long-lost daughter for the first time

   G. A friend meeting his/her best friend's new lover

5. **WHO AM I?** This activity allows students to learn about each other through self-disclosure in a nonthreatening way. Before the activity is to be scheduled, ask students to bring in a concealed object that they feel represents them in some way. Encourage your students to think about who they are as complex individuals. On the day of the activity, divide the students into groups of five to seven members. Next, ask each student to place his/her object in a large paper bag or box (the objects should remain anonymous). Now remove the first object; have the group name several characteristics of that item; and then see if the group can match the item with the student. Each student should then reveal to the group why he or she selected that particular object.

Be sure to discuss the role of self-disclosure in establishing relationships and communicating information about ourselves to others. Moreover, you could have students consider the characteristic of interpersonal communication that states, "Interpersonal communication begins with the self." What "self" is communicated by each object? How will that "self" influence how others respond?

CHAPTER 6
COMMUNICATING IN SMALL GROUPS

1. **SCAVENGER HUNT:** This activity is designed to illustrate to students how groups typically make decisions. Importantly, this activity should *precede* any substantive lectures or readings on how groups *should* make decisions. Divide your class into groups of five to seven members. Provide each group with a list of items to collect on their scavenger hunt. Below is a sample list; you may wish to revise this list to include items that are available on your campus. You should allow about 20 to 30 minutes for this activity. The group that collects all the items first "wins." After all the groups have returned, discuss how they decided to proceed. For example, did they all just run out the door? Or did they plan who would collect which items and so on? This activity is a good way to introduce the topic of group process.

   Scavenger List

   A. One flat stone
   B. One library book with a red cover, checked out from the library today
   C. Today's copy of the school's newspaper
   D. One full book of matches
   E. One small bag of potato chips purchased today (receipt required)
   F. One sheet of graph paper with 3 signatures on it that no one who belongs to the group may sign
   G. A safety pin, large or small
   H. One white leather sport shoe, with laces tied
   I. A photograph of someone in your group

   You may then want to lead a discussion, asking students the following:

   (1) Why did X group win and yours did not?
   (2) What could you have done differently to make your group more efficient?
   (3) Who was the leader in your group? How was she/he selected, or did she/he just emerge? What qualities must a group leader have?
   (4) What role did you assume in your group? What roles did others serve in your group? What role(s) was missing? How is it that people just "assume" a role or position in a group?

2. **SARGENT AND MILLER LEADERSHIP SCALE:** Ask your students to complete the scale on page 178 in their text. Instructions for calculating and interpreting their scores are provided with the scale. Discuss the three styles of leadership (authoritarian, democratic, and laissez-faire). Then lead class discussion around the following questions/issues:

   A. Which style is most/least efficient?
   B. Which style is most/least fair?
   C. Which style allows the most/least input from others?
   D. Which style is likely to result in a higher-/lower-quality decision overall?
   E. If you were not the leader in your group, which style of leadership would you like to see your group leader have? Why/why not? Is that style the same or different from your own?

3. **GROUP VERSUS INDIVIDUAL PROBLEM-SOLVING:** Provide each student with a copy of the questions listed below (without the "key"). Ask each student first to try answering each question on his/her own. Then have your students form groups of four to five members. Ask the groups to share their answers and attempt to solve any disputed or unanswered questions together. Then "grade" the answers by having students keep track of both their individual and group scores. Next, students should "compare" their own individual scores with those obtained with their group. Which score, individual or group, resulted in the better "grade"? Why do you suppose groups often reach a higher-quality decision (better grade) than individuals working alone?

(1) What actor starred as Frankenstein in the original version of the movie? (Key: Boris Karloff)

(2) What was Beaver's first name on the television sitcom "Leave It to Beaver"? (Key: Theodore)

(3) What swimmer holds the record for earning the most gold medals in the Olympics? (Key: Mark Spitz)

(4) Do they celebrate Thanksgiving in Canada? (Key: No)

(5) What religion was the actor Al Jolsen? (Key: Jewish)

(6) What was Gilligan's ("Gilligan's Island") first name? (Key: Willie)

(7) What famous comedy team is known for their rendition of "Who's on First"? (Key: Abbott & Costello)

(8) What U.S. president won an Olympic gold medal for swimming? (Key: None)

(9) What was the date of John F. Kennedy's assassination? (November 22, 1963)

(10) What U.S. president held four terms in office? (Key: Franklin D. Roosevelt)

(11) What now famous actor was Mr. Olympia? (Key: Arnold Schwarzenegger)

(12) What U.S. president played football for the University of Michigan? (Key: Gerald Ford)

CHAPTER 7
COMMUNICATING IN ORGANIZATIONS

1. **BEHAVIOR ALTERATION TECHNIQUES (BATS) AND MESSAGES (BAMS):** Have your students complete the scale on page 198 in their text. Instructions for calculating and interpreting their scores are provided with the scale. Follow through with their results with these discussion questions:

   A. How "satisfied" are you with your supervisor's (or boss's) methods for handling you? Does your level of satisfaction coincide with the research? (See Figure 7.1.)

   B. What suggestions might you give your boss on how to handle you effectively in order to gain your compliance?

   C. Do you think there are some employees who work better with antisocial-oriented bosses? Why/why not?

   D. Do you suspect that there are gender differences in the approach we take to influence others at work? If so, what are some potential differences you might hypothesize?

2. **PERFORMANCE APPRAISALS:** This activity is designed to help students deal with performance appraisals at work. There are few jobs that don't require some type of formal evaluation. Sometimes performance appraisals occur during regular intervals (every 6 months, for example); sometimes they occur only when needed (when the employee does something wrong). This role-playing activity should help students deal effectively with their own performance appraisals.

   Eight students should "pair up" in dyads of four. For each dyad, one student will role-play the evaluator or supervisor; the other will role-play the employee. Assign one of the following performance appraisal tasks to each dyad:

   A. The employee is continually late for work.

   B. The employee spends too much time "goofing off."

   C. The employee does not dress "appropriately" for the position.

   D. The employee is not well liked by the supervisor's secretary. The secretary complains that the employee treats her/him like a subordinate; that is, the employee apparently acts rude, obnoxious, and demanding.

   Have each dyad role-play the performance appraisal in front of the class. The rest of the students should carefully observe and offer suggestions for how both the supervisor and the employee could manage the interview successfully. Consider the following issues/questions in the discussion that ensues:

   (1) How did the interview go? How successful was the supervisor in accomplishing his/her goal? Do you think the employee will change his/her behavior as a function of this interview?

   (2) How did/should the supervisor open the performance appraisal session? How did/should it close?

   (3) Did the employee become defensive? Why or why not?

(4) What could the supervisor do or say differently to make the appraisal process a little easier on himself/herself? Easier on the employee?

(5) What was the ratio of supportive versus critical/defensive comments made in the interview? Why is the ratio important to consider?

3. **GUEST SPEAKER:** This unit of instruction provides an excellent opportunity to bring in a guest speaker to discuss his/her experiences working within a professional organization. It is especially helpful if you could elicit someone from the local community (potential employers) to speak with your group. The following is a list of topics you may want your speaker to address:

A. What type of organization do you represent?

B. How are decisions made in your organization?

C. What are you looking for in potential employees?

D. What types of training programs are available?

E. How would you describe your organizational subculture?

F. What do you value the most/least about your organization?

G. How can students find out more about your organization?

H. What communication problems do you face in your organization?

I. How important are both written and oral communication skills in your organization?

CHAPTER 9
COMMUNICATING WITH MEDIA

1. **COMMUNICATION TECHNOLOGY AVOIDANCE:** Ask students to complete the scale on page 228 in their text. Instructions for calculating and interpreting their scores are provided with the scale. Lead a discussion about students' feelings toward using high-tech communication media by having them respond to the following issues/questions:

   A. Why have you avoided (or approached) using high-tech media?

   B. What problems have you had using high-tech media?

   C. Do you know people who like to have or own the technology but really don't know how to use it? Who, in your home, is the media "expert," the person who can hook up or use most or all of the technology you own?

   D. Do you think we may have gone *too far* in our attempts to be technologically oriented? In what way(s)?

   E. Are you looking forward to even more technology? What inventions are you anticipating using yourself in the future?

   F. What excuses do technology avoiders give when they refuse to use media technology? Why do you suppose they became fearful in the first place? What recommendations might you give to someone who is afraid of using some of our more advanced technology today? How do we "cure" them of their anxieties? Should we?

2. **GROUP TV NEWS ANALYSIS:** This activity can be used as an exercise to introduce the topic of television effects. To save valuable time, the instructor should bring to class two current edited newscasts (i.e., commercials omitted) that are videotaped from two different local affiliate stations (preferably a top-rated and a low-rated). This means that the national, state, and local news coverage will constitute approximately 20 minutes or less.

   Activity: Divide the class into groups of five to seven members. Each member of the group is responsible for tracking a different facet of the news program (e.g., arrangement of stories, time devoted to each story, visuals used within stories).

   Equipment Required: You will need to have a room equipped with at least two monitors and two VCRs. Usually these can be ordered 2 to 3 days in advance of the exercise through a university media center. If you have more than two groups of students, have two groups analyze and view one monitor and two groups analyze and view the other.

   Instructions for Students

   A. Each group member is responsible for tracking one element throughout the national, state, and local news.

   B. Each member of the group reports on his or her findings after the news analysis. Findings should be summarized on the board according to the following five questions or issues:

      (1) How were the stories "arranged"? In general, what type of story came first, second, . . . , and last? Where were the "important" stories centered in the newscast?

      (2) How many minutes/seconds were devoted to national stories? Local stories? Weather? Sports? Entertainment (soft news)? Compute averages. What was the "average" time spent on each national story? On each local story? Compute.

(3) When were visuals used? In what way(s)? How do visuals help tell a story?

(4) How much time was spent telecasting "on the scene" reporting? Which type of story had no reporter on location? Which type did?

(5) How did the anchors relate to one another? How much actual time (minutes/seconds) was spent with reporters talking to each other? What did the anchors talk to each other about, generally?

(6) And, if more than five in a group, have the sixth member note how the entire newscast began and how it ended. How did the anchor/reporter switch to commercials; return from commercials? In other words, what strategy was used each time? And, if you have talented media students in class, one or more of them may want to comment on production techniques employed in the newscast, including the number of cuts, zooms, pans, and so on.

Discussion Questions: After these issues are summarized on the board, have the entire class respond to the following questions/issues:

1. What, if any, are the major differences between the two newscasts?

2. What do these differences mean in terms of potential audience effects? Which newscast would you rather watch and why?

3. Given the arrangement of stories, what priorities do station managers have? What is the "bottom line" for station managers? What do they care most about? How does their concern for gaining audience attention in order to make money potentially undermine our "need to be informed on the issues"?

4. Given the average amount of time devoted to any given national or local news story, how much "information" do viewing audiences receive? How much "depth" of information do we receive?

5. We know that the American public relies heavily on television for news coverage—more so than on the newspaper, radio, or news magazines. Given the coverage devoted to the average national or local news story, what does that say about the public's actual awareness of what's going on?

6. Why do newscasters talk to one another on the show? Why is the "happy talk" format necessary, or is it not necessary?

7. Were the visuals that were used essential? If not, why were they used?

8. How often was "on the scene" reporting used? Why is it used? How does being on the scene change the potential impact of the story on the viewing audience?

3. **TELEPHONE ETIQUETTE QUIZ:** Ask students to answer True or False to the following quiz. Afterward, discuss the importance of following proper telephone etiquette in the business context.

A. Business calls can be made at any time of the day. (False; business calls should be restricted to business hours.)

B. While in your office with another coworker, the phone rings. You should immediately answer the phone and accommodate the caller. (False; such calls should not be allowed to intrude. The caller can wait his/her turn.)

C. You should attempt to return phone calls immediately. (True.)

D. If you want to chat, ask if the receiver has time. (True.)

E. When you answer the phone, there is no need to identify yourself; after all, someone has called you. (False; assuming the speaker will recognize your voice can cause misunderstandings and embarrassment.)

4. **THE SOCIAL INFLUENCE OF MEDIA:** Discuss with your class the influence of television and newspaper coverage of crime stories on the moral condition of the public. Discuss how your students feel about watching/reading these accounts. Has this flood of information changed their daily behavior in any way? In other words, are they more cautious? Are they more fearful? Are these outcomes (caution and fear) good or bad?

5. **AT THE BEEP:** This activity is designed to allow students to creatively use an answering machine. Divide your class into groups of three or four members. Each group is responsible for coming up with a clever message they can use on their answering machines at home or at work. Each group will present their taped message to the class. Then have students address the following issues/questions:

A. What does each message "say" about the owner/group?

B. What kinds of messages annoy callers? Why?

C. What kinds of messages did you enjoy? What kinds of messages seemed more appropriate for work than for the home? Are they also the ones you enjoyed? Why or why not?

D. How does "safety" enter into your decision about what kind of message you can/should use?

E. What kinds of recommendations or guidelines might you suggest for answering-machine owners?

CHAPTER 9

PRESENTING ONESELF EFFECTIVELY

1. **SELF-DISCLOSURE SCALE:** Ask students to complete the scale on pages 272 and 273 in their text. Instructions for calculating and interpreting their scores are provided with the scale. Lead a discussion with your class on each of the five dimensions of self-disclosure: intentional/unintentional, amount, positive/negative, honesty/accuracy, and depth/intimacy. Below is a list of questions to get them started with the discussion:

   A. We know that intentional self-disclosure is just that—disclosure given on purpose. Can information about yourself ever "leak out"? If so, how?

   B. The book talks about verbal self-disclosure. Can self-disclosure ever be nonverbal? Give examples.

   C. Is it better to self-disclose positive or negative information to others? Can you be too positive about your disclosures? Can you be too negative? What perceptions might people have of us when we try to disclose positive information about ourselves? When we disclose negative information?

   D. Can we ever self-disclose too much? Too little? How do you know when enough is enough?

   E. Are there occasions when, or people with whom, we should not self-disclose? Are there people or events that suggest we should be dishonest in our disclosures?

   F. What do we think of individuals who seem to self-disclose too much too soon? Do you know people like that? How have you responded when this has happened to you?

2. **WHO AM I?** Ask your students to make a list of adjectives that best describe themselves. Next, ask students to circle the three adjectives they like most about themselves and to asterisk the three they like least. Now, divide the class into groups of four or five members. Have students (voluntarily) share with their respective group the list of adjectives they created. Afterward, ask students as a whole the following questions:

   A. How easy was it for you to self-disclose the adjectives you liked the most? Do you find we often downplay our successes and achievements? If so, why? What's the difference between being confident and being boastful?

   B. Do "conceited" individuals have a healthy self-concept? Why not? How do healthy self-concept individuals communicate? In other words, how do you know when someone has a positive self-concept?

   C. How easy was it for you to self-disclose the things about you that you liked the least? Why is it sometimes easier to tell people what's wrong with us, rather than what's right?

   D. How important is it for you to "screen" or "preselect" the impression you make on others? How did you do that with your group in this activity? What impression(s) did you try to "create" and why?

3. **AFFINITY-SEEKING STRATEGIES:** Have your students refer to Table 9.1 on pages 268–269 in their text. This table refers to 25 specific strategies that people report using to get others to like them. Ask your students to review the list and to indicate on a separate piece of paper the five strategies they personally use the most and five strategies they use the least. Follow up with these questions:

A. Which strategies are the most successful? Why?

B. Which are least effective at gaining affinity? Why?

C. Which strategies may be better at maintaining, rather than gaining, affinity over time?

D. Do you think there are/should be differences between males and females in the strategies they select? Why?

E. How many *different* strategies do you suppose popular versus lonely people use? Does diversity of strategy use influence popularity?

Finally, have students select one or two strategies that they have *never* used before. Then ask them to try it out on someone with whom they would like to gain affinity. Have them mentally "record" what happened and report back to the class next time.

4. **STEREOTYPES AND ATTRIBUTIONS:** This activity asks students to identify the stereotypes and attributions that they hold about others and how these stereotypes and attributions may interfere with their communication encounters. Ask students to individually write down characteristics that they feel best describe each of the following groups of people.

(Note: This list can be substituted for a list of your own that may reflect the surrounding university community or classroom.)

A. Native Americans

B. Unwed mothers

C. Sorority and fraternity members

D. Muslims

E. Middle-aged males

Collect the descriptions, and for the next class prepare an overall list of all the students' responses (omit names). Distribute or read them aloud and follow with these questions/issues:

(1) Where did you get these descriptions? That is, how do you know what you think you know about these groups?

(2) Do you think these descriptions are generally accurate: Why or why not?

(3) Why do we form stereotypes? When do we use them? Are they fair?

(4) How could some of these stereotypes interfere with successful communication encounters?

(5) Are stereotypes ever helpful? When? How?

(6) Were you ever treated like a stereotype yourself? How did that make you feel? How did you feel about the other person?

(7) How can we prevent stereotyping from occurring?

5. **ATTRIBUTIONS AND IMPRESSIONS:** Ask students to identify at least three different physical or behavioral attributes that serve as anchors for their overall first impressions of others. For instance, someone may intensely dislike fat. Whenever he/she sees someone who is fat, he/she automatically assumes that the fat person is lazy, powerless, sloppy, and unclean. For someone else, the critical attribute that makes a difference might be smoking, so that whenever she/he sees a smoker, she/he automatically assumes a negative first impression. And so on. After students identify their own personal biases, have them discuss the validity of those first impressions. How fair are they?

CHAPTER 10
INFLUENCING OTHERS

1. **STUDENT RESISTANCE SCALE:** Ask your students to complete the scale on pages 300 and 301 in their text. Instructions for calculating and interpreting their scores are provided with the scale. Lead a discussion on how students attribute their resistance responses to their teachers as either teacher-owned or student-owned. For example, you may want to ask the following questions:

   A. What kinds of teacher behaviors or demands are you most likely to resist? Most likely to comply with?

   B. Do you think you generally use student-owned or teacher-owned resistance—when you do resist?

   C. Are there certain teachers that you might be more willing to comply with (or resist?) than others? If so, what characteristics of those teachers do you think influence your decision to resist or comply?

   D. How resistant to teacher demands do you feel you are in general? Do you tend to comply, or are you more likely to resist?

2. **CREDIBILITY AND PERSUASION:** Identify three to five nationally known television personalities. Videotape brief segments of each personality. Show the segments to the class, and have the students identify the strategies that each speaker uses to establish his/her credibility. Compare and contrast the various speakers. You might want to videotape television personalities, such as Phil Donahue, Barbara Walters, Ted Koppel, Oprah Winfrey, or guests on "CNN Crossfire."

3. **DO THE MEDIA PERSUADE?** Ask your students to collect four or five advertisements or commercials (video or print). Ask them to identify which of the following three audience responses is being encouraged:

   (1) Constructing/reconstructing meaning,

   (2) Shaping or altering beliefs, or

   (3) Creating or modifying meanings.

   Be sure to have students provide their reasoning for each selection. This exercise can be done as either a class discussion or a writing assignment.

4. **FEAR APPEALS:** Divide the class into groups of five to seven members. Ask each group to develop three separate fear appeals for the following topics. The first appeal should be low fear; the second, moderate; and the third, a high fear appeal.

   A. Safe sex

   B. The Japanese moving ahead of the United States in world power

   C. All elementary and secondary schools switching to tuition funding

   D. Proper diet

   E. Environmental contamination

   F. Signing a living will

For each fear appeal, ask students to develop a print media campaign, a video campaign, or a skit.

Have students identify why high fear appeals may be more effective at gaining compliance than either low or moderate fear appeals.

5. **CREATING TWO-SIDED MESSAGES:** Ask students to select a controversial topic such as right to life, gun control, use of contraceptives by teenagers, euthanasia, motorcycle helmet laws, or social welfare programs. For the topic they select, ask them to present orally or in writing a two-sided message designed to persuade others to their point of view. Encourage class members to evaluate whether both sides were presented "fairly."

Another variation on this activity is to have students identify their own position on a controversial topic. But instead of developing a persuasive argument that supports their own position, have them develop an argument that supports the "other side." Afterward, talk about how counterattitudinal advocacy really works!

CHAPTER 11
COPING WITH CONFLICTS

1. **ARGUMENTATIVENESS SCALE (ARG):** Ask your students to complete the scale on page 322 in their text. Instructions for calculating and interpreting their scores are provided with the scale. Lead a discussion on how an individual's personal degree of argumentativeness may influence his/her conflict style and communication encounters in general. Moreover, you could ask the person the following:

   A. Do you find argumentative people interesting and attractive? (Make sure that students understand that you're talking about a positive attribute here—argumentativeness does NOT refer to someone who is hostile and aggressive.)

   B. Under what circumstances might you find an argumentative person *un*attractive? In other words, would you like someone who is argumentative at work, in social situations, or at home?

   C. Why do you think highly argumentative people enjoy a good argument? Do you suppose they "win" more often than low argumentatives? In other words, what reinforces that predisposition?

   D. In your opinion (we have no data on this), who would you hypothesize would be happier individuals overall, high or low argumentatives? Why do you think so?

2. **CAN CONFLICT BE PRODUCTIVE?** Conduct a class discussion in which the idea of conflict being good or productive is discussed. Do class members agree that conflict is usually productive? Why? Why not? Under what circumstances do they see conflict as being functional? Dysfunctional?

3. **MY CONFLICT STYLE:** Ask students to write a short paper that analyzes their own personal style of conflict management. Ask students to describe their style, how they feel using this style, and how they think others feel when they use this style. Would they describe their conflict-management style as predominantly a win-win, lose-lose, or win-lose strategy? Do they think the relationship between them and the "other" person is strengthened or weakened when they argue?

4. **CONFLICT NEGOTIATION:** Divide the class into groups of five to seven members. Present each group with a copy of the scenario listed below. Each group should discuss the problem and decide on how a solution can be attained.

   > A group is discussing the problem of cheating. One member of the group claims, "There's nothing wrong with a little cheating in the classroom. Everyone does it. Teachers expect too much from students, so they are forced to cheat to survive." Another group member retorts, "I disagree, and I can't believe you would readily admit to such a thing. Don't you understand that cheating only hurts the cheater? Besides, there is more to personal ethics than doing what everyone else is doing!" You know that both participants believe strongly in their positions. How can you help these two manage this conflict and reach an agreeable solution?

5. **CONFLICT IN ACTION:** Ask students to focus on a conflict they are currently involved in—or anticipate being involved in sometime soon. Have them write a two- to three-page analysis paper on the conflict by responding to the following issues:

A. What is the nature of the conflict? Describe what is happening (or what you think could happen). Who are the principal actors in the conflict? What is your position? What is his/hers?

B. What was/were the potential cause(s) of the conflict?

C. What have you tried to do so far to manage the conflict?

D. What is your goal? What do you want?

E. Based on your reading of Chapter 11, what ways could you resolve the conflict? In other words, plan in detail the negotiation strategies you will try to implement.

CHAPTER 12

OVERCOMING SHYNESS AND APPREHENSION

1. **PERSONAL REPORT OF COMMUNICATION APPREHENSION:** Ask your students to complete the scale on page 350 in their text. Instructions for calculating and interpreting their scores are provided with the scale. Then discuss with your students the concept of communication apprehension, its causes, and its consequences.

2. **PROFESSIONAL MANAGEMENT OF STAGE FRIGHT:** Ask your students to interview someone who gives public presentations as part of his or her job (e.g., actor/actress, business representative, lawyer, politician, minister, or teacher). Have each student pose the following questions to that professional:

   A. Do you ever experience stage fright? How often? How is it manifested; that is, do you get red blotches on your neck, clammy hands, and so on?

   B. What do you do to quell your stage fright—to reduce your apprehension *before* the actual presentation? Are there special clothes you wear, routines you practice, calming music you play, and so on?

   C. During your presentation, you must also occasionally experience some degree of stage fright. What do you do then?

   D. What happens when you lose your train of thought during a speech?

   E. What do you do when someone asks a question and you don't know the answer? How do you respond to someone who doesn't agree with you, doesn't believe you, or just seems to want to hassle you?

   F. Do you consider yourself a "good" speaker? Why is that? Do others consider you a "good" speaker as well?

3. **RESEARCH ON COMMUNICATION APPREHENSION:** Ask students to bring in a recent article on communication apprehension, anxiety, stage fright, or shyness to share with the class. Have them present an oral summary of the article.

4. **COGNITIVE RESTRUCTURING:** This activity is designed to demonstrate how cognitive restructuring techniques work at reducing someone's apprehension about communicating. This is a good assignment to use just before students know they will have to be giving a major speech to the class (Chapters 13, 14, and 15). The assignment may be written, or it may be done as a group project. Provide students with the following instructions:

   A. First, identify a particularly apprehensive-producing situation that you would like to remedy (public speaking, engaging in small talk at parties, speaking up in a group, or interviewing for a job). Make sure the situation you select is especially troublesome to you.

   B. Next, identify and list on paper those negative self-statements you make about that situation. In other words, what do you say to yourself before, during, and after the communication event? (Example: "I know I will forget the first main point." "No one is paying attention to me and what I have to say." "I am terrible at doing this!")

   C. Third, analyze each of those negative self-statements for errors in logic or overgeneralization. That is, how reasonable or realistic are they, anyway? Aren't most or all of them a little "dramatic" and overstated?

D. Fourth, for every negative self-statement, substitute a positive coping statement. Instead of saying, "I am terrible at doing this," try "I can do this and, with a little practice, I can do this well! In fact, I can be darned good at this!"

E. Finally, practice or rehearse your new list of coping statements. Just as your former list of negative self-statements have been committed to memory over the years, you will need to commit these new, positive ones to memory as well. Only through rehearsal can you do that.

5. **LUCY AND LAURA: PERCEPTIONS OF CA:** This activity demonstrates how we all selectively perceive and attribute more negative motives and traits to high communication apprehensives (CA's) and, at the same time, attribute more positive ones to low CA's. In order to do this activity effectively, it should be done *before* students read Chapter 12. Distribute the following profiles of either Lucy or Laura to each student in class. Half of the students should receive and read only the Lucy profile; the other half should receive and read only the Laura one. Ask them *not* to share their profiles with one another at this time.

PROFILES

Lucy: Lucy works at Lotterdale Electronics in their inventory department. Her job requires that she check stock inventory and enter the data onto a central computer. Lucy has been with the company 10 years, and even though she has never been promoted, she does her job efficiently and effectively. She gets high marks on her performance appraisals every 6 months, and when asked, she reports that she likes what she does very much. Lucy often eats lunch at her desk, seldom participates in coffee breaks with her coworkers, and does not socialize with any of them after work.

Laura: Laura works at Lotterdale Electronics in the human resources department. Her job requires that she screen all potential employees for positions in the company and orient new employees in on-the-job training. Laura has been with the company 10 years; she started as a receptionist and, after repeated promotions, emerged as head of an entire department. Laura gets high marks on her performance appraisals every 6 months and often tells people how much she enjoys working at Lotterdale. Laura makes a habit of inviting different people to lunch with her every day, knows everyone who works at the firm, and will occasionally socialize with people after work.

Instructions: After students have read their own respective profile of either Lucy or Laura, have them complete the following scale by indicating their perceptions of either Lucy or Laura. These bipolar adjectives can be read aloud to the class; have students record, on a scale of 1 to 5, their perceptions of the woman they have just read about.

5 . . . . . 4 . . . . . 3 . . . . . 2 1

1. Warm   Cold

2. Friendly   Aloof

3. Interesting   Boring

4. Fun   Dull

5. Open   Restrained

6. Competent   Incompetent

7. Calm   Anxious

8. Responsible   Unreliable

9. Leader   Follower

10. Personable   Detached

11. Likable   Distasteful

12. Attractive   Unattractive

13. Pleasing   Annoying

14. Assertive   Passive

15. Accommodating   Disagreeable

Scoring: Have students compute their own scores by adding together their responses to all 15 word pairs. Scores should range from a high of 75 to a low of 15. The median or mid-point for the scale is 45. The higher the score, the more positive the perception. Scores above 45, then, indicate fairly positive perceptions of the target woman whereas scores below 45 indicate fairly negative perceptions. Average students' scores on the board—all of those for Lucy and then all of those for Laura.

Interpretation: Compare and contrast students' responses to Laura and Lucy. Based on recent research that has examined individuals' perceptions of high CA and low CA others, we would expect students' perceptions of Lucy (high CA) to be significantly more negative (lower scores) than Laura's (low CA). Compared to Laura, Lucy (high CA) is likely to be viewed as aloof, uncommunicative, restrained, remote, somewhat less competent, and so on. On the other hand, Laura should be perceived as overwhelmingly positive. People would find her friendly, extroverted, polite, sociable, a leader, competent, fun, approachable, and so on.

Then discuss how easily those negative or positive perceptions were formed and on the basis of very little information. After all, why should anyone conclude that Lucy was cold or incompetent or unfriendly—simply because she is shy? By the same token, why should anyone conclude that Laura is competent, credible, accommodating, or responsible—just because she's talkative and outgoing? In other words, our perceptions may not be fair and we know they certainly aren't all that objective.

CHAPTER 13
PREPARING THE CONTENT

1. **AUDIENCE ANALYSIS SURVEY:** Ask students to complete the survey on pages 372–373 in their text. After each student has completed the questionnaire, discuss as a class (or in groups) their responses to each question. This activity may be completed in class as a group, or you may simply ask students to turn in the completed survey and calculate the means and percentages yourself. Either way, you should lead a class discussion on the importance of doing an audience analysis in terms of speech topic selection, preparation, and delivery. Moreover, ask students if there are other relevant audience characteristics in your classroom that the survey failed to tap. Finally, ask students what other way(s) they might obtain the same or similar data about their audience(s).

2. **CHOOSING A TOPIC:** One of the biggest problems for students in public speaking classes is selecting a topic. They spend so much time "searching" for the *best* topic that they can't afford to spend the time "researching" and "rehearsing." This activity is to help them get started.

   Bring to class the day's newspaper, a current weekly news magazine, and the campus newspaper. Divide the class into groups of five to seven members. Ask students to leaf through one of the above news media (you may want to divide the daily paper into sections). Have students list the topic areas presented in their paper/magazine. Then discuss with your students the wealth of topics that could be developed into a speech by simply reviewing these easily obtainable sources.

3. **ORGANIZING A SPEECH TO INFORM:** Ask students to select five topics from the following list. For each topic, have each student write a purpose statement, a central idea, and three main points. Also, have students identify the organizational pattern they would use to organize those main points.

   A. Protecting endangered species

   B. Being an organ donor

   C. How to make your own beef jerky

   D. Balancing the federal budget

   E. Solving the homeless problem

   F. The funding of AIDS research

   G. Responsible pet ownership

   H. Three well-known exercise programs

   I. Subliminal advertising

   J. Vivisection

   K. Weekend vacation trips

   L. Federal regulations of child-care facilities

4. **ORGANIZING A SPEECH TO PERSUADE:** This activity is designed to help students understand Monroe's motivated sequence. Before students try to develop their persuasive speech on their own, it helps to have them get some direction and support from their peers in a practice session.

Divide your class into groups of five students. Ask each group to develop a 5-minute persuasive speech. As a group, they should select a topic and define a clear central idea statement. Ask each group member to develop one step in the Monroe Motivated Sequence with the assistance of the entire group. Allow 25 minutes for the group to develop the speech. At the end of the planning time, have each group present their speech. Discuss as a class how well the motivated sequence was developed. What were the strengths and weaknesses in each group's message? How could each speech be improved?

5. **MONROE'S MOTIVATED SEQUENCE:** Ask students to watch or videotape several TV commercials (or you may want to bring in several videotaped commercials yourself). Ask students to identify the five steps of the motivated sequence used in each commercial. Which steps appeared to be emphasized or de-emphasized? Why? What recommendations would you give to advertisers of that commercial?

CHAPTER 14
SPEAKING BEFORE A GROUP

1. **NONVERBAL IMMEDIACY BEHAVIORS (IMM):** Ask each student to complete the scale on page 418 in their text. Have each student calculate his/her own nonverbal immediacy score. Discuss the range of responses and how the degree of immediacy may influence students' speech outcomes. Moreover, you may want to introduce the fact that intercultural differences may mediate those outcomes. In other words, you might ask them to what extent Asian-American students "value" immediate speakers? What about Mexican-American students? How difficult or easy is it for individual students to be immediate—given their cultural background? Discuss.

2. **PUBLIC SPEAKING AS EXTENDED CONVERSATION:** Have students make an audio recording of themselves. Ask each student to make two types of recordings:

   A. *Spontaneous speaking:* Instruct students to select a topic they feel comfortable talking about for 3 to 4 minutes (e.g., a vacation trip, their friends or family, pet peeves, or a social issue they care about). Because the purpose of this first recording is to analyze their characteristics (not the subject matter), encourage them to have some fun with it.

   B. *Short prose reading*: Ask students to select a paragraph or two of written prose or literature they enjoy. After selecting their prose, encourage them to read it a few times, trying to really understand the author's ideas. After a few rehearsals, students should then record their reading of the prose.

   After both types of speaking have been recorded, instruct students to listen to their tapes. They should be listening for similarities/differences in vocal characteristics. Based on their comparisons, did they notice anything different about each recording? Special attention should be made to their volume, articulation, pitch, rate, pauses, and overall vocal variety. Finally, discuss the implications of those differences on "reading" a manuscript, as opposed to speaking "with" an audience. Which is preferred by the speaker? By the audience? Why?

3. **CREDIBILITY: WHO HAS IT AND WHO DOESN'T?** Lead your class with a discussion about elected officials and their perceived credibility. Ask students for their perceptions of various personalities (select current figures). How did they arrive at these perceptions? How do they judge the former/current president of the United States? How about the vice-president? Using the president and vice-president, ask students to comment on the five dimensions of source credibility: competence, trustworthiness, composure, sociability, and extroversion. Which dimension is most important for political figures? Which is least important? Next, compare and contrast those credibility dimensions with television entertainment personalities. Now, which dimension is most (and least) important?

4. **IMPROMPTU SPEAKING:** Impromptu presentations help students learn to organize their ideas quickly and provide them with experiences to "think on their feet." Make up a list of easy, dichotomous topics (e.g., writing a paper versus giving a speech; eating a hamburger versus a hot dog). Place each set of adversarial topics on separate note cards. Have students select one of your cards, read it to himself/herself, and then give a 2-minute impromptu speech.

   Because students are usually thinking so hard about "what" to say, the delivery comes across naturally. This activity probably should not be "evaluated" in the traditional grading sense. Instead, you may want to just provide them with some supportive feedback on delivery skills.

Sample Topics:

A. Summer vs. winter
B. Morning classes vs. evening classes
C. Male teachers vs. female teachers
D. IBM computers vs. Macintosh computers
E. Sweaters vs. sweatshirts
F. Going out to a movie vs. staying home and renting a movie
G. Your favorite holiday: Your birthday versus Christmas (or another holiday)
H. Writing a letter vs. talking on the phone
I. Renting vs. buying a home
J. Diet Pepsi vs. Diet Coke
K. Dogs vs. cats
L. Home state vs. another state (e.g., California vs. Florida)
M. American Express vs. Visa credit cards
N. Airplane travel vs. train travel
O. Living in the city vs. living in the country
P. Objective tests vs. essay tests
Q. Ice cream vs. frozen yogurt
R. Walking vs. jogging
S. Beer vs. wine
T. Foreign cars vs. American cars
U. Pens vs. pencils
V. TV watching vs. reading a book
W. Live plants vs. artificial plants
X. Living together vs. marriage
Y. Going to the beach vs. going to the mountains
Z. Apples vs. oranges

5. **EVALUATING INFORMATIVE AND PERSUASIVE SPEECHES:** Below are two sample critique forms we have used in evaluating students' informative and persuasive speeches. You may want to try these or modify one for your own use.

SAMPLE A

INFORMATIVE SPEECH CRITIQUE
(20 Points)

	Strong	OK	Weak
INTRODUCTION (3)			
Effective attention-gainer	——	——	——
Explicit central idea statement	——	——	——
Specific preview statements	——	——	——
BODY (3)			
Main points are clear/signposted	——	——	——
Discussion supported with evidence	——	——	——
Clear, logical organization (Internal summaries & transitions)	——	——	——
CONCLUSION (3)			
Summary of main points presented	——	——	——
Memorable statement is creative	——	——	——
Created a sense of closure	——	——	——
DELIVERY (4)			
Sustained eye contact	——	——	——
Provides vocal variety	——	——	——
Used effective physical movements (gestures, movement, posture)	——	——	——
Immediate/extemporaneous delivery	——	——	——
QUALITY (4)			
Credible and informative speech	——	——	——
Minimal note cards used	——	——	——
Audience analysis/topic selection appropriate	——	——	——
Timing (within the assigned limit)	——	——	——
OUTLINE (3)			
Format (purpose statement, intro, body, and conclusion, references)	——	——	——
Turned in on time	——	——	——

SAMPLE B

PERSUASIVE SPEECH CRITIQUE
(20 Points)

	Strong	OK	Weak
GAINING AUDIENCE ATTENTION (2)			
Interesting and relevant	____	____	____
Effective transition	____	____	____
IDENTIFYING UNFULFILLED NEEDS (5)			
Need stated explicitly	____	____	____
Need illustrated	____	____	____
Need supported with evidence	____	____	____
Need related to audience	____	____	____
Need clearly developed	____	____	____
IMPLYING SATISFACTION BY OFFERING A SOLUTION (4)			
Solution stated explicitly	____	____	____
Solution solves earlier needs	____	____	____
Solution supported with evidence	____	____	____
Potential objections are countered	____	____	____
VISUALIZING WHAT SATISFACTION WILL MEAN (2)			
Futue projection (with/without proposed solution)	____	____	____
Visualization is concrete and vivid	____	____	____
DEFINING SPECIFIC ACTIONS (3)			
Call for action/adoption of idea	____	____	____
Steps necessary to take action are presented	____	____	____
Memorable statement presented	____	____	____
DELIVERY (5)			
Appearance is appropriate	____	____	____
Sustained eye contact	____	____	____
Provides vocal variety	____	____	____
Used effective physical movements (gestures, posture, movement)	____	____	____
Extemporaneous/immediate delivery	____	____	____

PERSUASIVE SPEECH CRITIQUE
(20 Points)

	Strong	OK	Weak
QUALITY (5)			
Credibility established/persuasiveness	＿＿	＿＿	＿＿
Smooth transition between steps	＿＿	＿＿	＿＿
Minimal note cards used correctly	＿＿	＿＿	＿＿
Audience analysis/topic selection appropriate	＿＿	＿＿	＿＿
Timing (within assigned time limit)	＿＿	＿＿	＿＿
OUTLINE (4)			
Format (purpose statement, used MMS format, and references)	＿＿	＿＿	＿＿
Neat professional appearance	＿＿	＿＿	＿＿
Turned in on time	＿＿	＿＿	＿＿

CHAPTER 15

PUBLIC SPEAKING: POLISHING AND FINE-TUNING

1. **HUMOR ORIENTATION SCALE (HO):** Ask students to complete the scale on page 438 in their text and to calculate their scores as directed. Then lead a discussion on how humorous they think they really are. Ask students how important they believe humor is for public speaking. Can anyone be humorous? Is all humor funny? Who determines what's funny or not funny? Under what circumstances should sarcasm be avoided? Follow up with what cautions speakers should keep in mind when using humor.

2. **USING METAPHORS AND SIMILES:** As a class or in groups, have students brainstorm and list metaphors and similes they commonly use (or have heard used). Next, ask them to create new metaphors and similes for every trite one they included on their initial list. Share them with the class. Discuss how metaphors and similes can be useful to a speaker.

3. **ADDING EXCITEMENT TO YOUR LANGUAGE:** Develop a list of words for your students. The only criterion for your list is "common usage." As an individual or as a class activity, ask students to substitute each word with another word (synonym) or phrase that is more concrete, animated, or intense. To help get them started, here is a list they can work on:

A. rich	N. tax increase
B. said	O. money
C. building	P. cheap
D. cold	Q. tall
E. wrong	R. blue
F. decrease	S. hungry
G. love	T. sad
H. asked	U. nervous
I. tired	V. polite
J. good	W. fat
K. bad	X. a "difficult" child
L. ill	Y. spoiled
M. poor	Z. angry

4. **SOUND BITES:** Chapter 15 includes the entire text of First Lady Barbara Bush's commencement speech. Have students assume the role of newspaper reporter/editor covering Barbara Bush's speech to the Wellesley College graduates and their families. Have them respond to the following questions:

A. What sound bites would you use in your newspaper coverage? List as many as you might use.

B. What criteria did you use to determine your selection of sound bites?

C. Of the sound bites you selected, which are best and why?

D. What functions do sound bites serve?

E. Do you think sound bites primarily distort or illuminate the facts?

5. **ANALYZING YOUR COMMUNICATOR STYLE:** Have students videotape one of their speeches for your class. After privately viewing the playback of their own individual videos, students should provide a written critique of their communicator style by responding to the following questions and issues:

A. In one word or phrase, how would you "label" your own rhetorical or communicator style? Why do you think so?

B. Based on what you have learned in this course, what do you believe are three of your strengths as a public speaker?

C. What are two of your weaknesses?

D. How might you improve your weaknesses or capitalize on your strengths as a public speaker? Be specific and behavioral in your answer.

E. Finally, how much of your "true" personality emerged in your presentation? Did you sound sincere, personable, and *real*? Why or why not?

CHAPTER 13
COMMUNICATING IN A MULTICULTURAL SOCIETY

DISCUSSION TOPICS AND ACTIVITIES

Discussion Topics

1. It is important for students to understand how disposed *all* of us are to being ethnocentric in our responses to people who appear to be different from us. Facilitate a discussion that encourages students to defend why they think the ways they do important things in their lives are better than the ways people in a different culture might do the same kinds of things. For example, students might discuss why having separate toilet facilities for males and females is necessary. Or why have toilet facilities at all? Why is exercising our right to vote essential; what about those cultures whose voting policies exclude the common person? What functions do clothes serve in our culture? In other cultures? Who is "right" and who is "wrong"?

2. Students are not always aware that the ways they think and act in any given situation are the result of the cultural orientations of their parents and grandparents. Moreover, parents and grandparents frequently represent a diverse set of cultural backgrounds. Facilitate a discussion wherein students are encouraged to indicate that they are the descendants of people of differing backgrounds, and discuss as a class how these orientations influence how they behave more generally; during the holidays. Discuss how their backgrounds influence how they handle conflict, guests in their homes, elders, and others.

3. Those who are "English as the primary language" communicators often fail to realize how difficult it is for people who speak "English as a second language." Facilitate a discussion around this topic the objective of which is to generate a list of the difficulties associated with communicating in English as a second language. There may be students in this language situation in the class who can contribute to this discussion. In any case, most students have met or are related to someone who is in this situation. Discuss the anxieties, frustrations, and resulting misperceptions associated with communicating in English as a second, as opposed to a first, language.

Activities

1. Have each student interview at least one person on campus who is from a co-cultural background that is different from his/her own. The interviewers should attempt to identify some of the most and least obvious co-cultural differences. As a class, consider these co-cultural differences in terms of the difficulties and anxieties associated with communicating with people from different backgrounds.

2. Have students interview someone from an underrepresented group or an ethnic minority. The interviewers should attempt to identify some of the characteristics that can serve as a basis of misconceptions about the particular group of people. Moreover, interviewers should attempt to determine what misconceptions the individual has about the general or mainstream culture. As a class, discuss the origins of such misconceptions and generate a list of alternative ways to extinguish them.

3. Have students go out on campus and observe women talking with women, men talking with men, and women talking with men. With as much accuracy as possible, have students document the co-cultural styles of people relating to individuals of the same gender and those associated with cross-gender communication. Back in class, consider how gender acts as a powerful co-cultural influence when people attempt to relate to each other.

CHAPTER 14

UNDERSTANDING MASS COMMUNICATION

DISCUSSION TOPICS AND ACTIVITIES

Discussion Topics

1. It is important for students to understand how the "profit-making motive" has contributed to the development of the media as they exist in the world today. Facilitate a discussion around the money-making histories of various media in America. This discussion will help students grasp the connection between the advances in media technology that we experience today and the large-scale profits that are realized by the media industries.

2. It is important for students to understand both the limited and the long-term effects of the media. Encourage students to think of and list as many examples of both types of effects as they can. Once four or five examples of each type of effect have been generated and listed on the board, facilitate a discussion explaining how different types of media produce short-term and long-term effects.

3. The meaning construction function of the media parallels what was discussed about human communication more generally in Chapter 1. Discuss the similarities and the differences in the ways meanings are constructed during different modes of communication.

Activities

1. Have students bring to class several examples of how the television and magazine media attempt to persuade us to model through product purchasing the appearance and behaviors of popular people. For example, students could tape and bring in a video of several of the clothing commercials they viewed, or they could cut out and bring in cosmetic or clothing advertisements from a magazine. These examples can be shared with the class and serve as bases for understanding how the media attempt to manipulate consumers into buying particular kinds of products. In fact, the media often *create* wants and needs for their advertised products.

2. Assign groups of students the task of actually putting together a product line (e.g., like a toy or a cordless telephone) to be marketed via specific media. Students would construct a "product prototype," formulate a plan for the media marketing of the product, and make a presentation to the entire class. This activity would give students a feel for the design, fabrication, and media marketing of different types of products.

3. Have students keep a viewing log of the numbers of positive and negative stories presented on the national news over a week. They could also keep track of the amount of actual time of each type of news story. Classwide analysis of these data would give students an understanding of the kinds of news materials the media present and whether there is a preference for positive over negative stories or vice versa.

4. In dyads or small groups, have students generate opinions regarding the following media trivia issues:

(a) How has the "Donna Reed Show" stereotyped women? What effects does this show and others like it have on our own stereotypes of women today?

(b) Does sex in advertising, the movies, and other media promote sexual promiscuity? If so, how? To what extent?

(c) Name five children's role models from TV today that are prosocial and unoffensive.

(d) Do the media pay too much attention to the personal lives of politicians? How far should reporters go in their search for "truth" behind the public lives of our politicians?

(e) What impact do you think "Beverly Hills, 90210" has on today's adolescents? How about "Married . . . With Children"?

(f) Do you believe that radio disc jockeys are given too much freedom in what they are allowed to say and do over the air? Why or why not?

After students have addressed these issues in their groups, the class as a whole should discuss the theoretical explanation (or research) that supports (or fails to support) their opinions. Students may want to reconsider their opinions in light of this discussion and the chapter readings.

CHAPTER 15
CONDUCTING COMUNICATION RESEARCH

DISCUSSION TOPICS AND ACTIVITIES

Discussion Topics

1. When consuming research-based recommendations regarding effective communication, it is important for students to understand the assumptions communication scientists operate from when they conduct research that leads to such recommendations. Facilitate a classroom discussion wherein students are encouraged to provide examples that illustrate (1) the assumption of an orderly universe, (2) the assumption of cause-effect relationships, and (3) the assumption of scientific integrity. Although students may find these assumptions abstract and hard to understand at first glance, their eventual comprehension of these postulates will make for a more enjoyable and smooth-running introductory course.

2. It is important for students of human communication to think about the comparative advantages of qualitative versus quantitative observations. Facilitate a class discussion wherein students are encouraged to think of as many communication variables as possible that would best be assessed by both qualitative and quantitative types of observations. This discussion will help students learn the appropriateness of making specific types of observations given specific kinds of circumstances.

3. It is important that students of human communication understand that research *must* be conducted in an ethical manner. Facilitate a discussion wherein the issue of "being ethical" when conducting and interpreting research is defined, and stimulate examples of how researchers who operate unethically confuse what we can learn about effective communication as opposed to advancing our knowledge base. This discussion can add a great deal of interest to the topic of conducting communication research.

Activities

1. Assign students to groups, give each group two variables, and have them generate arguments explaining why their respective set of variables ought to be related (e.g., self-disclosure and intimacy). This activity helps students understand how developing logical reasons for why things are probably related leads to the formulation and eventual testing of research hypotheses. This activity also helps students understand why research projects are designed to test hypotheses.

2. Next, have students "design a study" testing their communication hypotheses defined in Activity #1. While it may be unreasonable to expect students to accomplish this task without some difficulty, the *process* is worth the try. That is, students can begin to learn the problems associated with conducting an experiment, a survey, or an observation. The process may "look easy," but clearly, it's not. Moreover, you can discuss with students the trade-offs between feasibility (being able to conduct the study in real life) and validity (the perfect world!).

FUNDAMENTALS OF
HUMAN COMMUNICATION

3. It is important for students of human communication to understand the pervasive influence of surveys on their lives. Have students search out examples of political, media viewing, and other commercially sponsored surveys that are currently being conducted and reported. In-class discussion of these surveys should focus on purpose, quality, costs, and influence on students and on society generally. This activity adds exciting material to the class.

4. Students frequently have a hard time distinguishing among nominal, ordinal, interval, and ratio types of measures. These are important differences for students to understand. In addition to the material in this chapter on these levels of measurement and that which is provided in lecture, have students bring to class examples of each type of measurement. For example, for nominal have them bring in apples and oranges; for ordinal, a rank ordering of political candidates; for interval, an attitude questionnaire; and for ratio, an oral thermometer.

5. Have competing groups of students generate hypotheses from the following "bogus" variables. One group should argue one way; the other group should argue the opposite. Compare and contrast the arguments they generate. Then discuss the importance of *observation* and *testing* in their efforts to determine who is right.

   (a) Shoe size and intelligence (e.g., the greater the shoe size the higher the intelligence, or the smaller the shoe size the lower the intelligence)

   (b) Mother's height and number of offspring

   (c) Number of words in an essay and grade on a test

   (d) Age and persuasibility

   (e) Writing pen (Bic vs. Mont Blanc) and creativity

PART V

EVALUATION AND FEEDBACK

EVALUATING STUDENTS: FORMATIVE FEEDBACK

All teaching involves evaluation. At the heart of evaluation is making judgments about how to measure achievement. To be sure students have learned, a teacher must observe or test students' performance in some way. Bloom, Hastings, and Madaus (1971) divide measurement of achievement into two categories: formative and summative.

Formative measurement occurs before or during instruction. It has two basic goals: to guide the teacher in planning and to help students identify areas to study. Tests or observations of performance closely related to learning objectives are useful for this purpose (Woolfolk & McCune-Nicolich, 1984). *Summative* measurement occurs at the end of a sequence of instruction. Its purpose is to let the teacher and students know the level of achievement acquired. The final comprehensive exam and teacher evaluations given at the end of the course are examples of summative feedback.

The difference between formative and summative evaluation is one of purpose or use. If the goal is to obtain information about achievement in order to plan future lessons, the testing is formative. If the purpose is to measure final student achievement or the teacher's overall performance, the evaluation is summative. As mentioned earlier, it is the use of the results that determines whether a test is formative or summative. Let's now look at some common formats of formative tests: objective and essay exams.

WRITING EXAMINATION QUESTIONS

Objective Testing. Multiple-choice, true/false, short-answer, fill-in items, and matching exercises are all part of objective testing. This simply means that the items are not open to many interpretations, or the questions are not "subjective." When objective tests are used, the most difficult part is writing the items. Essay tests also require careful construction, but you will most likely find that grading the completed answer is generally the major difficulty with essays. Before we turn to essays, let's discuss some guidelines for constructing and grading multiple-choice (not multiple-guess) tests. The guidelines we have provided rely heavily on Gronlund (1982) and Woolfolk and McCune-Nicolich (1984).

1. The *stem* of a multiple-choice item is the part that asks the question or poses the problem. The choices are called *alternatives*. The wrong answers are called *distractors* because of their purpose.

2. The stem should be clear and simple and present only a single problem. Nonessential details should be left out.

> *INCORRECT:* There are several stages in small-group development. The emergence of conflict may occur in any of these stages, but conflict is most likely to start in the _____ stage.

> *CORRECT:* The stage in which conflict starts to emerge in small-group development is _____.

3. The problem in the stem should be stated in positive terms. Negative language is confusing. However, if you must use words such as *not, no, false,* or *except,* underline them and/or type them in all capitals.

> *INCORRECT:* Which of the following is not an advantage of writing a letter as a communication medium?

> *CORRECT:* Which of the following is *NOT* an advantage of writing a letter as a communication medium?

4. As much wording as possible should be included in the stem so that phrases will not have to be repeated in each alternative.

> *INCORRECT:* The collaborative style of conflict is:
>
> A. A strategy for handling conflict in which people narrowly view all conflicts as win-lose events.
> B. A strategy for handling conflict in which people jointly or willingly cooperate with their opponent.
> C. A strategy for handling conflict in which people "give in" to their opponent.

> *CORRECT:* The strategy for handling conflicts in which people work jointly or willingly in cooperation with their opponent is characteristic of individuals with a _____ conflict style.
>
> A. Competitive
> B. Collaborative
> C. Compromising

5. Do not expect students to make extremely fine discriminations.

> *INCORRECT:* Most researchers claim that _____ of a message's impact is due to nonverbal factors.
>
> A. 93%
> B. 95%
> C. 85%

> *CORRECT:* Most researchers claim that approximately _____ of a message's impact is due to nonverbal factors.
>
> A. 90–95 %
> B. 60–65%
> C. 35–40%

6. Each alternative answer should fit the grammatical form of the stem so that no answers are obviously wrong.

> *INCORRECT:* The statement "the world is round" is an example of a:
>
> A. Fact
> B. Attitude
> C. Belief
>
> *CORRECT:* The statement "the world is round" is an example of a(n):
>
> A. Fact
> B. Attitude
> C. Belief

7. Categorical words such as *always, all, only,* or *never* should be avoided unless they can appear consistently in all alternatives. Using these categorical words is an easy way to make the alternative wrong, but most smart test takers know they ought to avoid categorical answers.

> *INCORRECT:* High communication apprehensive students:
>
> A. Never receive extra help or prompts from the teacher.
> B. Are always perceived as more intelligent.
> C. Are perceived as detached and apathetic toward school.
>
> *CORRECT:* High communication apprehensive students:
>
> A. Receive extra help or prompts from the teacher.
> B. Are perceived as more intelligent.
> C. Are perceived as detached and apathetic toward school.

8. The distractors (wrong answers) should be the same length and in the same detail as the correct alternative.

> *INCORRECT:* Which function of a speech does the phrase "In summary" fulfill?
>
> A. To remind your audience to pay attention so that they can remember what they are supposed to do
> B. The conclusion
> C. To remind the audience of your main points
>
> *CORRECT:* Which function of a speech does the phrase "In summary" fulfill?
>
> A. To end the speech in an upbeat manner
> B. To sign off, leaving the audience wanting more
> C. To remind the audience of your main points

9. Avoid including two wrong answers (distractors) that have the same meaning. If only one answer can be right and two answers are the same, then they both must be wrong. This narrows down the choices.

10. Avoid using exact wording found in the textbook. Poor students may recognize the answers without knowing what they really mean.

11. Overuse of "all of the above" and "none of the above" should be avoided. Such choices may be helpful to students who are simply guessing. In addition, "all of the above" may trick a quick student who sees that the first alternative is correct and does not read on to discover that the others are correct, too.

12. Obvious patterns also aid students who are guessing. The position of the correct answer should be varied, as should its length. The correct answer should sometimes be the longest, sometimes the shortest, and more often neither the longest nor the shortest.

13. In your directions to students, you may want to suggest that they select the "best" answer to each question, as opposed to the "right" answer. This may help to avoid those lengthy discussions about whether the correct answer was really correct or whether several of the other options might be correct as well.

Essay Testing. Essay testing allows students to create the answers on their own. Some learning objectives are best measured by this type of evaluation. The most difficult part of essay testing is judging the quality of the answers, but writing good, clear questions should not be easily dismissed. We will now focus our attention on the writing, administering, and grading of essay tests.

1. Essay tests should be limited to the measurement of more complex learning outcomes (synthesis, application, and evaluation)—that is, outcomes that cannot be measured by short objective questions.

   EXAMPLE: Explain why a persuasive speech needs a different format than an informative speech for maximum effectiveness.

2. An essay question should give students a clear and precise task. It should indicate the elements to be covered in the answer.

   EXAMPLE: Explain Monroe's Motivated Sequence. Be sure to include the five steps in order of arrangement.

3. Give students ample time for answering. If more than one essay is being completed in the same class, you may want to give suggested time requirements for each.

   EXAMPLE:
   1. Discuss how speech and language distinguishes humans from animals. (10 minutes)
   2. Explain the index of fidelity and how we can live with limited accuracy in our lives. (15 minutes)

4. Do not include a large number of essay questions. It is better to plan on more frequent testing than to include more than two or three essay questions in a single class period.

5. Combining an essay question with a number of objective items is one way to avoid the problem of limited sampling.

Essays: Taking the Subjectivity Out of Testing. Prior research has demonstrated that subjectivity in grading essays and papers is widespread among educators. For example, Starch and Elliott (1912) completed a series of studies that found that papers (essays) given to different teachers to evaluate produced scores ranging from 64% to 98%. That is, the grades for the same papers ranged from "D" to "A." Neatness, spelling, punctuation, and communication effectiveness were evaluated differently by each teacher. Follow-up studies found that these results were not confined to one subject area. Rather, the individual standards of the grader (teacher) and the unreliability of scoring procedures caused the primary problems (Starch & Elliott, 1913a, 1913b; cited in Woolfolk & McCune-Nicolich, 1984).

Furthermore, certain qualities of an essay itself were found to influence grades. For example, in a study of grading practices of 16 law schools, Linn, Klein, and Hart (1972) found that neatly written, verbose, jargon-filled essays, with few grammatical and construction errors were given the best grades. Other research indicates that teachers often reward quantity (verbosity) rather than quality in essays (Woolfolk & McCune-Nicolich, 1984, p. 552).

There are several ways to avoid problems of subjectivity and ensure fairness and accuracy in grading essays:

1. Construct a model answer first. That is, you should outline the answer you expect your students to provide.
2. Next, you may want to preassign various points to each part of the answer.
3. You may also want to assign points for the organization and internal consistency of the answer.
4. Once you have assigned points, you may then translate the points into grades such as 1 to 5 or A, B, C, D, and F.
5. Finally, sort the papers into piles by grade. The papers in each pile should be skimmed to see if they are relatively comparable in quality. What you're searching for here is "internal consistency" or reliability in your grading.

   Other helpful tips for checking objectivity include the following:

6. Grade all responses to one question before moving onto the next.
7. After you finish reading and scoring the first question, shuffle the papers so that no students end up having all their questions graded first, last, or in the middle (Hill, 1976).
8. You may have greater objectivity if you ask students to put their names on the back of their papers so that grading is anonymous.

HOW TO ASSIGN GRADES

There are a variety of ways you can compute and assign grades for your class. We have outlined some of the more common ways teachers determine final course grades. The first, norm-reference grading, is used by most teachers and understood best by most administrators, students, and parents. However, it may not be the most appropriate grading method, particularly if your class is small and your students do not reflect the entire range of abilities evidenced in the normal population. College students, on the whole, represent a skewed distribution of abilities and achievements—most have a history of obtaining C's or better in school. Thus, to impose a normal curve onto students who are already "abnormal," that is, high achievers, would be inappropriate.

Criterion-reference grading is one of the best approaches, as you will see below. After all, this method requires that students achieve at some standard that you set beforehand. The criteria are spelled out before the student even enters the classroom so that both you and the student know what it takes to make an A, B, C, D, or F. Finally, the point system for grading is an alternative that can be used in conjunction with either norm- or criterion-reference grading systems. It's an easy way for both you and your students to keep track of grades as the semester goes along—simply by keeping score; adding points earned throughout the course.

NORM-REFERENCE GRADING

In norm-reference grading, the major influence on a grade is the student's standing in comparison with others who also took the course/test. One very popular type of norm-reference grading is "grading on a curve" or a "normal distribution." If grading were done strictly on the normal curve, there would be an equal number of A's and F's, a larger number of B's and D's, and an even larger number of C's.

CRITERION-REFERENCE GRADING

In criterion-reference grading, the grade represents a list of accomplishments. If clear objectives have been set for the course, the grade may represent a certain number of objectives that have been met satisfactorily. When a criterion-reference system is used, criteria for each grade are set in advance. It is then up to the student to strive for and reach a level that matches the grade she or he wants to achieve. Theoretically, in this system all students can achieve an A if they master the necessary number of objectives. And, of course, theoretically, all students could fail to achieve any or all objectives, depending on the inherent difficulty of the tasks involved. Criterion-reference grading has the advantage of relating judgments about a student to the achievement of clearly defined learning objectives.

POINT-SYSTEM GRADING

The point system is a popular method for combining grades from many assignments. Each test or assignment is given a certain number of total points, depending on its importance. A test worth 25% of the final grade could be worth 25 of 100 total potential points earned in a course (or 50 of 200 points). Points are then awarded on the test or assignment based on specific criteria. In many cases, the criterion-reference and point-system methods may be combined. In fact, you will notice on our own sample syllabus, that we use a point system based on a percentage criterion-reference system. Using a point system has several advantages. First, it is easy to calculate final grades. Second, it is easy for the students to keep track of their own progress. Finally, it helps teachers determine the relative weights or worth of each class activity or assignment.

GUIDELINES FOR GRADING

We know that calculating and assigning grades is the least agreeable activity for any teacher. We can have a really good class, generate a lot of enthusiasm, and build positive affect with students—up until the first evaluation/exam. At that point, students may become irritable, angry, even hostile, if they feel we have been unfair or unreasonable in our grading practices. To save yourself some of this very negative feedback and to ensure that everyone understands your grading policies, we suggest you practice the following tips. These recommendations are modified from Drayer (1979, pp. 182–187).

1. Explain your grading policies to students the first day or the first week of the course. Remind them of your policies regularly; students may forget or need to be told more than once. Be sure to include your grading policy on your course contract or syllabus.
2. Set reasonable standards.
3. Base your grades on as much objective evidence as possible. Grading on "participation" is considered subjective and may suffer from teacher bias. For example, we know that attractive, outgoing students receive more attention and better grades than do unattractive, quiet students. However, in some cases, the talkative student is perceived as a "problem student" whereas the quiet one is thought to be the "perfect" student. Obviously, then, the communication behaviors of

students in the classroom affect the perceptions made about them, and thus their "participation" grade. If you want to grade "participation," perhaps you should consider doing "in-class" activities, with each activity representing a certain number of points in the class.

4. Be sure students understand test and assignment directions. You may want to write out the instructions on a handout or outline the directions on the board.

5. Ask clear questions focusing on important material that has been taught.

6. Watch for cheating during tests. Do not leave the classroom. Walk around the room; let your students know you're attentive, but not "hounding" them. Be firm but reasonable when you encounter cheating.

7. Correct, return, and discuss test questions as soon as possible. Turn-around time should be no longer than 1 week. Remember: Students like (and expect) immediate feedback.

8. As a rule, do not change a grade unless you make a clerical or calculation error. Make sure you can defend the grade assigned in the first place.

9. Guard against bias in grading. You may want students to put their names on the back of their papers, or you may want to use an objective point system when grading essays or papers.

10. Keep students informed of their class standing. Of course, if you use a point system, students can easily keep track of their own records.

11. Give students the benefit of the doubt. All measurement techniques involve error. Unless there is a very good reason not to, give the higher grade in borderline cases.

12. Review your exam questions or assignment. If a larger number of students miss the same question or part of an assignment in the same way, revise the question or assignment for the future and consider throwing it out for that testing/assignment. When you admit your errors to students (writing a bad test item), students are more likely to perceive you as being flexible, responsive, and ethical.

EVALUATING TEACHERS: SUMMATIVE FEEDBACK

Students aren't the only ones who are evaluated; teachers, too, are "graded" on their performance in the classroom. Sometimes the "grades" or evaluations students assign to us may not seem all that fair. Some students, for instance, may complain that you are not available during office hours when, in fact, you are always there. The point is, you may be right, but if students don't *perceive* that you are available (at *their* convenience), then they may indicate on your evaluations that you are not. Other responses, however, may be more accurate than we may want to admit. Treat your evaluations and students' written comments as constructive criticism to help you become better at what you do. Try not to get too ego-involved and defensive. We know negative feedback hurts, but we still want to know what we do wrong and how to become more effective teachers in the long run.

Remember, also, that teaching is not a popularity contest. Not all students will like us. Not all students will appreciate our sense of humor. Not all students will learn from us. Even so, we must develop a certain "thickness to our skin" by shrugging it off and doing better next time—with the next group. All of us have had bad classes; all of us have had one or two students that seem to ruin it for the rest of the class. Sometimes it only takes one or two students to keep us from enjoying our teaching experience. Fight it off—try not to give in to the perceptions of a few, and instead, approach each day with renewed energy and commitment to do the best you can.

In this section, we discuss the entire teaching-evaluation process in some detail. We hope you find teaching a rewarding and valuable experience. Teaching evaluations are the best and only way we can discover what we should or should not be doing. Teaching evaluations, in the final analysis, are the best and only way of becoming the kind of teacher we want to be. After all, teaching evaluations are a form of feedback—a way of discerning if students are receiving the message we intend.

FORMAL STUDENT FEEDBACK

Most universities, colleges, and departments require you to have students rate your teaching performance. Chairs and personnel committees will often use student ratings of your teaching as the primary source of information about your teaching effectiveness. However, you may also want to elicit summative or final course feedback to help plan for future course development and teaching strategies.

Prior research indicates that students seem to learn more with instructors they rate high in clarity of presentation, organization, and planning. Students who perceive themselves as having learned also tend to learn more. Of course, academic learning is not the only important criterion for assessing teaching effectiveness. As a teacher you will want your students to enjoy their college experience, be absent less often, develop positive self-concepts, and feel a certain confidence in dealing with the material you present. You may want them to take more courses or choose a career in your subject area. Information obtained from student questionnaires can be a great help in reaching these goals. Results may also provide ideas about how to make changes in course content.

INFORMAL STUDENT FEEDBACK

During the course, you may want to elicit informal feedback from your students as well. That is, why wait until the end of the term to determine what you did wrong (or right)? For example, you may ask them once a week or every 3 weeks to write down on a piece of paper some constructive feedback about how the course is going and your own teaching. The critical point of collecting this feedback is to *use* the feedback. That is, show your students that you are concerned about their learning experience. For example, if your students complain that they need extra time with you, you may want to consider changing your office hours, or you may need to come in early or stay late after class to accommodate your students. The key is to respond to the feedback you receive from your students.

GUIDELINES TO HELP YOU IMPROVE YOUR TEACHER RATINGS

Finally, we have provided a few suggestions to help you improve your teacher ratings and, at the same time, improve your overall teaching effectiveness.

1. Obtain a copy of the teacher-evaluation form used by your department. Examine each of the items carefully. Think of them as "criteria" for teaching effectiveness. Then read them over again before you enter the classroom—each and every day. This procedure will help you keep in mind the important and relevant criteria that students will be asked to judge your teaching effectiveness. In this way, you will be in a better position to try to match your own teaching performance with the criteria your department has determined as critical.

2. Organize your lessons/lectures carefully. You may want to put your outline on an overhead or on the board. Students will quickly get the idea that you are, in fact, organized. At the same time, you will have available your notes for teaching.

3. Strive for clarity in your explanations by using concrete examples and illustrations. Try to think of examples and stories *before* class. Sometimes applying the principles and concepts is harder than defining them. Immediately after giving your own illustration, ask your students to supply one or two more. In this way, they become actively involved in the learning experience and it provides you with the opportunity to see if they truly understand the concept.

4. Communicate an enthusiasm for your subject and students. *Look* like you are excited to see them. Tell them so. No matter how tired you really are, no matter how depressed you may be, you are still obligated to give students your best in your role as a professional instructor. No student looks forward to entering a classroom when they can predict the teacher will be unpleasant, boring, and apathetic. Show them instead that you are committed to teaching, excited about the material, and anxious to be with them. Learn their names and then use their names frequently in class. Make them feel special.

5. Keep all students involved. Try to elicit comments from everyone. Let them know that no matter what they say, their comments will be treated with respect. By example, show them that they can feel "safe" communicating with you and in front of their peers in your class.

6. Balance goals for student learning and goals directed toward encouraging students to like your subject and school in general. In other words, make sure they learn the content, but at the same time, try to get them to enjoy the material and learning process as well. Students' college experience should be exciting, challenging, and rewarding—help them believe that it is all of that and more.

7. Constantly broaden your knowledge in your area. Read the latest books; subscribe to and read the journals in communication. We can't impress upon you enough the importance of staying current in the field. Information changes so fast; what we thought was true yesterday may not be today. But more important, we are always learning new and interesting things about human communication behavior. There is so much to learn. There is so much we should know.

SAMPLE TEACHING EVALUATIONS

We have included two sample teaching evaluations. As a new teacher, you should obtain a copy of the teaching evaluation form used at your school or department. Be sure to "learn" this evaluation form early in the course so that you will know what your peers perceive as important and thus be able to meet their expectancies.

1. Department of Communication Studies, West Virginia University. (See Model 1.)
2. Department of Speech Communication, California State University, Long Beach. (See Model 2.)

INTERPRETING YOUR OWN TEACHING EVALUATIONS

1. Compare your overall mean score with those obtained across all teachers in your department and school. Most departments provide that information for you. Examine individual item means, as well as the overall mean, to determine areas you need to work on. Importantly, you should emphasize also those areas that students really appreciated. Sometimes we forget to examine and reflect upon those issues that students liked about us.

2. Consider the standard deviation from the mean for the department and school. This standard deviation tells you the range of differences around the mean. You should compare your mean, then, to see if you fall into this range.

Let's consider a hypothetical example. Let's say your mean score on a 5-point scale for the item "Rate the overall effectiveness of this teacher" is 4.2. Next, you'll want to compare your mean with the collective or overall mean for the department or school—let's say that mean is 4.5. Is the difference between 4.2 and 4.5 (.3) meaningful—significant enough to warrant some concern from your chair or director? The standard deviation becomes critical here. If the standard deviation is greater than .3 (and it probably will be), then you don't have to worry. If the standard deviation is smaller, then you should feel compelled to work harder to increase your rating.

3. Written feedback: Read all of your written comments, but don't let a single isolated negative comment embedded within a lot of other positive feedback trigger a backlash. Keep isolated comments in perspective. Once again, not everyone is going to like you (even if they should!). But, if others validate those negative perceptions, then of course you must treat them as legitimate, honest, and worth your scrutiny.

MODEL 1*
INSTRUCTOR-COURSE EVALUATION

DIRECTIONS: Please respond to each item below by marking the appropriate space on the IBM sheet you will receive. Do not identify yourself on the IBM sheet. Note that in some cases the most positive score is an A while in the other cases it is an E.

INSTRUCTOR CONTENT:

1. Did the instructor introduce significant ideas?

   DID   A   B   C   D   E   DID NOT

2. Did the instructor seem to be well informed and up-to-date in his/her field?

   YES   A   B   C   D   E   NO

INSTRUCTOR METHOD:

3. Did the instructor use enough examples or illustrations to clarify the material?

   SUFFICIENT   A   B   C   D   E   INSUFFICIENT

4. Did the instructor present material in an interesting manner?

   VERY INTERESTING   A   B   C   D   E   VERY DULL

STUDENT/TEACHER INTERACTION

5. Considering the size of the class, did you feel free to ask questions, express ideas, and so on?

   FREE   A   B   C   D   E   NOT FREE

6. Was the instructor responsive to feedback from the class?

   RESPONSIVE   A   B   C   D   E   UNRESPONSIVE

---

* Developed and used by the Department of Communication Studies at West Virginia University.

MY INSTRUCTOR IS**

7. SOCIABLE	A	B	C	D	E	UNSOCIABLE
8. CHEERFUL	A	B	C	D	E	GLOOMY
9. GOOD-NATURED	A	B	C	D	E	IRRITABLE
10. NERVOUS	A	B	C	D	E	POISED
11. TENSE	A	B	C	D	E	RELAXED
12. ANXIOUS	A	B	C	D	E	CALM
13. UNSELFISH	A	B	C	D	E	SELFISH
14. KIND	A	B	C	D	E	CRUEL
15. SYMPATHETIC	A	B	C	D	E	UNSYMPATHETIC
16. MEEK	A	B	C	D	E	AGGRESSIVE
17. QUIET	A	B	C	D	E	VERBAL
18. TIMID	A	B	C	D	E	BOLD
19. EXPERT	A	B	C	D	E	INEXPERT
20. RELIABLE	A	B	C	D	E	UNRELIABLE
21. QUALIFIED	A	B	C	D	E	UNQUALIFIED

** Responses to items 7–21 measure overall *teacher credibility* in the classroom. Specifically, items 7, 8, and 9 assess the *sociability* dimension of credibility, or how friendly the teacher is perceived to be. Items 10, 11, and 12 refer to *composure,* or how relaxed the teacher is. Items 13, 14, and 15 measure teacher *character.* Items 16, 17, and 18 assess *extroversion,* or how verbally outgoing the teacher is. And finally, 19, 20, and 21 determine the level of *competence,* or how informed students perceive the teacher to be. Importantly, teacher credibility has been linked positively to a variety of student learning outcomes.

TESTS AND GRADES

22. Was the testing fair?

    UNFAIR   A   B   C   D   E   FAIR

23. Were the grades assigned fairly?

    UNFAIR   A   B   C   D   E   FAIR

TEXT AND READINGS

24. How interesting were the assigned text/readings?

    VERY DULL   A   B   C   D   E   VERY INTERESTING

25. How valuable were the assigned text/readings?

    WORTHLESS   A   B   C   D   E   VERY VALUABLE

GENERAL COURSE EVALUATION

26. In general, how valuable was the material presented in the class?

    VERY VALUABLE   A   B   C   D   E   WORTHLESS

27. In comparison to other courses you have taken, how does this course rate?

    ONE OF THE BEST   A   B   C   D   E   ONE OF THE WORST

28. In terms of your career and personal needs, how relevant was this course?

    HIGHLY RELEVANT   A   B   C   D   E   HIGHLY IRRELEVANT

29. Knowing what you know now, how likely would you be to take this course if you had it to do over again?

DEFINITELY WOULD TAKE   A   B   C   D   E   DEFINITELY WOULD NOT TAKE

COURSE OUTCOMES

30. As a result of this course, do you believe you have a better understanding of human communication?

    YES   A   B   C   D   E   NO

31. Do you believe you will be more effective in your career as a result of this course?

    YES   A   B   C   D   E   NO

OVERALL EVALUATION

Considering everything, how do you evaluate this class and instructor?

32. VALUABLE	A	B	C	D	E	WORTHLESS
32. GOOD	A	B	C	D	E	BAD
33. PLEASANT	A	B	C	D	E	UNPLEASANT

MODEL 2*

STUDENT EVALUATION OF INSTRUCTOR

This form is provided for you to use in evaluating the instructor of this course. A summary of the evaluation from all the students in this class and this evaluation will be read by your instructor only after the semester grades have been submitted. Please be candid in your responses. These evaluations are used to assess the quality of teaching by this instructor as perceived by students. Responses may be used in making personnel decisions regarding your instructor.

Do not put your name on this form. You must use a #2 pencil. If errors are made, please erase completely. Make no written comments on the front of this form. Written comments may be made on the back.

If any person has tried to influence your ratings on this evaluation through substantive advice or instruction as to what ratings you should give, you should report that person(s) to the department chair, or other university administration, so that appropriate administrative action may be taken.

1. The instructor provided clear and accurate information regarding the course objectives, requirements, and grading procedures.

   STRONGLY   5   4   3   2   1   STRONGLY   N/A**
   AGREE   DISAGREE

2. The instructor's grading was consistent with stated criteria and procedures.

   STRONGLY   5   4   3   2   1   STRONGLY   N/A
   AGREE   DISAGREE

3. The instructor provided assignments/activities that were useful for learning and understanding the subject.

   STRONGLY   5   4   3   2   1   STRONGLY   N/A
   AGREE   DISAGREE

4. The instructor's expectations concerning work to be done in this course were reasonable.

   STRONGLY   5   4   3   2   1   STRONGLY   N/A
   AGREE   DISAGREE

5. The instructor was well prepared for classes.

   STRONGLY   5   4   3   2   1   STRONGLY   N/A
   AGREE   DISAGREE

6. The instructor was effective in presenting subject content and materials in the class.

   STRONGLY   5   4   3   2   1   STRONGLY   N/A
   AGREE   DISAGREE

---

* Used by the Department of Speech Communication at California State University, Long Beach.
** N/A = NOT APPLICABLE.

7. The instructor was available during posted office hours for conferences about the course.

STRONGLY   5   4   3   2   1   STRONGLY   N/A
AGREE   DISAGREE

8. Rate the overall teaching effectiveness of this instructor.

EXCELLENT   5   4   3   2   1   VERY POOR

PLEASE WRITE COMMENTS IN THE SPACE PROVIDED. COMMENT ON WHAT YOU LIKED BEST ABOUT THE INSTRUCTOR/COURSE, AND MAKE SUGGESTIONS FOR IMPROVEMENT IF ANY ARE NEEDED.

REFERENCES

Bloom, B. S., Englehart, M. D., Furst, E. J., Hill, W. H., & Krathwohl, D. R. (1956). *Taxonomy of educational objectives handbook I: Cognitive domain.* New York: McKay.

Bloom, B. S., Hastings, J. T., & Madaus, G. F. (1971). *Handbook on formative and summarized evaluation of student learning.* New York: McGraw-Hill.

Branan, J. M. (1972). Negative human interacting. *Journal of Counseling Psychology, 19,* 81–82.

Check, J. F. (1979). Classroom discipline: Where are we now? *Education, 100,* 134–137.

Drayer, A. M. (1979). *Problems in middle and high school training: A handbook for student teachers and beginning teachers.* Boston, MA: Allyn & Bacon.

Good, T. L., & Brophy, J. E. (1987). *Looking in classrooms* (4th ed.). New York: Harper & Row.

Gronlund, N. (1982). *Constructing achievement tests* (3rd ed.). Englewood Cliffs, NJ: Prentice-Hall.

Harrow, A. J. (1972). *A taxonomy of psychomotor domain: A guide for developing behavioral objectives.* New York: McKay.

Hill, J. R. (1976). *Measurement and evaluation in the classroom.* Columbus, OH: Charles E. Merrill.

Hurt, H. T., Scott, M. D., & McCroskey, J. C. (1978). *Communication in the classroom.* Reading, MA: Addison-Wesley.

Kaplan, R. (1974). Effects of learning with part vs. whole presentation of instructional objectives. *Journal of Educational Psychology, 66,* 787–792.

Kaplan, R., & Rothkopf, E. Z. (1974). Instructional objectives as directions to learners: Effects of passage length and amount of objective relevant content. *Journal of Educational Psychology, 66,* 448–456.

Kaplan, R., & Simmons, F. G. (1974). Effects of instructional objectives used as orienting stimuli or as summary/review upon prose learning. *Journal of Educational Psychology, 66,* 614–622.

Katzer, J., Cook, K. H., & Crouch, W. W. (1982). *Evaluating information: A guide for users of social science research.* Reading, MA: Addison-Wesley.

Kearney, P., & McCroskey, J. C. (1980). Relationship among teacher communication style, trait, and state communication apprehension and teacher effectiveness. In D. Nimmo (Ed.), *Communication yearbook 4* (pp. 533–552). New Brunswick, NJ: Transaction.

Kemp, J. E. (1985). *The instructional design process.* New York: Harper & Row.

Krathwohl, D. R., Bloom, B. S., & Masia, B. B. (1956). *Taxonomy of educational objectives handbook II: Affective domain.* New York: McKay.

Lashbrook, V. J., & Wheeless, L. R. (1978). Instructional communication theory and research: An overview of the relationship between learning theory and instructional communication. In B. D. Rubin (Ed.), *Communication yearbook 2* (pp. 439–456). New Brunswick, NJ: Transaction.

Linn, R., Klein, S., & Hart, F. (1972). The nature and correlates of law school essay grades. *Educational and Psychological Measurement, 32,* 267–279.

McKeachie, W. J. (1986). *Teaching tips: A guidebook for the beginning college teacher* (8th ed.). Lexington, MA: D. C. Heath.

Mehrabian, A. (1971). *Silent messages.* Belmont, CA: Wadsworth.

Mouly, G. J. (1973). *Psychology for effective teaching*. New York: Holt, Rinehart, & Winston.

Nash, P. P., Richmond, V. P., & Andriate, G. (1984). *Advanced instructional communication instructor's manual* (rev. ed.). West Virginia University.

Nungester, R. J., & Duchastel, P. C. (1982). Testing versus review: Effects on retention. *Journal of Educational Psychology, 74,* 18–22.

Popham, W., & Baker, E. (1970). *Establishing instructional goals*. Englewood Cliffs, NJ: Prentice-Hall.

Rothkopf, E. Z., & Kaplan, R. (1972). Exploration of the effect of density and specificity of instructional objectives on learning from text. *Journal of Psychology, 63,* 295–302.

Starch, D., & Elliott, E. C. (1912). Reliability of grading high school work in English. *School Review, 20,* 442–447.

Starch, D., & Elliott, E. C. (1913a). Reliability of grading work in history. *School Review, 12,* 676–681.

Starch, D., & Elliott, E. C. (1913b). Reliability of grading work in mathematics. *School Review, 21,* 676–681.

Woolfolk, A. E., & McCune-Nicolich, L. (1984). *Educational psychology for teachers* (2nd ed.). Englewood Cliffs, NJ: Prentice-Hall.